THE I TATTI
RENAISSANCE LIBRARY

James Hankins, General Editor

DECEMBRIO

LIVES OF THE
MILANESE TYRANTS

ITRL 88

PIER CANDIDO DECEMBRIO

◆ ◆ ◆

LIVES OF THE MILANESE TYRANTS

TRANSLATION AND
INTRODUCTION BY

GARY IANZITI

LATIN TEXTS EDITED BY

MASSIMO ZAGGIA

THE I TATTI RENAISSANCE LIBRARY
HARVARD UNIVERSITY PRESS
CAMBRIDGE, MASSACHUSETTS
LONDON, ENGLAND
2019

Series design by Dean Bornstein

First printing

Library of Congress Cataloging-in-Publication Data

Names: Decembrio, Pier Candido, 1399–1477, author. | Ianziti, Gary,
translator, author of introduction. | Zaggia, Massimo, editor. | Container
of (expression): Decembrio, Pier Candido, 1399–1477. Philippi Mariae
Vicecomitis Mediolanensium ducis tertii vita. | Container of (expression):
Decembrio, Pier Candido, 1399–1477. Philippi Mariae Vicecomitis
Mediolanensium ducis tertii vita. English. | Container of (expression):
Decembrio, Pier Candido, 1399–1477. Annotatio rerum gestarum in vita
Francisci Sfortiae IV Mediolanensium ducis. | Container of (expression):
Decembrio, Pier Candido, 1399–1477. Annotatio rerum gestarum in vita
Francisci Sfortiae IV Mediolanensium ducis. English. 2019.
Title: Lives of the Milanese tyrants / Pier Candido Decembrio ; translated
and with an introduction by Gary Ianziti ; edited by Massimo Zaggia.
Other titles: I Tatti Renaissance library ; 88.
Description: Cambridge, Massachusetts : Harvard University Press, 2019. |
Series: The I Tatti Renaissance library ; 88 | Text in Latin with English
translation on facing pages ; introduction and notes in English. |
Includes bibliographical references and index.
Identifiers: LCCN 2018017736 | ISBN 9780674987524 (alk. paper)
Subjects: LCSH: Filippo Maria Visconti, Duke of Milan, 1392–1447 —
Biography — Early works to 1800. | Francesco Sforza, Duke of Milan,
1401–1466 — Biography — Early works to 1800. | Milan (Italy) — History —
To 1535 — Early works to 1800. | Milan (Italy) — Kings and rulers —
Biography — Early works to 1800.
Classification: LCC DG657.5 .D43 2019 | DDC 945/.2050922 — dc23
LC record available at https://lccn.loc.gov/2018017736

Contents

࿗࿗࿗

Introduction

࿐ᏕᏕᏦ

I know not whether he be more dear to the prince
for his loyalty and diligence, or more pleasing to the people
at large for his kindness and good character.

Lorenzo Valla on Pier Candido Decembrio[1]

The two works published in this volume were written at different times and under widely different circumstances. They also represent two very different moments in the career of their author, the once famed but now too often forgotten Milanese humanist Pier Candido Decembrio (1399–1477).[2] The first work — a life of the Duke of Milan Filippo Maria Visconti (1392–1447) — was essentially a product of Decembrio's twenty-eight years of service, from 1419 to 1447, as secretary, envoy, and personal literary factotum to Duke Filippo Maria and his advisors.[3] During most of this time, Milan was the central focus of Italian politics and the source of tensions that repeatedly led to armed conflict with rival powers, such as Florence and Venice. At the heart of the intrigue lay the mysterious figure of the Duke of Milan himself, ambitious, all-powerful, and inscrutable in his intentions. As a bona fide member of the inner circle, Decembrio enjoyed the privileged position of being able to view court life at close quarters. It is generally agreed that with his biography of Filippo Maria Visconti he produced a masterpiece, distilling decades of direct experience into a vivid portrait of a Renaissance prince. Most specialists of the period today would no doubt concur with the ringing endorsement of the nineteenth-century Swiss cultural historian Jacob Burckhardt, who proclaimed: "The picture of the fifteenth century would be incomplete without this unique biography, which is characteristic down to its minutest details."[4]

The second work published here has attracted much less acclaim. It is an account of the deeds in arms of the condottiere Francesco Sforza (1401–66), who through a combination of guile, force, and sheer willpower managed to secure for himself and his immediate heirs the succession to the Duchy of Milan.[5] Decembrio wrote this second biography in the early 1460s, at a critical moment in his career.[6] Sforza's accession to power in February/March 1450 had coincided with a decision on Decembrio's part to leave Milan and to seek his fortunes elsewhere. It was a fateful move, dictated by circumstances that will be explored in due course. Decembrio's path led him first to Rome and to service in the curia of the humanist pope Nicholas V. Later, he gravitated to Naples, where he was engaged in the secretariat of King Alfonso of Aragon. By the time he returned to Milan in the late 1450s, Decembrio found himself a virtual outsider in his native land. His composition of a life of the new prince Francesco Sforza was part of a concerted effort on his part to reverse his personal fortunes and to enter into the good graces of the new regime. The plan failed miserably, however, and Decembrio subsequently sought refuge in Ferrara, where he spent most of the remaining years of his life at the court of the Este family.

Even so brief a summary as this brings into high relief the very different dynamic governing the composition of these two biographies. In his life of Duke Filippo Maria, Decembrio wrote as an insider with firsthand knowledge of the events and people he was describing.[7] His portrait of Filippo Maria Visconti has an immediacy that derives in large part from its character as eyewitness testimony. To this considerable advantage we can add another: we know from the surviving documentation that Decembrio composed this biography in the months following Filippo Maria's death, on August 13, 1447. The sudden disappearance of the prince he had faithfully served for so long probably provided Decembrio with the stimulus to record his impressions. But it also offered him the opportunity to pursue a more detached and objective approach than might otherwise have been possible. While ever the Visconti partisan in his chapters on political and military events, Decembrio did not hesitate for example to dip his pen in darker colors when depicting Filippo Maria's private life. The result is a rather odd combination of devotion to the memory of the duke, Milanese patriotism, and lurid court scandal. Such a mix may appear puzzling to modern eyes, but it had—as we shall see—a worthy classical precedent in the Suetonian biographies that had long been popular at the Visconti court, and which Decembrio consequently adopted as his literary model.

The biography of Francesco Sforza lies at the opposite end of the spectrum to that of Filippo Maria in almost every respect. Here Decembrio had no insider's view of the action he set out to describe. He was neither a camp follower behind the Sforza entourage, nor was he one of those who rallied to the condottiere's cause late in the 1440s, as the struggle for the Milanese succession intensified. The latter course was the one chosen by many of Decembrio's closest friends, as well as not a few of his enemies, including his archrival and fellow humanist Francesco Filelfo (1398–1481).[8] Such men ended up coming to terms with Sforza and spent the decade following his installment as duke consolidating their own positions. Decembrio, on the other hand—as we have already seen—was abroad during the crucial period of the 1450s. While he made every effort to maintain his Milanese contacts, and even tried to be of service to the Sforza regime, he inevitably fell out of favor. More seriously still, the plan he hatched on returning to Milan in the late 1450s—to regain the lost ground by writing a biography of Francesco Sforza—was doomed from the start. His was not a biography commissioned by the regime,[9] and he was consequently given no access to written records or to sensitive documents. Instead, he had to rely on hearsay and on whatever oral sources of information he could scare up. Not surprisingly, the final product failed to satisfy those it had been so carefully crafted to please. It was riddled with too many omissions, too many egregious errors, to pass muster with the members of the new ruling elite.

Later readers too have judged the work severely, though for different reasons. The consensus view is that it lacks the crisp and brutal honesty of Decembrio's account of Filippo Maria Visconti.[10] It is certainly true to say that the life of Francesco Sforza suffers by comparison with the earlier biography. Yet it is also possible to question whether such a comparison is really fair, or at least whether it offers the only viable option for achieving an understanding of the work. An alternative is to accept that there are fundamental differences between Decembrio's two biographies and that they were produced at different times, under very different conditions and for very different purposes. Such an approach would imply treating the two works separately, paying particularly close attention to at least three main issues: the circumstances of composition, the classical models in play, and the critical response of the readership, both at the time and more recently. It is fortunately quite possible to mount a brief investigation of this kind, thanks in large part to the abundance of information contained in Decembrio's published and unpublished correspondence.

Filippo Maria Visconti

Decembrio's first and most important biography is also his most controversial one. Here, briefly, is a work ostensibly written to praise its subject yet also laced with its fair share of less than flattering commentary. Perhaps the most notorious instance comes in chapter 46, where Decembrio dwells at some length on Filippo Maria's penchant for surrounding himself with beautiful young boys, whose unique privilege it is to share the duke's most intimate moments. But other passages are equally telling. In chapter 63, for example, Decembrio discusses Filippo Maria's attitude toward the men of letters who graced his court. The best Decembrio can say on this point is that Filippo Maria neither held his literary men in contempt nor showered them with honors and rewards. Not a few modern critics have tended to see in such remarks a thinly veiled allusion to Decembrio's own frustrations at failing to secure what he regarded as an adequate level of patronage for his literary efforts.[11] By no means however are the negatives in Decembrio's portrait of the duke limited to these well-known examples. Throughout the biography—but particularly in the later chapters—Decembrio paints in vivid colors the picture of a man suffering from paranoia to the point of being quite literally fearful of his own shadow, prone to superstitions of the most bizarre kind, vindictive, hiding his true feelings from his closest collaborators, seeming to delight in playing cruel tricks on the weak and defenseless, shrinking from physical contact with other human beings, including most especially his own wife, living in almost total isolation from the outside world, in short, a physical and mental wreck of the most pathetic kind imaginable.

Various interpretations have been offered to explain the inconsistencies in Decembrio's portrayal of the duke. Perhaps none is more compelling that that devised by Decembrio himself, in his answer to a query from his very first reader, the highly cultivated Marquis of Ferrara, Leonello d'Este. Leonello's letter to Decembrio, written on October 22, 1447, makes it clear that Decembrio had sent his biography to the marquis in order to obtain his approval, prior to publication. The marquis responded with warm praise for the work yet also confided that he had serious misgivings about the contents of chapter 46, the one detailing Filippo Maria's indulgence in his taste for young boys. It was highly inadvisable, Leonello felt, to write such an explicit account of matters that were best passed over in silence. Decembrio would thus do well to suppress the chapter altogether, or at the very least to express his meaning in language so allusive as to become impenetrable. Leonello concluded by adding that, although contemporaries were already well aware of Filippo Maria's particular vice, this was no reason to pass that knowledge on to posterity.[12]

Decembrio responded to Leonello's letter on October 31. He began by expressing his pleasure at receiving such broadly favorable comments on his new work. He also professed himself glad to have Leonello's frank appraisal as to whether it was appropriate to canvass the issues covered in chapter 46. Decembrio then moved on to reassure Leonello on the key point: he wanted to dispel any impression he might have conveyed that his biography was meant to harm Duke Filippo Maria's reputation. On the contrary, its whole purpose was to praise and glorify the man to whom he felt he owed everything he had managed to achieve. "I loved that prince of mine," he wrote to Leonello, because "he took me under his wing from my earliest childhood; he provided me with the leisure and means to pursue my studies. . . . This is why I decided to write his biography . . . not . . . to cover my prince with opprobrium, but to spread his fame and glory."[13] The question remained however as to why, in a work ostensibly designed with such a clear encomiastic intent, Decembrio had dared to raise the curtain on Filippo Maria's secret vices. The answer had to do with the biographer's duty to maintain a semblance of devotion to historical truth. "Nothing is more reprehensible in a historian than lying," Decembrio wrote to Leonello. "My fear therefore was that if I failed to mention these notorious things you refer to, my account would lack credibility when it came to treat the areas where my prince was deserving of praise and commendation."[14] Decembrio was nevertheless ready to concede that while this argument might be valid in regard to contemporary readers, Leonello was right to be concerned about the advisability of passing such potentially damaging information on to posterity. Decembrio therefore announced that he would accede to Leonello's wishes and rewrite the offending passages. For the sake of contemporaries he would retain the contents of chapter 46, but at the same time he would compress their meaning so drastically as to make sure that the matters treated there were suggested rather than openly stated, thus protecting Filippo Maria's reputation in the eyes of the generations to come.

A subsequent letter from Leonello to Decembrio, written on August 19, 1448, proves that Decembrio kept his promise.[15] Chapter 46 as it stands today is undoubtedly the second version, revised to Leonello's satisfaction. But while the Leonello-Decembrio correspondence can be called into play to illuminate the issues surrounding chapter 46, it does not necessarily explain the more general problem: why are there so many other dark shadows marring Decembrio's portrait of a prince whose memory he intended to honor? If the whole purpose of the work was to erect a literary monument to the deceased duke, why cast aspersions of the kind one still finds so generously scattered throughout the text? The question is especially pertinent in the light of a further fact: Leonello was not the only early reader to detect a note of negativity in the biography. Decembrio's "warts and all" approach left him open to attack from his enemies. Francesco Filelfo, for example, a humanist in the service of Francesco Sforza, accused him of deliberately defaming the memory of Duke Filippo Maria.[16] The allegation stuck and was repeated by others. Down to the end of his life, Decembrio was frequently called upon to defend himself against those who felt he had betrayed his erstwhile patron by focusing on his vices rather than on his virtues. Decembrio's response to such slurs was consistent with what he had always maintained: his biography was meant as an act of homage, and this was how readers should perceive it. Thus in a letter of 1473 Decembrio observed that although he had so far published ninety-seven books, only his life of Filippo Maria Visconti had achieved universal notoriety: "everyone knows it, reads it, and commends it as portraying accurately the character and genius of that most worthy prince."[17]

Yet despite such efforts at clarification, the accusations did not go away. They received a sort of canonical formulation with Paolo Giovio in the following century[18] and have continued to condition modern critics. There is a lingering feeling that the negatives in Decembrio's portrait of the duke outweigh the positives. Some readers have suggested that this strong undercurrent of negativity may reflect the brief period of republican government that Milan experienced immediately following the death of Filippo Maria Visconti.[19] Filippo Maria had left behind no legitimate male heir. In the immediate aftermath of his demise (August 13, 1447), a group of Milanese patricians — all former associates of the Visconti regime — met to devise a new constitution for their city. Within a matter of days a republic was proclaimed and approved by popular acclamation. Because it was placed under the protection of Milan's patron saint, Ambrose of Milan, the newly minted polity subsequently came to be known as the Ambrosian Republic. Executive power was vested in twenty-four "Captains and Defenders of Liberty," elected on a rotating basis. While this supreme organ was a novel creation, other elements of the governing apparatus were either revitalized versions of existing Milanese communal institutions (such as the Council of the 900), or they were survivals of the Visconti ducal administration (e.g., the treasury officials, or *maestri delle entrate*).[20]

The Ambrosian Republic began life with high hopes, but circumstances militated against its long-term survival. These circumstances included most notably the ongoing war of aggression being waged against Milan by neighboring Venice, and the wily behavior of the generalissimo the new city government had hired to manage its defense, Francesco Sforza. In spite of such obstacles, the republic remained intact with varying fortunes for over two and a half years before finally ceding full powers to Sforza on February 26, 1450. But to return to the main point, how is Milan's republican interlude supposed to have affected Decembrio's portrait of Filippo Maria Visconti? The key lies in the chronological overlap: as we know from the correspondence with Leonello, Decembrio wrote his biography in the immediate aftermath of his master's death. Since it has traditionally been thought (rightly or wrongly) that the Ambrosian Republic was founded on a wave of popular animosity against the Visconti,[21] scholars have naturally been tempted to read the negatives in Decembrio's portrait of Filippo Maria as so many barbs directed against the last ruler of that house.[22] Viewed in this light, the Decembrio of 1447–48 becomes at one and the same time a denouncer of Visconti tyranny and an apologist for the nascent republic. But where does this leave Decembrio's protestations of loyalty to Filippo Maria in his letter to Leonello? Were such declarations a mere smokescreen? And if they were, why send the *Life* for perusal to another Renaissance prince like Leonello? And what about the many passages in the *Life* where Filippo Maria appears in heroic guise? In the early chapters Decembrio portrays the young Filippo as an energetic prince bent on reconstructing the duchy once ruled over by his father, Gian Galeazzo Visconti. A key passage lodges an exaggerated claim: that of all the Visconti rulers who preceded him, Filippo Maria alone was forced to acquire power through his own efforts (chap. 25). That he succeeded in his bid for supremacy is proof in Decembrio's eyes of the man's qualities. Moreover, once firmly in control of Milan itself, Filippo gradually and systematically unseats the various warlords who have abusively occupied the Lombard cities. He possesses the stuff of a true leader: Decembrio cites in particular Filippo's clemency in prosecuting war (chap. 31), his fame (32), and the care with which he manages affairs of state (33). More praise is showered on the man in later chapters: Decembrio highlights Filippo Maria's mild character, his kindness, his "greatness and generosity of spirit" (70), and the skillful way he is able to transform enemies into friends and supporters (45).

In my view the "republican" interpretation of Decembrio's biography is based on a highly selective reading of the text. A more balanced reading would easily yield a quite different picture, one more in conformity with the ideas expressed in the letter to Leonello;[23] in addition to which there are also Decembrio's personal inclinations to consider. Ever the staunch defender of princely government, he seems an unlikely candidate for a sudden swing to republicanism.[24] Indeed, the evidence suggests that his reactions in the weeks immediately following the death of Duke Filippo Maria were quite the opposite of republican grandstanding. News of the events of mid-August 1447 caught him entirely unawares. In fact, at the time, Decembrio was not in Milan at all but in Ferrara, where he was acting as one of Filippo Maria's chief negotiators at a general peace conference convened under the auspices of Pope Nicholas V. Contrary to what is often believed, Decembrio was not among the founders of the Ambrosian Republic and was not chosen as one of its initial leaders. In fact, his first reaction on hearing the news from Milan was to try to persuade the new republican government to persevere in the negotiations Filippo Maria had undertaken with the other Italian powers in Ferrara. When his advice was ignored, he was furious and wrote several letters expressing fierce criticism of the government's decision, even going so far as to accuse its leaders of blatant stupidity and inexperience in matters of statecraft.[25] While he hastened to patch over these early differences in a letter of September 7, offering to serve the new regime as faithfully as he had served under Filippo Maria, he did not begin his official period of service until nearly a year later, when he was appointed secretary of the Ambrosian Republic on September 1, 1448.[26] By this time, of course, he had already published his biography of Filippo Maria Visconti in its final version.

For all of these reasons, it seems unlikely that the darker shadows in Decembrio's treatment of Filippo Maria were fueled by anti-Visconti republican sentiment. Rather, it seems logical to give credence to Decembrio's claim that he wrote the work as a tribute, a reading that is consistent not only with his own declarations but also with what we know about his long career as a loyal servant to his former master. But why then include so many flaws in the portrait? More convincing than republicanism as an explanation are the circumstances of composition themselves, rooted as they are in the troubled months that followed the definitive demise of the Visconti ascendancy. While others were busy planning the future, Decembrio looked into the past: his life of Filippo Maria was also a meditation on an era that had just come to an end. With the duke now buried and his line extinct, the time was no longer ripe for the sorts of panegyrics that Visconti apologists had been churning out for decades.[27] Rather, what was required was a more honest account of the recent past, a reckoning up of the balance sheet that would stand as an accurate record of what had actually transpired at the very center of power.

The literary model Decembrio chose for this operation was a highly appropriate one: Suetonius's *Lives of the Caesars*. Decembrio himself had long been an admirer of Suetonius. As he made clear in an early letter to Cambio Zambeccari (1428/29), he believed that ancient biographers such as Suetonius and Plutarch provided the best guides as to how one should go about writing the lives of outstanding contemporary figures. Consistent with this position, Decembrio issued a scathing assessment of Guarino Veronese's recently published oration (1428) in praise of the mercenary captain Carmagnola. Although Guarino had promised to deliver a biography of his subject, wrote Decembrio, he had really served up little more than a list of abstract virtues. Where, he asked, was the information on Carmagnola's lineage, his paternal and maternal ancestors, his manner of speaking and behaving in the private sphere? Where were the anecdotes that would give the reader an insight into the military leader's true character? These were the staples of biographical writing as exemplified by Suetonius and Plutarch, and Guarino had clearly failed to respect them.[28] The subtext to be supplied here was that Decembrio himself *would* respect these ancient models in his own as-yet-to-be-written biographies. That he continued to be particularly taken with Suetonius is proved by an oft-cited passage in his *Zibaldone*, where he praised the Roman author's style and genius and proclaimed him to be the supreme practitioner of the art of biography.[29]

Decembrio's taste for Suetonian biography had strong roots in Visconti culture going back to Petrarch.[30] It also corresponded perfectly with the authoritarian style of princely government that prevailed in Milan. What could be more natural in such an environment than the tendency to see history as the story of all-powerful, larger-than-life political and military leaders? As Decembrio wrote in his biography (chap. 62), there was nothing Duke Filippo Maria himself enjoyed more than listening to readings relating the deeds of the great men of antiquity. The tastes of the duke, the court, and Milanese humanists such as Decembrio thus converged on the biographical mode of telling history as epitomized by the ancients, and especially by Suetonius. Out of this convergence came a major Milanese cultural project of the 1430s, sponsored by Filippo Maria, but apparently supervised by Decembrio himself: the translation into the vernacular not only of the lives of the Caesars by Suetonius but also of Quintus Curtius' *Historia Alexandri*, as well as of Julius Caesar's *Commentarii*. The latter two translations were both executed by Decembrio himself.[31] He prefaced his translation of Caesar's *De bello gallico* with a dedication to Filippo Maria, in which he reiterated his conviction that Caesar was indeed to be seen as the author of Books 1 to 7 of that work as well as of the *De bello civili*.[32] To his translation

of Curtius' *Historia Alexandri*, Decembrio added a little work of
his own, also addressed to Filippo Maria: a *Comparatione de Caio
Iulio Cesare imperadore maximo et d'Alexandro Magno*, where he ar-
gued strenuously—largely on the basis of Suetonius—that Caesar
should be seen as superior in every way to Alexander the Great.

As Massimo Zaggia has noted, the great translation project of
the 1430s illustrates the close ties that connected a certain type of
classical biography to the political ideology that was predominant
in Visconti Milan. This ideology often goes under the name of
"Caesarism," meaning a belief in the superiority of a political system based on strong leadership provided by an exceptional individual, whose abilities place him above the law. It was the *mise en
place* of just such a system that formed the subject of Suetonius's
early lives, particularly those of Julius Caesar and Augustus. Can it
be any wonder then that when Decembrio came to pen his tribute
to the recently deceased Filippo Maria he chose Suetonius as his
model and guide?

The full consequences of this choice need to be taken into account in any discussion of the shape the biography was finally to
assume. If Decembrio dwells on what seem to us trivialities, such
as Filippo Maria's eating habits—a feature of his biography that
has drawn severe censure—this reflects a concern with detail that
is typical of the Suetonian manner.[33] The same may be said of the
"balance-sheet" approach, which results in Decembrio giving full
coverage to the vices of his prince, as well as to his virtues. Suetonius himself never shrank from reporting on the sexual exploits of
his subjects, including the reputed homosexual adventures of the
young Julius Caesar (*Iul.* 49) or the long list of adulteries committed by Augustus (*Aug.* 69, 70, 71). Suetonius thought such information to be pertinent to the evaluation of a ruler's character. He
thus divided his biographies into two major sections: that concerning public life, and that concerning the private sphere. Decembrio adopted the same organizational principle.

Other aspects of Suetonian biography too are helpful in clarifying the character of Decembrio's life of Filippo Maria Visconti.[34] It is especially important to note that Suetonius did not write panegyric: his approach was a rigorously analytical one, based on weighing up the pros and the cons to achieve an overall assessment.[35] His ability to write with critical detachment was no doubt due to his belonging to a period somewhat removed in time from that of the emperors whose lives he chronicled. Decembrio enjoyed a similar immunity, given that he wrote after the demise of the Visconti line, and was thus able to indulge more freely on the negative side of the ledger than might otherwise have been possible. But the correspondence with Leonello d'Este suggests that denigration was no part of Decembrio's agenda. Rather, his failure to adhere to a strict code of panegyric was a matter of choice, dictated on the one hand by the times, and on the other by the Suetonian literary model that had received Filippo Maria's enthusiastic endorsement. By choosing the Suetonian form, Decembrio was thus able to perform an act of homage toward his former master, while at the same time legitimizing a discursive path that led almost inevitably to the same ambiguities, doubts, and shadows that characterized the imperial Roman portraits sketched by Suetonius himself.[36]

The Suetonian stamp on Decembrio's *Life of Filippo Maria Visconti* is perhaps most visible in the way the biographical material is distributed. In accordance with the model, there is no preface, and Decembrio's incipit rephrases the first sentence of Suetonius' *Augustus*. As in Suetonius, Decembrio's opening chapters (1–8) present an account of his subject's ancestry, parents, birth, infancy, and early years up to and including his seizure of power. At chapter 10 Decembrio changes tack: using words that echo those of Suetonius (*Aug.* 9), he announces that "having briefly reviewed" his prince's life to this point, he will next provide a summary of Filippo Maria's deeds. What follows is essentially a rapid review of Filippo's wars: first those fought against his internal enemies (chap. 11), then those aimed at recovering the territories and towns lost to his family's control after the death of his father, Gian Galeazzo (12–14), and finally the great wars of expansion and conquest that led to Milan's protracted state of conflict with rival Italian states, especially Florence and Venice (15–25). Chapters 11 to 25 of Decembrio's biography thus correspond to Suetonius, *Augustus* 10 to 23. The next chapters (26–37) discuss various topics: as in Suetonius, these cover military organization, the prince's style of leadership, his building projects, and other matters belonging to the public arena. At chapter 38 Decembrio makes another important thematic announcement, again couched in terms that clearly reflect the Suetonian precedent (*Aug.* 61). "Having thus far related what pertains to Filippo's actions in peace and war," Decembrio writes, "I will next proceed to tell of the inner man and to detail his private life." What we have here is the typical Suetonian turn toward coverage of the subject's most intimate doings. From this point on we are treated to a long series of chapters dealing with topics that will be familiar to any reader of Suetonius' *Lives of the Caesars:* these topics include marriages, sexual relations, children, household management, style of governance, jokes and sayings, games and pastimes, physical appearance, preferred clothing, eating habits, daily routine, general health and illnesses, tastes in literature, superstitions and fears, and signs and omens foretelling the subject's imminent death. At the end of the biography, Decembrio continues to follow Suetonian principles in describing in detail his prince's death, funeral, and burial, not forgetting to add a brief allusion to the events that ensued thereafter.

It would nevertheless be quite wrong to present the *Life of Filippo Maria Visconti* as a mere formal exercise: as a matter of one more humanist aping one more classical author. Decembrio's priority at all times is to render as accurate a picture as possible of his subject. Suetonius provides him with the template, but in the end much of the substance is his own. Numerous features could be cited to show how Decembrio's treatment diverges from that of his Roman predecessor, starting from the obvious point that Filippo Maria was no Roman emperor at all, but rather a Renaissance prince with a very different set of priorities and prerogatives. Decembrio correspondingly invests his protagonist with a sharp sense of political realism and endows him with the appropriate measure of cunning intelligence, cynicism, and lack of scruple. Qualities such as these, he seems to imply, are the necessary attributes required of a prince who hopes to survive in the turbulent world of fifteenth-century Italian politics. There are words of praise and admiration for the devious means Duke Filippo developed to test the loyalty of his dependents (chap. 41). "Never," Decembrio writes, did he dare "trust any of his people so completely that he forgot to distrust them even more" (28). Filippo accordingly devised elaborate ways and means of finding out "not just what each man was doing, but even what he was thinking" (34), all the while keeping his own thoughts entirely to himself (43). The duke's sphinx-like public demeanor is clearly a mask worn to deceive, but in Decembrio's eyes such deception is not a vice but rather a tool designed to maintain princely power. This realistic approach to politics stands in stark contrast to the more formalized lists of virtues and vices canvased by Suetonius,[37] although Decembrio can also occasionally deal in these as well (31).

Another major difference between the two authors is that Decembrio, unlike Suetonius, wrote on the basis of "autopsy," using in the main what he had been able to observe about his subject at firsthand. Again the contrast is striking, since Suetonius, writing about emperors who lived before his time, tended to work in bookish fashion, compiling what he had learned from his reading, and often citing his sources verbatim.[38] The result is a strong divergence in the respective modes of presentation. Drawing mainly on his personal experience, Decembrio seldom if ever relies on citation from written sources. When he quotes the words of Filippo Maria, they are words he has actually heard spoken.[39] When he describes his former master pacing up and down in the palace followed by his dog (chap. 53), he conveys a picture of something actually seen, and seen time and time again.

The value of Decembrio's biography ultimately lies neither in its imitation of Suetonius nor in its supposed articulation of any precise ideological position. It lies rather in the work's transparency as a record of things lived and experienced. Filtered though they may be through the lens of Suetonianism, Decembrio's pictures of life at the Visconti court leave us with the impression that he has drawn a brutally honest portrayal of a Renaissance prince in action. At times Filippo's behavior verges on the tyrannical, as in his treatment (including torture) of political prisoners. The man has a warped sense of humor, and his conduct of affairs is to all appearances erratic and unpredictable. With rare exceptions he successfully manages to hide his inner feelings from even his closest collaborators: he veils his plans in secrecy and deliberately keeps everyone guessing as to his true intentions.[40] But in Decembrio's portrait one senses too the presence of an underlying coherence: there is method in the prince's apparent madness. At a deeper level Filippo's very inscrutability is a strategy bent on instilling a kind of Hobbesian awe in friend and foe alike. The man's primary aim is simply to maintain his state; and to do so in this particular environment he knows he must rule by fear.

Moving from chapter to chapter, but especially from chapter 26 onward, Decembrio gradually reveals the various technologies of power that his prince deploys to this end: he details the vast network of informers that kept Filippo up to date with everything that was happening throughout the city (chap. 55); he describes the techniques of surveillance that operated within the court itself, the protocols, the rules and regulations that governed access to the prince's person (41 and 47); above all, as we have already noted, he stresses the shroud of secrecy that surrounded sensitive areas of policy development. In presenting such material to the reader, Decembrio neither condemns nor condones; he simply describes. The tone is matter-of-fact: this is how it was. What we are left with is an absolutely unique view of what was going on behind the scenes in one of Renaissance Italy's most brilliant courts. Decembrio's biography lifts the veil, so to speak, and shows us the naked reality of princely power at its most arbitrary and uncompromising. To tell the truth, we are thematically not far here from Machiavelli's *Prince*, the classic treatise that was to be penned over half a century later, in 1513.[41] If Machiavelli was to present the theory, Decembrio had already made manifest the reality of Renaissance *Realpolitik*. This is why even a twentieth-century student of politics like Elias Canetti could still find in *The Life of Filippo Maria Visconti* a rich source of inspiration.[42]

Francesco Sforza

The coming to power of Francesco Sforza in early 1450 was by all accounts a highly significant event. In Milan, it settled the question of the succession that had been open since the death of Duke Filippo Maria Visconti. As such, it also spelled the end of the ill-fated Ambrosian Republic. Not long after its inception, in fact, the republic had entered troubled waters. Pressed by its enemies on all sides, riven by party strife, and with dwindling financial resources to draw on, the government had lurched from crisis to crisis. Not least among its worries was the behavior of Francesco Sforza himself. Originally captain general of the republic, Sforza had from the beginning made his intentions quite clear: he aimed at nothing less than to assume total control of the duchy. In part, his claim to power rested on his skill at arms, and thus on his being Milan's only hope of keeping its enemies, mainly Venice, permanently at bay. In part too, Sforza's claim rested on his marriage to Bianca Maria Visconti, Filippo Maria's daughter and only surviving child. Neither argument was sufficient to convince the leaders of the Ambrosian Republic, and so began a long duel of wits, which the republic was doomed to lose. Sforza indeed did not hesitate, at the opportune moment, to betray his masters and to place himself and his forces at the service of the Venetians (Treaty of Rivoltella, October 18, 1448), hoping thereby to gain a significant advantage. When the Milanese, in desperation, tried to outmaneuver him by making their own peace with Venice (September 24, 1449), Sforza reacted by mobilizing his armies in a siege action that eventually succeeded in starving the city of Milan into submission.

Francesco Sforza's takeover of Milan has often been characterized as a conquest. Yet it was conquest not by main force, but by attrition. Working patiently over a period of two and a half years, Sforza and his collaborators gradually drew the net around their objective. They used every opportunity to undermine the republic, shutting down its alternatives one by one, until only one solution remained open. In the end, while military operations had their role to play, the final settlement had as much to do with accommodation as with force. The dire straits to which the city had been reduced by early 1450 gave the elements favorable to Sforza the leverage they needed to deliver him power. But it was power negotiated rather than power seized. The conditions agreed between the condottiere and the delegation of eminent Milanese citizens who met with him between February and March 1450 contained some significant concessions. These included the acknowledgment on Sforza's part of many of the institutional arrangements that had prevailed under the Visconti. What this meant in practice was a high degree of continuity with previous city traditions, a feature that suited the condottiere as much as it suited the Milanese. Sforza was in fact banking on his credentials as the logical successor to the Visconti—through his marriage, but also through appealing to a dubious "testament" supposedly left behind by Filippo Maria—in order to gain acceptance as the new ruler of Milan. As a further concession, Sforza also guaranteed a certain continuity of personnel: those prominent citizens who had supported his takeover of the city were to be rewarded with positions of honor, if not necessarily of real power.[43]

As we already know, Pier Candido Decembrio was not among those who received this preferential treatment. He opted instead to leave Milan, slipping quietly out of the city early in 1450, probably well before Francesco Sforza's official installation as duke on March 22, 1450.[44] The reasons for this departure have been variously interpreted. They have sometimes been mythologized into the republican narrative alluded to earlier: on this reading Decembrio left Milan because he preferred exile to servitude under a new prince. The problem with this hypothesis is that there is a distinct lack of credible evidence to back it up.[45] More likely explanations can be gleaned from other sources, including Decembrio's own correspondence. A letter of November 17, 1449, for example, shows how desperate he had become to flee his homeland. By this time the situation in Milan had deteriorated beyond repair, chaos reigned supreme, and starvation and misery were rampant. Decembrio must have felt trapped. He thus wrote to his contact in Ferrara, Ludovico Casella, soliciting his aid in finding a new position in a suitably equipped Italian court.[46] In actual fact, Decembrio had prospects in several locations.[47] Is it any wonder that he subsequently chose to take up an offer at the Roman curia, where his old friend and fellow humanist Tommaso Parentucelli now reigned as Pope Nicholas V?

The appointment in Rome did not mean that Decembrio cut off all contact with his homeland. On the contrary, the evidence shows that he cultivated ties with the leading members of the Sforza regime, most particularly with the powerful head of the Sforza chancery, Cicco Simonetta. The letters exchanged were cordial and continued throughout the 1450s. They show Decembrio doing his best to make himself useful to the new masters of Milan, particularly as a conduit of information about what was going on behind the scenes in both Rome and Naples. His reports were appreciated.[48] He also undertook missions to Milan on behalf of Nicholas V, suggesting that he retained his credibility as a valid channel of communication between the pope and Francesco Sforza. Thanks to this diplomatic activity, Decembrio managed to spend significant periods of time in his home city. In a letter addressed to the pope from Milan on February 22, 1452, he expressed his joy at finding his house and library intact after an absence of two years.[49] This must have come as a great relief given the circumstances that had prevailed at his departure.

While there were frequent visits and professed attachment on Decembrio's side, there was nevertheless a certain reticence on the part of the new regime to accept him back into the fold. This alone can explain Decembrio's decade of wandering: his absence from Milan was to last until the end of 1459. Even then he failed to secure a position for himself. The Sforza held him at arm's length: why? The answer can be found by examining more closely the latter stages of Decembrio's period of service (September 1, 1448–early 1450) as secretary to the Ambrosian Republic. It should be stressed that Decembrio's sin was not one of simple involvement; plenty of those who had played leading roles in Milan's experiment with self-government made a smooth transition into the Sforza apparatus.[50] If Decembrio's case was different, this was owing to a certain number of specifics. In order to grasp these, one needs to return once again to consider the events that unfolded after the death of Filippo Maria Visconti and the proclamation of Milanese self-rule in August 1447.

The demise of the Visconti line had as one of its consequences the dismemberment of the duchy over which the princely family had long ruled. A number of major Lombard cities used this golden opportunity to reclaim their status as independent self-governing units, very much along the lines followed by Milan itself. Among these was the important center of Pavia. Other places, including Lodi, Piacenza, and Parma, declared their adherence to the Venetians, whose armies continued to press forward into Lombardy. Threatened with extinction, the Milanese hired the condottiere Francesco Sforza as commander of their military forces. Over the next year or so, Sforza's successes in the field became the stuff of legend. But his motivations were suspect: was he fighting to defend Milan, or to further his own claim to become the successor to the Visconti dominions? The answer became clear on October 18, 1448, when it was announced that he had entered into an alliance with Venice. He was now turning his troops around to attack his former employers and make himself the lord and master of Milan.

The news undermined the authority of the Milanese government, which up to this time had been dominated by a membership largely selected from the most prominent families. A revolution in governing personnel ensued at the beginning of the following year as popular elements took charge and initiated a campaign of violent recriminations against the patricians, a number of whom were suspected of plotting to turn the city over to Francesco Sforza. Arrests and executions followed, ushering in what is usually referred to as the radical phase of the republic's history. Hostility to Francesco Sforza ran high in this period, and the new government spared no effort to hunt down and prosecute those Milanese citizens who favored him.[51] A search was also on to recruit military support for the war effort to come. Facing the combined might of Sforza and Venice, the Milanese authorities naturally turned for help anywhere they thought it might be found. Letters went out to Pope Nicholas V, to Emperor Frederick III, to the king of France, to the dauphin, to the Duke of Savoy, to Alfonso of Naples, to Charles (Duke of Orléans). Along with appeals for help, these letters portrayed Francesco Sforza as a traitor, as a disturber of the peace, and as a scoundrel whose only aspiration was to establish tyranny over Milan.[52]

At this point we need to remember that Pier Candido Decembrio was at this very time serving as secretary to the Milanese government. He had, in other words, continued to serve in this capacity under the radical, anti-Sforza regime that took control at the beginning of 1449. It was indeed none other than Decembrio who penned the letters mentioned above: letters intended to destroy Francesco Sforza's reputation. Unfortunately, these same letters, duly countersigned by Decembrio, subsequently fell into the hands of Sforza agents. In the Sforza camp, Decembrio's name henceforth became associated with the most intractable elements within the Milanese populace, those "Guelfs" who remained to the end adamantly opposed to a Sforza takeover of their city. Whether such an association was legitimate can be questioned. To what extent did Decembrio share the views of the extremists, to what extent was he simply acting as a loyal civil servant who continued to perform his secretarial duties? But ultimately Decembrio's deeper convictions are not really the issue here. What counts is the impact his political involvement at this stage had on perceptions within the Sforza circle. There are signs that the animosity sparked by his actions was not only keenly felt at the time but continued to boil away long after the events. Years later the incident of the intercepted letters was considered important enough to figure prominently in the official account of Sforza's career written by his secretary Giovanni Simonetta, showing that it had still not been forgotten even in the 1470s.[53]

Decembrio's continued performance of his secretarial duties under the radical government that took charge in 1449 would in itself provide a sufficient explanation for his status as persona non grata after the Sforza takeover. Consider too that he had continued to serve while the radicals were engaging in their campaign of violence against the wealthier citizens, many of whom were imprisoned, exiled, and in some cases executed. A number of these persecuted "Ghibellines" did indeed favor the Sforza cause, or soon came to. After 1450 it was easy enough for the Sforza camp to distinguish between those Milanese citizens who had sided with them in 1449 and those who had not. There can be little doubt that Decembrio fell into this second category.

An inkling of how Decembrio was viewed in Sforza circles in the early 1450s can be gleaned from the writings of Francesco Filelfo. True, the famed Hellenist had been Decembrio's archenemy since arriving at the Visconti court in 1439. Throughout the 1440s, theirs had been a battle for supremacy between the two dominant humanists resident in Milan, one homegrown, the other a product of Renaissance cosmopolitanism. In contrast to Decembrio, Filelfo had navigated the turbulent years of the Ambrosian Republic with skill, keeping his options open and cultivating to the extent possible all parties, including those who leaned toward the Sforza solution. After 1450 he became the leading humanist at the Sforza court. While his writings may not have shaped, or even influenced, opinion, they probably retailed — with due allowance for humanist bombast and exaggeration — something akin to a commonly held set of prejudices.

Of particular interest in the present context is the way Filelfo portrays Decembrio, especially the Decembrio whose actions during the crucial years of the republic were already notorious. An eloquent example can be found in the *Odae* (3.4), where he describes Decembrio as "a man polluted by a thousand vices."[54] According to Filelfo, Decembrio was guilty of the most heinous crimes. It was Decembrio who in 1449 had urged the plebeian rabble to track down and massacre dozens of honorable men. It was Decembrio who was responsible for the mass starvation that had eventually set in and caused misery that was only alleviated by the timely arrival of the city's savior, Francesco Sforza. Such a

portrait is clearly out of all proportion to what is known of Decembrio's role in these events. Yet it also corresponds in its broad
outlines to a general impression that has not subsided to this day:
the impression that Decembrio can be classified as one of the most
fanatical leaders of the Ambrosian Republic, a sort of Robespierre
more than ready to resort to extreme measures in the service of the
republican cause.

Even more serious allegations were yet to come. Throughout
the 1450s, Filelfo was at work on his magnum opus, an epic poem
known as the *Sphortias*. The work purported to chronicle the
events of 1447 to 1450. The first four books were completed and
circulated by 1456. They contained a passage (4.15–50) relating
events that supposedly followed Sforza's taking of Piacenza in
November/December 1447. According to Filelfo, a meeting of the
Milanese citizenry ensued, in which Decembrio harangued the
crowd. Filelfo's summary of the speech has Decembrio branding
Francesco Sforza as Milan's most treacherous enemy because the
faithless condottiere shows all the signs of fighting not for his employers but for his own aggrandizement. Filelfo then has Decembrio counsel that Milan's best option is to make a separate and
secret peace deal with Venice. Only by implementing such a plan
will the city fathers manage to defend themselves against their
headstrong generalissimo. To keep faith with him would be to
nourish a serpent in their midst.[55]

It would of course be a mistake to take Filelfo's account as anything like an accurate picture of Decembrio's activities during the
crucial years of the Ambrosian Republic. It is all too clear that
long-standing enmity heavily conditioned Filelfo's portrait of his
hated former rival. But again the question of accuracy is not para-
mount here. What really counts is that such allegations were being
put about unchallenged in the 1450s. Nor were they being put
about by just anyone, but by the man who had become the court
poet and historian of the Sforza. High-profile works like the

Sphortias and the *Odae* not only enjoyed official backing and patronage, they were addressed directly to the leadership of the regime and were deliberately crafted to meet the tastes of its members.[56] The conclusion seems inescapable: the prevailing view in Sforza circles after 1450 was that Decembrio had taken a hard line, anti-Sforza stance after Rivoltella (October 18, 1448) and that he had subsequently done everything in his power to prevent a Sforza occupation of Milan. Quite beyond Filelfo's ravings, there was evidence for this view in the intercepted letters of March 1449, which we have seen were later cited by Sforza's official historian, Giovanni Simonetta. So it becomes quite understandable why, when he returned to Milan at the end of the 1450s, Decembrio faced a steep uphill battle to regain favor.

The composition of a biography of Francesco Sforza was clearly a major plank in Decembrio's push to obtain pardon and reinstatement. But the idea was not simply to please the new duke of Milan. The work had a more subtle purpose, which had to do with rehabilitating Decembrio's image in the eyes of the new rulers of the duchy. The biography was meant to show the extent to which the former adversary from the latter days of the Ambrosian Republic had come to his senses, changed his spots, and embraced the new status quo. This operation involved some acrobatics. Fortunately, the biography offered Decembrio the opportunity to rewrite the history of the fateful years, 1447 to 1450. A significant proportion of the work (chaps. 31–39) is dedicated to the coverage of these three years alone. Not surprisingly perhaps, Decembrio never mentions his role as secretary and loyal servant of the Ambrosian Republic. Instead, he uses the opportunity to condemn the bloodthirsty rampage of the populist government of 1449. He justifies Francesco Sforza's separate peace with Venice as an act of mercy toward Milan (chap. 35), thus distancing himself from what was widely perceived to have been his earlier view: that the Sforza-

Venice alliance signed at Rivoltella represented nothing less than an open betrayal. Of course, he avoids mentioning his authorship of the letters of March 1449 inviting foreign powers to rush to Milan's aid against Sforza. In fact, he does not mention the matter at all, except to condone the prevailing official Sforza policy of the day, that foreign (especially French) military aid is both unreliable and dangerous (37).

This rewrite of recent history then was no simple panegyric; it was intended to correct perceptions about Decembrio's own political convictions and actions during the crucial years that preceded the Sforza takeover of Milan. Perhaps the most eloquent example of this concerns the question of Sforza's claim to be seen as the legitimate heir to the Visconti dominions. One of the chief arguments advanced by the regime in support of this claim was Francesco Sforza's marriage to Filippo Maria Visconti's only daughter and heir, Bianca Maria. It was by virtue of this marriage that Sforza was supposed to have initially acquired the right to accede to the Visconti dominions. But Decembrio, in the final chapter of his biography of Filippo Maria, had correctly pointed out the inconvenient fact that Bianca Maria had never been made heir to the duchy (chap. 71). He had even gone so far as to validate the rumor that Filippo Maria had made out a last will and testament in favor of King Alfonso of Naples. Such a position, publicly stated and circulated in 1448, was clearly anathema to Sforza. It played directly into the hands of his enemies, since it was tantamount to delegitimizing his every action in the period 1447 to 1450. Only if one were to accept that Sforza was fighting for what was his by right of his marriage was it possible to justify his betrayal of the Ambrosian Republic in October 1448 and his final campaign against Milan itself. In his biography of Francesco Sforza, Decembrio accordingly made haste to revise his previous position: his systematic justification of Sforza's actions required that he adopt the official line on the issue of legitimate succession, whether true or not. Decembrio's Sforza biography thus repeatedly and explicitly states that Francesco Sforza was — in 1447 to 1450 — motivated only by the desire to obtain what was rightfully his by virtue of his marriage to Filippo Maria Visconti's nominated heir, Bianca Maria. Indeed, Decembrio goes even further by implying that Filippo Maria originally fostered the marriage as a way of ensuring a smooth transition of the duchy to his son-in-law Francesco Sforza (chaps. 14, 19, 31, 35).

As it pertained to his own actions during the republican period, Decembrio could not stretch the truth too far. He could hardly portray himself as having been a Sforza partisan, even when he came to narrating the events of the crucial years, 1449 to 1450. He thus places other protagonists in the forefront of the pro-Sforza groundswell (chap. 38), maintaining on the whole a discreet silence as to his own activities. There is, however, one point at which Decembrio manages to polish up his own image and make it more palatable to the new masters of Milan. This is where he relates how in the summer of 1449 the Ambrosian Republic, in despair at its prospects of survival, decides to send an envoy to the imperial court in order to negotiate the submission of the city to the Holy Roman Empire (37). The government's idea is that placing the city under imperial protection will enable it to fend off its powerful enemies, namely Francesco Sforza and the Venetians. Decembrio himself is chosen as the Milanese envoy to the emperor, but he refuses to accept the commission, on the grounds that he does not wish "to become the instrument whereby the ducal title would be returned to the empire." Decembrio then reminds his readers that it was his own father, Uberto Decembrio, who had initially helped secure the imperial investiture for Gian Galeazzo Visconti in 1395.

Here Decembrio manages to chalk up a number of points in his favor. The incident, if it really happened, would suggest that Decembrio—whatever his personal political orientation in the summer of 1449—remained adamantly opposed to the idea that Milan might be reclaimed by the empire, a plan that was actually being floated at the time by imperial agents such as Enea Silvio Piccolomini.[57] The episode would also serve to remind the post-1450 regime—then heavily engaged in secret negotiations to obtain the imperial investiture for Francesco Sforza—that the name Decembrio was forever associated with the initial obtaining of the ducal title for the Visconti. If Pier Candido Decembrio, according to his own account, had refused to carry out the proposed mission, this was because, as the son of Uberto Decembrio, he was congenitally unable to do so. Perhaps too, Pier Candido hoped thereby to make the Sforza leadership see that he might well be of service in their own ongoing efforts to secure the coveted title.

There is indeed a broader sense in which Decembrio's biography of Francesco Sforza can be read. In its general thrust, the work reproduces a set of arguments identical to those being compiled by the regime to justify its seizure of power. Alongside the considerable diplomatic efforts being made in the 1450s, the production of historical accounts of recent events had an important role to play, since historical narrative could cogently present the rationale behind Sforza rule in Milan. Historical narrative could, for example, by recapitulating Francesco Sforza's career in arms, document his skills as both soldier and statesman. The point was not simply to praise the man but to show why he and he alone deserved to become the successor to the Visconti. To this end historical narrative could stress the marriage tie to Bianca Maria. More important still, it could extol Sforza's campaigns to keep the Duchy of Milan intact. Without the condottiere's efforts, according to this logic, the lands once ruled by the Visconti would have been in danger of complete disintegration (read: they would have been gobbled up by Milan's aggressive neighbors Venice and Savoy). Through historical narrative, Francesco Sforza could truly be shown to have saved the duchy from total annihilation at the hands of its enemies.

During the 1450s such arguments were being pitched to the imperial court in the hopes that they might convince the emperor to invest Francesco Sforza with the ducal title. The granting of the title would provide the ultimate seal of approval in support of Sforza's right to rule. Negotiations at the imperial level, however, did not achieve the desired result, leaving the regime open to accusations of illegitimate seizure of power. It was the absence of the imperial sanction that led the regime to focus more heavily on the production and dissemination of historical accounts geared to convince public opinion of the righteousness of the Sforza cause. The same arguments that were being formulated in the negotiations with the emperor could be repackaged and circulated more widely in the form of historical narrative. Thus codified, they constituted an arsenal of persuasive weapons that could be drawn on wherever and whenever the legitimacy of the Sforza regime was questioned.[58]

The man initially tasked with producing an official Sforza history of the kind required was none other than Decembrio's old rival and nemesis, Francesco Filelfo. Filelfo's brief included the composition not only of the aforementioned epic poem *Sphortias* but also that of a history in prose of much broader scope. Where the *Sphortias* was meant to focus on the decisive three-year period (1447–50) that saw Francesco Sforza conquer Milan, the projected history was meant to chronicle all of Sforza's deeds from his earliest beginnings. But while Filelfo made steady progress with his epic poem, his efforts in history had, by the time Decembrio returned to Milan at the end of the 1450s, yielded next to nothing.[59]

Decembrio must surely have been aware of his rival's failure to produce the desired Sforza history. One has only to look at his correspondence of the early 1460s. Several of his letters are addressed to members of the Sforza inner circle. In a number of these, alongside the announcement that he has taken it upon himself to write a biography of the man who now rules Milan, Decembrio indulges his taste for polemics. In a letter of 1461 to Mattia Triviano, he notes that Francesco Sforza has long wished to see written a proper history of his deeds. But unfortunately (continues Decembrio) those tasked with the job, having promised much, have failed to come up with the goods. All their boasting and bravura have served only to highlight their inadequacy. Now the modest and unassuming Decembrio is about to achieve what these cosseted, officially commissioned hacks have failed to achieve: a fully-fledged Sforza history written in the high-flown Latinate style of the humanists.[60] The reference to Filelfo remains implicit here, but Decembrio makes it explicit later on in the postscriptum to a letter sent to the Sforza ambassador in Florence, Nicodemo Tranchedini. In conveying to Tranchedini the news that he has written his own biography of Francesco Sforza, Decembrio underlines the fact that Filelfo, despite being on the payroll, has neither written, nor will ever write, such a work: he is too busy gorging himself on the nectar of court life.[61]

Decembrio's intention then was to preempt his rival by furnishing the regime with the history it had hoped to conjure out of its wayward court poet. Significantly, Decembrio's biography begins by dismissing Filelfo's recently published *Sphortias* as wholly inadequate to the task at hand: what good can come of "some silly little verses"? Only a prose history can satisfy the demands of the moment, and this history is what Decembrio has set himself to deliver (chap. 3). But are we dealing here with a history or with a biography of Sforza? In truth, the distinction between the two genres does not seem to have been so clear-cut to Decembrio himself, or to his contemporaries. In his correspondence, Decembrio refers to his work on Sforza as a biography (*vita*), yet it clearly represents a type of biography that verges on history. Unlike the

Visconti biography, with its deeply Suetonian imprint, the Sforza work eschews the description of the prince's private life, to focus instead on his deeds, or *res gestae* (see chap. 1, "The Preface of Pier Candido"). The title itself indicates this: *A Record of the Deeds of Francesco Sforza*. The overall organization is chronological, rather than — as in the *Life of Filippo Maria Visconti* — thematic. Comparison of these two works by Decembrio shows that nascent humanist biography was malleable enough to allow for a wide degree of adaptation to particular circumstances. With the Sforza biography, Decembrio clearly hoped to supply the regime with what it had long sought to obtain: a suitable apology (couched in the appropriate humanist style) for its occupation of Milan. This explains why this biography veers so sharply toward history, and why it differs so dramatically in character from the Suetonian format familiar to readers of the biography of Filippo Maria Visconti.

Pier Candido Decembrio

Decembrio's Sforza project reached fruition in 1462 with the submission of the completed manuscript to the first secretary of the Sforza chancery, Cicco Simonetta. The exchange of letters between the two was cordial in tone, and Cicco offered some hope that Decembrio's efforts would be crowned with success.[62] But it was not to be. There followed an ominous silence. The following year brought a hammer blow in the form of a lengthy "review" of Decembrio's biography written by yet another important Sforza official, Vincenzo Amidano. Amidano meticulously and mercilessly pounced on what he and no doubt other members of the inner circle saw as serious flaws in the work: its omissions, its faux pas, its blatant errors of fact and judgment.[63] Wounded to the core, Decembrio responded a week later. Pleading his innocence and good intentions, he stressed that he had done his very best despite a distinct lack of support and guidance from the leadership of the regime. How indeed could he have done better, he wrote, given that his frequent requests for clarification on difficult points of interpretation had all been met with evasive silence?[64]

Such excuses were of course not likely to wash. By 1463 the regime had already turned to other means of generating the desired official history. The Filelfo protégé and chancery employee Lodrisio Crivelli had been designated to supply what his master had failed to deliver.[65] And when Crivelli fell out of favor in the following year, the history project devolved to Cicco Simonetta's brother Giovanni, also employed in the chancery. The project, in other words, had been internalized. It was to be Simonetta's task, working from documents housed in the chancery archives, to compile the long, detailed account of Francesco Sforza's career that had been foreshadowed since the Sforza seizure of power in 1450. The *Rerum gestarum Francisci Sfortiae commentarii*, Simonetta's signature work, was completed by the mid-1470s and eventually published early in 1482.[66] As for Decembrio's Sforza biography, it was quietly shelved and largely forgotten until its rediscovery in the eighteenth century, when it was enshrined along with the *Life of Filippo Maria Visconti* in Ludovico Antonio Muratori's multivolume *Rerum italicarum scriptores*.

And Decembrio himself? After the exchange of letters with Amidano, he made a few more feeble attempts to curry favor with the Sforza. But he must soon have realized that his chances of returning to his pre-1450 glory days were next to nil. This hard lesson learned, he began yet another round of searching for a position elsewhere. Feelers went out in all directions, wherever there was some hope that his high reputation as a humanist might secure some advantage. As we already know, one of his best contacts happened to be in Ferrara, where he had close ties with the prominent humanist and secretary Ludovico Casella. There was some delay, but by the beginning of 1467 Decembrio's pleas for assistance had finally been answered.[67] He therefore settled his affairs in Milan and decamped to the court of the Este, where he became a revered and respected figure. His gratitude knew no bounds. Typically, he gave it expression in yet another princely biography, a life of Ercole d'Este, written after the latter's elevation as Duke of Ferrara in 1471.[68]

Decembrio nevertheless returned to Milan as a private citizen late in life and died there in 1477. His body was placed in the sarcophagus that still stands at the entryway to the Church of Sant'Ambrogio. There one can read his funerary inscription, with its declaration that he was the esteemed author of no less than 127 books.[69] Today, most of his works have long since been forgotten, many justifiably, others much less so. It is to be hoped that the two biographies here published, the first an undisputed masterpiece, the second of interest for other reasons, will go some way toward rekindling interest in one of humanism's lesser-known major figures. Perhaps the final word on Decembrio's status as a humanist should be left to his lifelong friend and comrade in arms Lorenzo Valla: "There is no man of letters that I would rate higher than you," Valla wrote to Decembrio in the early 1440s, "and no friend of mine that I hold dearer. . . . I have yet to publish a book, nor shall I ever, without your prior seal of approval."[70]

NOTES

1. Lorenzo Valla, De vero falsoque bono, ed. Maristella De Panizza Lorch (Bari, 1970), 3: "Candidus December, qui dubito an principi propter fidem et industriam sit gratior an populo propter humanitatem et mores iucundior."

2. Decembrio was the second son of the prominent Lombard humanist Uberto Decembrio (d. 1427) and the elder brother of the author of the Politia litteraria, Angelo Decembrio. The best general overview of all three members of the family can be found in DBI 33:483–503. Pier Candido is perhaps most often remembered today for his Panegyric in Praise of Milan (on which see Petraglione, "Il De laudibus"; Lentzen, "Die Rivalität") as

well as for having produced and circulated the first translation of Plato's *Republic* to appear in the Latin West (Zaggia, "La versione latina"; *I Decembrio*). For his career as a Visconti political operative, see Gabotto, "L'attività politica"; Borsa, "Pier Candido." (Full references to sources cited briefly in this Introduction can be found either in the Bibliography or in the Abbreviations at the beginning of the Notes to the Translations.)

3. Filippo Maria Visconti, the second son of Duke Gian Galeazzo Visconti (1351–1402), ruled Milan for over thirty-five years, from June 1412 down to his death in August 1447: see *DBI* 47:772–82; Cognasso, *Il ducato*.

4. Jacob Burckhardt, *The Civilization of the Renaissance in Italy*, trans. Samuel G. C. Middlemore (New York and Toronto, 1960), 242. Burckhardt's thumbnail sketch of Filippo Maria Visconti, ibid., 63, is entirely dependent on Decembrio's biography.

5. On Sforza, see the convenient summary in *DBI* 50:1–15.

6. Zaccaria, "Sulle opere," 38–41, describes the circumstances of composition.

7. Decembrio himself makes this point in a letter of June 30, 1468, addressed to Ludovico Casella; see Genoa, Biblioteca Universitaria, MS C.VII.46, fol. 118r: "Philippi enim Marie olim heri mei vitam sic scripsi ut gnarus eorum que videram maiore ex parte" (Indeed years ago I wrote a biography of my lord and master Filippo Maria Visconti, fully informed as I was for having witnessed with my own eyes most of what I was describing). On the authoritative character of the Genoa manuscript, one of several containing Decembrio's voluminous correspondence, see Zaccaria, "L'epistolario," 97–98.

8. On Filelfo, see *DBI* 47:613–26. Daniela Gionta, "Tra Filelfo e Pier Candido Decembrio," in *I Decembrio*, 341–401, details his rivalry with Decembrio. Filelfo's most important Sforza writings are now available in Jeroen De Keyser, *Francesco Filelfo and Francesco Sforza* (Hildesheim-Zurich-New York, 2015).

9. Writing to Francesco Sforza's personal physician Guido Parato on February 8, 1462, Decembrio noted that he had undertaken to produce a

biography of the duke on his own initiative, unprompted by the promise of any pecuniary reward ("nullo premio ductus"): Genoa, Biblioteca Universitaria, MS C.VII.46, fols. 67r–67v. Zaccaria, "Sulle opere," 39, cites from this letter, but with a misattribution as to the addressee caused by overreliance on a faulty Milanese manuscript, i.e., Milan, Biblioteca Ambrosiana, I 235 inf., fol. 80v.

10. See, for example, the introductory remarks in Pier Candido Decembrio, *Leben des Filippo Maria Visconti und Taten des Francesco Sforza*, trans. Philipp Funk (Jena, 1913), liv–lvi; Ditt, "Pier Candido Decembrio," 67–68; Eric Cochrane, *Historians and Historiography in the Italian Renaissance* (Chicago and London, 1981), 113; *DBI* 33:494.

11. See, for example, Felice Fossati's lengthy commentary on this particular passage in Decembrio, *Vita Philippi Mariae*, 333–46.

12. Genoa, Biblioteca Universitaria, MS C.VII.46, fol. 6v. The full text of the letter, with English translation, is reproduced in this volume as Appendix, letter I.

13. Genoa, Biblioteca Universitaria, MS C.VII.46, fols. 6v–7r: "Amavi principem illum, qui me a pueritia aluit, qui studiorum quietem et modum mihi adhibuit. . . . Ob id vitam eius scribere institui, absolvique, ut vides. . . . Non enim ita edideram, ut infamiam pareret principi meo, sed laudem potius et gloriam." For the entire letter, see Appendix, letter II.

14. Ibid.: "Nihil in historico mendacio est turpius. Timui igitur si que notiora fuerant omitterem, minus fidei promererer in his que laudem et commendationem merebantur."

15. Genoa, Biblioteca Universitaria, MS C.VII.46, fol. 32r; Appendix, letter III.

16. See Francesco Filelfo, *Sphortias*, bk. 4, ll. 23–29, in De Keyser, *Francesco Filelfo*, 77.

17. Letter addressed to Nicodemo Tranchedini, May 24, 1473: see Marcello Simonetta, *Rinascimento segreto: Il mondo del segretario da Petrarca a Machiavelli* (Milan, 2004), 48 n. 44.

18. Paolo Giovio, *Vitae duodecim Vicecomitum Mediolani principum* (Paris, 1549), 186; Paolo Giovio, *Gli elogi degli uomini illustri*, ed. Renzo Meregazzi

(Rome, 1972), 50. On these works by Giovio, see T. C. Price Zimmermann, *Paolo Giovio: The Historian and the Crisis of Sixteenth-century Italy* (Princeton, NJ, 1995), 206–8, 224.

19. Federica Cengarle, *Immagine di potere e prassi di governo: La politica feudale di Filippo Maria Visconti* (Rome, 2006), 91 n. 6.

20. Current work on the Ambrosian Republic is largely indebted to a seminal two-part study by Marina Spinelli, "Ricerche per una nuova storia della Repubblica Ambrosiana," *Nuova rivista storica* 70 (1986): 231–52; and *Nuova rivista storica* 71 (1987): 27–48. Recent contributions include Beatrice Del Bo, *Banca e politica a Milano a metà del Quattrocento* (Roma, 2010), 63–94; and Patrick Boucheron, "Les combattants d'Ambroise: Commémorations et luttes politiques à la fin du Moyen Âge," in *La mémoire d'Ambroise de Milan: Usages politiques d'une autorité patristique en Italie*, ed. Patrick Boucheron and Stéphane Gioanni (Rome, 2015), 483–98.

21. For the traditional view that the Milanese populace was animated by "powerful resentment against signorial government," see Lauro Martines, *Power and Imagination: City-States in Renaissance Italy* (New York, 1980), 140–48, at 141. But as Spinelli points out, such views find no confirmation in the surviving documentation: "Ricerche," 244 n. 52.

22. Besides Cengarle, *Immagine di potere*, recent examples include Simonetta, *Rinascimento segreto*, 140; and Carol Everhart Quillen, "Humanism and the Lure of Antiquity," in *Italy in the Age of the Renaissance*, ed. John M. Najemy (Oxford, 2004), 37–58, at 50.

23. For examples of such a reading, see Philipp Funk's introduction to *Leben des Filippo Maria Visconti*, especially the remarks on p. liv; Zappa, "La Vita di Filippo Maria Visconti"; Viti, "Decembrio," 494.

24. A point made by Borsa, "Pier Candido," 369; and reiterated by Eugenio Garin, "La cultura Milanese nella prima metà del XV secolo," in *Storia di Milano* (Milan, 1955), 6:546–608, at 604–8.

25. See especially Borsa, "Pier Candido," 358–60, 429–31. Borsa publishes a letter of August 23, 1447, where Decembrio warns the new government against negotiating directly with Venice. The Venetians, he writes, "are ready to take full advantage of your inexperience" (Quaerunt enim omni celeritate . . . vos tamquam inexpertos per timorem inducere ad ligas).

"Or," he says provocatively, "are you so stupid as to think that they desire
to preserve your freedom?" (An ita insipientes eritis ut credatis eos cupere libertatem vestram?). A subsequent letter of August 29 is harsher
still: see Genoa, Biblioteca Universitaria, MS C.VII.46, fols. 11v–12r,
where Decembrio expresses his dismay at the Milanese government's
naiveté (*simplicitas*) and ignorance (*ignorantia*) in giving in to the Venetian
blandishments.

26. Borsa, "Pier Candido," 361–64, 432–33.

27. Among such panegyrics one can list various orations by Antonio
da Rho. See David Rutherford, "A Finding List of Antonio da Rho's
Works," *Italia medioevale e umanistica* 30 (1990): 75–108, at 96. Several of
Rho's unpublished orations are cited in Fossati's notes to Decembrio, *Vita
Philippi Mariae*, 141, 146, 202, 258, 282, 409–10. Also belonging to the
genre is an *Orazione di Francesco Filelfo in lode di Filippo Maria Visconti*, ed.
Giovanni Benadduci (Tolentino, 1898).

28. Battistella, "Una lettera inedita," 120–34, publishes the full text of
Decembrio's letter to Zambeccari. See especially 122: "nam si (Guarinus)
paternum genus ac maternum vel avitum paulo altius repetendo retulisset, qualesque in familiari sermone, inter domesticos denique illius mores
fuerint explicuisset, tum de vita ab eo recte distinctum esse concederem,
ut familiaris mihi Suetonius ac Plutarchus de illustribus viris scriptita-
runt" (now if Guarino had gone a bit further back into Carmagnola's
family history, informing us from what stock his parents sprang, if he
had provided some snippets of the man's daily conversations, and detailed his private life, then I would concede that his work might be called
a biography. Such indeed were the methods adopted by my own favorites, Suetonius and Plutarch, in writing the lives of great men). Guarino's
oration in praise of Carmagnola is published in Antonio Battistella, *Il
conte Carmagnola* (Genoa, 1889), 511–19. See in general Giuliana Crevatin,
"La *virtus* del condottiero tra retorica e romanzo," in *Federico di Montefeltro: La cultura*, ed. Giorgio Cerboni Baiardi, Giorgio Chittolini, and Piero
Floriani (Rome, 1986), 417–39.

29. Zaggia, "Appunti," 193.

30. Petrarch was resident at the Visconti court for eight years, from 1353 to 1361. On his importance in shaping Milanese literary culture, see Garin, "La cultura Milanese," 547–56; and Zaggia, "Linee," 8–20. Regarding Petrarch's fascination with Suetonius, see Guido Martellotti, *Scritti petrarcheschi*, ed. Michele Feo and Silvia Rizzo (Padua, 1983), 23, 484, 552–54; and Monica Berté, *Petrarca lettore di Svetonio* (Messina, 2011).

31. Zaggia, "Appunti," 189–205, 321–28. For further details see Ponzù Donato, "Il *Bellum Alexandrinum*," and Schadee, "The First Vernacular Caesar."

32. Decembrio had already correctly established Caesar's authorship in a letter of 1423 to Bartolomeo Capra: see Petrucci, *Petri Candidi*, 73–82.

33. Fossati, in his commentary to Decembrio, *Vita Philippi Mariae*, 334, takes Decembrio to task over his meticulous description (chap. 52) of the duke's culinary likes and dislikes. But see Suetonius, *Augustus* 76.

34. My coverage of Suetonian biography relies largely on the classic study of Andrew Wallace-Hadrill, *Suetonius: The Scholar and His Caesars* (London, 1983). Useful recent additions to the literature include Tomas Hägg, *The Art of Biography in Antiquity* (Cambridge, 2012), 214–34; and *Suetonius the Biographer: Studies in Roman Lives*, ed. Tristan Power and Roy K. Gibson (Oxford, 2014).

35. Wallace-Hadrill, *Suetonius*, 23–24, 142; G. B. Townend, "Suetonius and His Influence," in *Latin Biography*, ed. T. A. Dorey (London, 1967), 79–111, at 81–82.

36. Ditt, "Pier Candido Decembrio," 68, attempts to resolve the contradictions in Decembrio's portrait by claiming that he wrote the first third of the biography while Filippo Maria was still in power and the second two-thirds after the latter's death, but he presents no evidence to support this claim.

37. On which see Wallace-Hadrill, *Suetonius*, 142–74.

38. For some eloquent examples, see Alcide Macé, *Essai sur Suétone* (Paris, 1900), 117–27, 357–78.

39. See, for example, chapters 27, 41, 42, 55, 65, 67.

xlvii

40. See chapters 42 (political prisoners), 44 (warped sense of humor), 62 (erratic behavior), 43 (secrecy).

41. On this point in general, see Riccardo Fubini, *Politica e pensiero politico nell'Italia del Rinascimento* (Florence, 2009), 273–89.

42. Elias Canetti, *Crowds and Power*, trans. Carol Stewart (New York, 1973), 341, 557, 565.

43. On many of the points raised here, the bibliography is large: see, for example, Francesco Cognasso, "La Repubblica di S. Ambrogio," in *Storia di Milano* (Milan, 1955), 6:386–448; Franco Catalano, "La nuova signoria: Francesco Sforza," in *Storia di Milano* (Milan, 1956), 7:3–81; Martines, *Power and Imagination*, 143–47; Riccardo Fubini, *Italia quattrocentesca: Politica e diplomazia nell'età di Lorenzo il Magnifico* (Milan, 1994), 107–35; Franca Leverotti, *Diplomazia e governo dello stato: I 'famigli cavalcanti' di Francesco Sforza* (Pisa, 1992), 57–70; Maria Nadia Covini, *L'esercito del duca: Organizzazione militare e istituzioni al tempo degli Sforza* (Rome, 1998), 54–74; Jane Black, "Double Duchy: The Sforza Dukes and the Other Lombard Title," in *Europa e Italia: Studi in onore di Giorgio Chittolini* (Florence, 2011), 15–27.

44. A letter of Francesco Filelfo dated February 4, 1450, suggests that Decembrio was still in Milan at that time: see Franceso Filelfo, *Collected Letters: Epistolarum libri XLVIII*, ed. Jeroen De Keyser, 4 vols. (Alessandria, 2016), 1:375–76.

45. A letter of Francesco Barbaro to Decembrio dated April 30, 1453, testifies as to the latter's bona fide republican credentials, but the Venetian Barbaro appears to be putting words into Decembrio's mouth; Decembrio's response is characteristically evasive: see *Francisci Barbari . . . Epistolae*, ed. A. M. Quirini (Brescia, 1743), 315–17. In evaluating Barbaro's letter one must also bear in mind that in 1453 Venice was at war with Milan in an effort to unseat Francesco Sforza: see the comments of Gabotto, "L'attività politica," 260. The last twenty-five words of Decembrio's *Life of Filippo Maria Visconti* (chap. 71) have sometimes been read as a celebration of the nascent Ambrosian Republic; to my ear this famous passage does not sound like anything more than a simple statement of

fact. It seems in any case a very narrow basis indeed on which to build a theory of Decembrio's republicanism.

46. On Casella, secretary to Leonello d'Este and later to Borso d'Este, see *DBI* 21:310–12. Decembrio's letter can be found in Genoa, Biblioteca Universitaria, MS C.VII. 46, fol. 41r: "Fides tua et probitas, vir magnifice, et erga bonos affectio tuae caritatis me hortantur ut indubiam de te spem suscipiam. E contra negociorum multitudo et herilium curarum pondus addubitare cogunt, ne quoniam absens ex animo tuo excidam. Precor igitur ut ex solita virtute, pietate, humanitate, Candidi tui memor sis, eumque si potis est, ex his fluctibus in portum revehas tranquillitatis" (Your loyalty and probity, excellent man, and the affectionate esteem you show toward honest men, urge me to place high hopes in you. On the other hand the many tasks you face, and the weight of the responsibilities you carry, cause me to wonder whether my absence does not cause you to forget my plight. And so I beseech you, in the name of your accustomed goodness, compassion, and generosity, do not forget your devoted friend Pier Candido, and if possible, pull him from these troubled waters and convey him to some safe haven of tranquility). See Borsa, "Pier Candido," 372. Borsa, 434–36, also publishes a letter of the same year containing a similar appeal for help addressed to Federico da Montefeltro, Lord of Urbino.

47. Besides Ferrara and Urbino, Decembrio's options included Naples and Rome: see Borsa, "Pier Candido," 362, 375, 433.

48. Gabotto, "L'attività politica," 247–48, 251, 260–61, 268–69; Simonetta, *Rinascimento segreto*, 140–45. Both authors have published additional material documenting Decembrio's post-1450 correspondence with Sforza officialdom: see Ferdinando Gabotto, "Un nuovo contributo alla storia dell'umanesimo ligure," *Atti della Società Ligure di Storia Patria* 24 (1892): 1–331, at 29–30; Simonetta, "Esilio, astuzia e silenzio," 96–107.

49. Genoa, Biblioteca Universitaria, MS C.VII. 46, fol. 26v: "Deo duce et sanctitatis tue benedictione, iter meum tute emensus sum. Nam et Mediolanum incolumis applicui et domum intactam, libros integros reperi" (With God as my guide and the blessing of your Holiness, my

journey has been a safe one. I have reached Milan unharmed and found my house undisturbed and my library untouched).

50. Examples include such promoters of the Ambrosian Republic as Oldrado Lampugnani (d. 1460) and Guarnerio Castiglioni (d. 1460). For their respective career trajectories, which spanned with relative ease the Visconti, republican, and Sforza periods, see *DBI* 63:280–83, and *DBI* 22:161–66. A further example of such dexterity is provided by the figure of Pietro Pusterla: see Leverotti, *Diplomazia e governo*, 226–28.

51. The list of those arrested in 1449 included Giorgio Lampugnani and Teodoro Bossi. Both men were tortured, convicted of treason, and sentenced to death. Lampugnani was executed; Bossi's sentence was commuted to life imprisonment. He died a few months later. See, respectively, *DBI* 63:271–72 and *DBI* 13:338–39.

52. See Cognasso, "La Repubblica di S. Ambrogio," 425. W. Forghieri, "P. C. Decembrio e Francesco Sforza," *Archivio storico lombardo* 61 (1934): 648–50, publishes the letter to the dauphin. The letter, dated March 24, 1449, describes Francesco Sforza as "levis homo, dominandi cupidine inflatus" (a man of no weight, puffed up with desire for domination). It warns the dauphin not to be taken in by the lies: "viri nec aliud affectantis quam tyrannidem et oppressionem urbis nostre" (of a man whose aim is nothing else but to tyrannize and oppress our city).

53. Simonetta, 258. Simonetta specifically mentions Decembrio as the author of the defamatory letters: "Petro Candido viglebiense dictante."

54. Francesco Filelfo, *Odes*, ed. and trans. Diana Robin (Cambridge, MA, 2009), 179–85.

55. De Keyser, *Francesco Filelfo*, 77–78.

56. See most recently Jeroen De Keyser, "Picturing the Perfect Patron? Francesco Filelfo's Image of Francesco Sforza," in *Portraying the Prince in the Renaissance: The Humanist Depiction of Rulers in Historiographical and Biographical Texts*, ed. Patrick Baker, Ronny Kaiser, Maike Priesterjahn, and Johannes Helmrath (Berlin, 2016), 391–414.

57. Fabio Cusin, "Le aspirazioni straniere sul ducato di Milano e l'investitura imperiale (1450–1454)," *Archivio storico lombardo* 63 (1936): 277–369, at 308–17.

58. Fabio Cusin, "L'impero e la successione degli Sforza ai Visconti," *Archivio storico lombardo* 63 (1936): 3–116; Gary Ianziti, *Humanistic Historiography under the Sforzas: Politics and Propaganda in Fifteenth-century Milan* (Oxford, 1988); Covini, *L'esercito del duca*, 161–72; Silvia Fiaschi, "La cattedra, la corte e l'archivio: Umanesimo e produzione storiografica tra Milano e Pavia nel 400," in *Almum Studium Papiense: Storia dell'Università di Pavia*, ed. Dario Mantovani (Milan, 2012), 1.1:743–60; Maria Nadia Covini, "La fortuna e i fatti dei condottieri 'con veritate, ordine e bono inchiostro narrati': Antonio Minuti e Giovanni Simonetta," in *Medioevo dei poteri: Studi di storia per Giorgio Chittolini*, ed. Maria Nadia Covini, Massimo Della Misericordia, Andrea Gamberini, Francesco Somaini (Rome, 2012), 215–44.

59. For references to the Sforza history project, see Filelfo, *Collected Letters*, 2:522, 533–34, 541–42. Filelfo's last reference to the project comes in a letter addressed to Piero de'Medici (May 17, 1455) published in Carlo de'Rosmini, *Vita di Francesco Filelfo da Tolentino*, 3 vols. (Milan, 1808), 2:324–26.

60. Genoa, Biblioteca Universitaria, MS C.VII.46, fol. 67r: "Iam tandem venerabilem patrem, fratrem Joachinum nostrum certum reddere potes, me vitam principis nostri diu ab illo exoptatam, suo ordine, claro et puro stilo, nec a veritate ulla ex parte abhorrente, descripsisse, quod a nemine hucusque factum legi, quamquam nonnulli multa polliciti, sive impotentia deterriti, sive ignavia desierint ab incepto ut aiunt magnarum rerum. Ego vero qui pusillus sum, et ingenio et doctrina, nec tam magna polliceri soleo, gaudeo me consecutum esse parvitate mea quod illi sua magniloquentia et hiatu oris nequiverunt. Vale." (At last you may inform the venerable father, our Fra Gioacchino, that I have written our prince's biography, a work he has long desired, and I have written it according to his wishes, in a clear and pure style that in no way deviates from the truth. This is something that up to now, according to what I have read, no one else has succeeded in doing, though some have, after making big promises, soon given up on such a daunting task, deterred by their own inability, or by sheer laziness. But as for me, recognizing the limits of my intellectual gifts and learning, and thus unaccustomed to making such big promises, I am glad to have achieved with my modest means what

others, with all their boasting and bombast, have been entirely incapable of achieving. Farewell). Borsa, "Pier Candido," 441, publishes this letter from the defective manuscript, Milan, Biblioteca Ambrosiana, I 235 inf., fol. 80v. His translation of the letter, 402–3, contains a serious mistake as to the addressee. On Mattia Triviano, see Edoardo Fumagalli, "Per la biografia di Mattia Triviano, precettore di Galeazzo Maria Sforza," *Aevum* 70 (1996): 351–70. On the influential ecclesiastic "Joachinus" (Gioacchino Castiglioni), see Edoardo Fumagalli, "Francesco Sforza e i domenicani Gioacchino Castiglioni e Girolamo Visconti," *Archivium Fratrum Predicatorum* 56 (1986): 79–152.

61. Genoa, Biblioteca Universitaria, MS C.VII.46, fol. 67v: "Scripsi vitam huius principis nostri ab origine usque ad pacem ultimo cum Venetis factam, summa brevitate et veritate, annorum seriem imitatus, quod te latere nolim. Hoc nec Philhelcus (sic) tuus adhuc fecit, nec faciet aut facturus est, quia tamen mero huius aule se ingurgitat" (Here's some news for you: I have written a biography of our prince, a concise and accurate account that moves in chronological order from his birth down to the peace he recently concluded with the Venetians. Now there's something that your Filelfo has neither done, nor is about to do, nor indeed is ever likely do in the future, because he prefers to spend his time guzzling up the undiluted wine served at court). The letter is dated from Milan, March 29, 1462.

62. Zaccaria, "Sulle opere," 39–40.

63. Amidano's letter can be found in Genoa, Biblioteca Universitaria, MS C.VII.46, fols. 82v–83v. It is dated October 15, 1463. On Amidano (d. 1475), see *DBI* 2:792, and especially Leverotti, *Diplomazia e governo*, 113–14.

64. Genoa, Biblioteca Universitaria, MS C.VII.46, fols. 81v–82v. Decembrio's letter is dated October 22, 1463: Fossati publishes it in the preface to Decembrio, *Annotatio rerum gestarum in vita Illustrissimi Francisci Sfortie*, XIII.

65. On Crivelli, see *DBI* 31:146–52; and Leverotti, *Diplomazia e governo*, 154–57.

66. For the exact date of publication (January 23, 1482), see Gary Ianziti, "Storici, mandanti, materiali nella Milano sforzesca, 1450–1480," in *Il principe e la storia*, ed. Tina Matarrese and Cristina Montagnani (Novara, 2005), 465–85, at 466 n. 6.

67. On the details of these arrangements, see Borsa, "Pier Candido," 407–10.

68. On Decembrio's *Vita Herculis Estensis*, see Zaccaria, "Sulle opere," 42–43.

69. Zaccaria, "Sulle opere," manages to compile a list of some 120 "books" (as opposed to "works") by Decembrio, showing that the claim was no idle boast from beyond the grave. But studies such as that of Kristeller, "Pier Candido Decembrio," suggest that too often such productivity was purchased at the price of relying on hasty compilation.

70. Lorenzo Valla, *Correspondence*, ed. and trans. Brendan Cook, I Tatti Renaissance Library 60 (Cambridge, MA, 2013), 126: "Nam ut et sentio et sepe in cetu hominum dixi, nemo litteratorum est quem tibi anteponeam, nemo amicorum meorum quem non tibi posthabeam. Itaque unius tuo iudicio atque consilio contentum me esse existimabam ac fore existimo; nondum enim opus edidi neque edam, nisi arbitratu tuo." On the close relationship between Decembrio and Valla, see Riccardo Fubini, *Umanesimo e secolarizzazione da Petrarca a Valla* (Rome, 1990), 103–7, and Riccardo Fubini, *L'umanesimo italiano e i suoi storici* (Milan, 2001), 320.

LIVES OF THE
MILANESE TYRANTS

VITA PHILIPPI MARIAE
TERTII LIGURUM DUCIS

: I :

De origine Vicecomitum et viris ex ea illustribus.

Vicecomitum originem antiquam sane et praeclaram extitisse multi prodidere. Nomen autem sumpsisse putatur ab Angleriae comitibus, quibus a Federico expulsis, Vicecomites eorum loco dicti sunt. Procedente vero tempore etiam comites se appellarunt. Qui primus ex ea familia nomen meruit, Ubertus Vicecomes, Ottonem et Eriprandum filios genuit, quamquam nonnulli Eriprandum non Uberti filium fuisse memorent, sed illustrem parta victoria, ex qua viperae insigne retulit. Otto Mediolanensis Ecclesiae praesul electus, cum Turrianam factionem per vim expulisset, auctor suis in primis fuit adipiscendi principatus. Huius frater Oppizo, et ab eo Tebaldus genitus dicitur. Matheus Tebaldi filius Vercellas ac Novariam urbes a Libycis et Vocuntiis conditas, ut Plinius existimat, subegit; Novum praeterea Comum, quae Lario lacui magna ex parte sita est, adeptus urbem; ab Arnulfo Romanorum rege vicarius electus, principatu abdicatur.

THE LIFE OF FILIPPO MARIA
THIRD DUKE OF LOMBARDY[1]

∴ I ∴

The origins of the Visconti and their illustrious forebears.

Many writers have recorded that the origins of the Visconti were quite ancient and distinguished. It is thought however that the family derived its name from the counts of Angera.[2] When Frederick Barbarossa deposed these counts (*Comites*), their successors came to be called Visconti (*Vicecomites*). With the passage of time these Visconti too assumed the title of counts. The first member of the family to win a name for himself, Uberto Visconti, had two sons, Ottone and Eriprando, although several sources report that Eriprando was not Uberto's son at all, but a famous warrior whose victories earned him the right to bear the coat of arms depicting the viper.[3] Ottone was chosen archbishop of Milan. He used force to drive out the Della Torre faction, and then proceeded to establish Visconti supremacy.[4] Ottone had a brother named Obizzo, and this brother's son is said to have been Tebaldo. Tebaldo's son was Matteo. Matteo conquered Vercelli and Novara, cities that according to Pliny were founded respectively by the Libicii and by the Vocontii. Matteo also seized Como, a city located for the most part along the shores of Lake Larius. Appointed imperial vicar by Arnulf, king of the Romans, Matteo later abdicated.[5]

: 2 :

De maioribus Philippi Marie.

Maiores Philippi deinceps a Matheo editi: Matheum filii quinque secuti sunt, Galeaz, Iohannes, Luchinus, Stephanus ac Marcus. Galeaz a Placentinis evocatus, pulso Alberto e Scotorum familia, Placentiam possedit urbem. Idem militia insignem Azonem reliquit filium, qui primus Mediolanensis dominatus fundamenta iecisse creditur. Extant adhuc aetate nostra pleraque non ineptae elegantiae aedificia ab eo condita, ut ex portae Ticinensis menibus et Abiatis arce coniectari licet. Hic Pergamum ac Cremonam urbes maiorum suorum adiecit imperio. Luchinus deinde. Post Iohannes presulatu insignis Italiam fere omnem, et in hac Brixiam, Parmam, Bononiam et in primis Genuam, clarissimam cunctarum urbem, tenuit. Stephanus, Philippi proavus, Galeaz Bernabove et Matheo filiis superstitibus, decessit.

: 3 :

De Galeaz Philippi avo.

Galeaz, Philippi avus, vir gloriae appetentissimus, Papiam urbem bello subegit, veterem Logumbardorum regum sedem. Hic Carolum Galliae regem e captivitate ingenti pretio redemit, quo natam eius Iohanni Galeaz filio suo in matrimonium daret. Aedificandi autem sumptuositate adeo excelluit, ut non immerito a quibusdam

: 2 :

Filippo Maria's ancestors.

Filippo Maria's ancestors sprang in turn from this Matteo, who had five sons: Galeazzo, Giovanni, Luchino, Stefano, and Marco. Galeazzo was called to Piacenza, drove out Alberto Scotti, and took possession of that city. He left behind a son, Azzone, who was an outstanding soldier and is commonly credited with having first laid the foundations for his family's absolute rule over Milan. There are still extant in our own day a number of rather elegant buildings erected by Azzone, as can be gathered by examining the walls of Porta Ticinese and the Castle of Abbiategrasso. Azzone added Bergamo and Cremona to the Visconti dominions.[6] After him came Luchino, then the famous archbishop Giovanni, who held sway over practically the whole of Italy, including Brescia, Parma, Bologna, and above all Genoa, that most renowned of all cities. Stefano, Filippo Maria's great-grandfather, died leaving behind three sons: Galeazzo II, Bernabò, and Matteo.

: 3 :

Filippo Maria's grandfather Galeazzo II.

Filippo Maria's grandfather Galeazzo II, a man most eager to win glory, conquered Pavia, the ancient capital of the Lombard kings. He paid a huge ransom to free King Charles of France from captivity, in order to secure the marriage of the king's daughter to his son Gian Galeazzo.[7] His extravagance in building was such that I think certain writers were correct in saying that while he stood

scriptum existimem hunc, cum omnes aetatis suae virtute anteiret, se ipsum aedificandi magnificentia longe superasse. Conditae enim ab eo insignes arces visuntur aetate nostra in Ticini urbe et Mediolanensi; quamquam Mediolanenses post Philippi obitum arcem eam, quae Portae Iovis appellabatur, diruerint funditus.

<h2 style="text-align:center">: 4 :</h2>

<h3 style="text-align:center">De Iohanne Galeaz Philippi patre.</h3>

Iohannes Galeaz Philippi pater, cum adolescens adhuc esset, Helisabet Gallorum regis filiam duxit uxorem, ex qua Azonem aliosque filios genuit. Postmodum ea defuncta, cum nemo ex natis, filia excepta, superstes extitisset, veritus ne a patruelibus suis per vim opprimeretur, sumpta in uxorem Caterina Bernabovis filia, socerum subinde astu cepit, translataque in se potestate omni, primus Vicecomitum Mediolanensium dux creatus est. Hic fines imperii sui ad Adriaticum usque mare propagavit. Nam Veronam, Vicentiam, Paduam ceterasque urbes finitimas tenuit; in Tuscia vero Pisas, Senas, Perusium; tantique fuit apud exteros nomen eius, ut Soldanus Arabum rex basilicam ab eo aedificari concesserit in Iherosolomitana urbe. Ab hoc Iohannes et Philippus Maria geniti sunt. Iohannes cum parum prudenti consilio uteretur, suorum conspiratione oppressus interiit.

head and shoulders above all others of his age in sheer ability, he outdid even himself in the magnificence of his building projects.[8] The remarkable castles he constructed in Pavia and Milan are still admired in our own day, even though the Milanese completely destroyed the castle known by the name of Porta Giovia after the death of Filippo Maria.[9]

: 4 :

Filippo Maria's father Gian Galeazzo.

Filippo Maria's father Gian Galeazzo, while still an adolescent, married Elisabeth, daughter of the king of France.[10] From her he fathered Azzone and several other sons. After Elisabeth died, and seeing that none of their children, except for one daughter, had survived, Gian Galeazzo began to fear that he might be over-powered by the clan of his uncle Bernabò. So he took Caterina, Bernabò's daughter, as a wife, and then captured his father-in-law by trickery. He next concentrated all power in his own hands, and became the first of the Visconti to be made Duke of Milan.[11] Gian Galeazzo extended his dominions as far as the Adriatic Sea. For he held Verona, Vicenza, Padua, and other adjacent cities; in Tuscany too he held Pisa, Siena, and Perugia; such indeed was his reputation abroad that the Sultan, king of the Arabs, allowed him to build a church in the city of Jerusalem.[12] Gian Galeazzo had two sons: Giovanni and Filippo Maria. Giovanni failed to govern with prudence, was overthrown by a palace conspiracy, and perished.

: 5 :

De nativitate Philippi Marie et eius nutrimentis.

Hactenus Vicecomitum familia celebris et ad summum perducta columen substitit quinto ac vicesimo super centesimum quo ceperat anno, finemque propagandi imperii sui ulterius fecit. Philippus Maria natus est nono Kalendas Octobris, die lunae, post exortum solis per horam minutis amplius sex, anno Domini millesimo trecentesimo nonagesimo secundo, in ea arcis parte, quae Mediolanensi urbe occiduum solem spectat; in qua postea Iohannes Antonius Brixiensis habitavit, summo in honore habitus apud eum. Nutrimentorum eius locus Papiae magna ex parte fuisse ostenditur in arce avita; licet peregrinationis ociandique causa in oppidis finitimis plerumque diverteret, ut Laudem et Sanctum Angelum usque mandato patris.

: 6 :

De patris iudicio et astronomorum ab infantia eius.

Cum infans adhuc esset, adeo ingenii sui vim atque indolem ostendit, ut pater eum Iohanni Mariae natu maiori in successione praeponere optaret. Nempe cum ad eum salutandi gratia aliquando accessisset, pauloque ante abiisset Iohannes e conspectu patris, oculis in eum coniectis, aliquantulum siluisse, deinde dixisse fertur: mirari se eorum consuetudinem, qui filios natu maiores in principatu praeficerent quasi digniores; sibi enim condecentius

: 5 :

The birth of Filippo Maria and his upbringing.

One hundred and twenty-five years into its rule, the fabled Visconti family reached the peak of its power and brought its drive
toward further territorial aggrandizement to an end.[13] Filippo
Maria was born on the twenty-third of September, a Monday, at
more than six minutes into the hour after sunrise, in the year of
our Lord 1392, in the wing of the castle that from Milan looks toward the setting sun;[14] here in later years Giovanni Antonio of
Brescia would take up residence, he being a man Filippo Maria
held in high esteem.[15] Filippo was mostly brought up in the family's castle in Pavia, though he also had occasion to frequent nearby
towns in his wanderings, and sometimes went as far as Lodi and
Sant'Angelo Lodigiano, in accordance with his father's wishes.

: 6 :

*What Gian Galeazzo and his astrologers thought of
Filippo Maria.*

While still only a child Filippo Maria showed such strength of
character that his father wished to place him ahead of his older
brother Giovanni Maria in the line of succession. And once when
Filippo had gone to greet his father, and Giovanni had just left,
the duke gazed at the youngster in silence for a moment, and is
then reported to have expressed his wonderment at the practice of
according priority in princely succession to the eldest son, as if being first born were a guarantee of superiority; his own view was

videri, si ex omnibus ingenio virtuteque praestantis eligerent. Qua ex voce satis quid de eo conciperet, ostendit. Astronomi etiam, qui ea tempestate Papiae degebant, saepenumero prodidere eum, si ad aetatem summam pervenisset, totius familiae suae gloriam longe antecessurum. Ducebatur autem loro vinctus fibula a tergo reiecta quemadmodum circophetici solent, ne improvide concideret, trepidus ne titubaret. Qua ex re creditum est eum stirpis sue novissimum et veluti postremum futurum principem.

: 7 :

De primo dominatu eiusdem.

Nundum decenis patrem amisit; sortitusque Papiam ac Veronam testamento eius, cum frater Mediolani ducatum suscepisset, Papiae substitit, Comes declaratus; nec ulli deinceps maiori negocio sese exercuit, venationi dumtaxat et ocio indulgens. Mansitque per novem fere annos eodem statu; donec urbe a Facino capta, etiam sumissius degere coactus est, ut ex inopia geminatos anulos e paterno fisco eruerit; contemptior in dies et abiectior, ut saepe solus urbem vagaretur exercitareturque privatorum more.

that it would make more sense to choose the most able and talented of one's sons to be next in line. This pronouncement shows clearly enough what grandiose plans the duke had in mind for Filippo Maria. The astrologers at the court in Pavia too consistently predicted that the child, should he live into adulthood, was destined to surpass by far the glory of his forebears. But he used to be led around on a leash, which was fastened by a clasp to his back, as is done with circus monkeys, the idea being to prevent him from stumbling and tottering about in a state of trepidation. Because of this practice it was believed that the child was destined to be the last of his line and would bring the princely House of Visconti to an end.

: 7 :

His beginnings as a ruler.

Filippo lost his father when he was not yet ten years old. His part of the inheritance by his father's will included Pavia and Verona, while his brother took over the Duchy of Milan. Filippo Maria lived in Pavia as its titular count, but he did little more in this role than give himself over to hunting and leisurely pursuits. He continued in this way for nearly nine years, until Facino Cane captured the city.[16] At that point Filippo was forced to live in more straitened circumstances, reaching such a state of indigence that he was reduced to pilfering a pair of precious rings from his father's treasury. He subsequently became increasingly impoverished and unkempt, often wandering about the city alone and conducting his affairs like any other private individual.

: 8 :

De adeptione ducatus Mediolanensis per Philippum.

Iohanne Maria fratre defuncto, cum Facinus paulo post excessisset e vita, Iohannes Carolus una cum Hestore Mediolanum occuparunt. Erat autem Hestor Bernabovis filius, Iohannes nepos. Destitutus itaque omni spe, et quid ageret incertus, suadentibus amicis, Beatricem antea Facino nuptam sumpsit uxorem, quamquam aetate imparem nec satis congruentem claritati suae ob maiorum stirpem. Eius igitur opibus adiutus, non Papiam modo, sed Terdonam, Alexandriam, Novariam aliaque oppida sibi adiunxit. Inde Mediolanum admotis copiis, decimoseptimo Kalendas Iunias haud longe ab urbe metatus est, demumque per arcem excurrit armatus, sexto ac decimo Kalendas Iulias, in solemni die Iulitae martiris, cum vigesimum nundum attigisset annum, cunctorumque assensione dux appellatur: quem diem deinde quotannis celebrem ac solemnem haberi voluit.

: 9 :

De Philippi moribus in initio principatus.

Urbe adepta, nihil antiquius habuit, quam principis more cunctorum se votis mitem exhibere. Itaque aditus ad illum libere patebat omnibus. Deinde paulo post secessit e turba maioribus rebus in-

: 8 :

Filippo Maria obtains the Duchy of Milan.

The death of Filippo's brother Giovanni Maria, followed shortly thereafter by the death of Facino Cane,[17] allowed Giovanni Carlo and Estorre to take charge of Milan. Estorre was the son of Bernabò Visconti, while Giovanni Carlo was Bernabò's grandson. Filippo Maria meanwhile had lost all hope and was at a loss as to what he should do. Friends persuaded him to marry Beatrice, Facino Cane's widow, even though she was much older than he, and far inferior in family status to one who could boast Visconti ancestry.[18] Drawing on his wife's financial resources, Filippo Maria became ruler not only of Pavia, but also of Tortona, Alessandria, Novara, and other towns. Then moving his troops toward Milan, he set up camp not far from the city on May 16, and at last stormed the castle.[19] On June 16, the feast day of Saint Giulitta Martyr, he was universally acclaimed Duke of Milan, though he was not yet twenty years old. From that time forward he wanted the sixteenth of June to be celebrated each year with solemn festivities.

: 9 :

How Filippo Maria behaved at the beginning of his reign.

Once he had occupied Milan his priority was to show himself to be the mild ruler everyone was hoping for. And so he allowed all comers to approach him freely. Not long afterward however he withdrew into solitude, turning his mind to higher aims, until at

tendens animum, donec, posthabitis ceteris curis, belli dumtaxat consiliis et cogitationibus sese abdidit.

∶ 10 ∶

De rebus gestis per eum.

Descripta veluti summa parte vitae eius, deinceps quae ab illo gesta sunt, breviter expediam. Bella in Italia varie gessit, verum quae memoratu digna sunt: Genuense, Helvetium, Florentinum, Gallicum, Venetum, quae partim suo, partim aliorum auspicio egit. Etsi Gallorum auxilio confisus, tandem in reliquos arma moverit.

∶ 11 ∶

De origine bellorum eius.

Bellorum originem hinc primum duxit: vindicare fratris sui necem seque ab finitimorum periculis tutum reddere. Itaque post adeptam statim urbem in Hestorem ac Iohannem bellum movit, quorum opera Iohannes frater interemptus fuerat. Obsessa igitur Modicia, quo in oppido ambo confugerant, intra paucissimos dies oppidum cepit: Hestore in arcem compulso, demum oppresso vi machinae, Iohannes paulo ante per insidias oppido evasit.

last he dropped all other concerns and hid himself away, focusing his thoughts exclusively on his war plans.

: 10 :

The deeds of Filippo Maria.

Having briefly reviewed our prince's life to this stage, I will now summarize his deeds.[20] He conducted various wars in Italy, the most memorable being those he fought with Genoa, with the Swiss, with Florence, with Savoy, and with Venice. These wars were partly directed by himself and partly by his captains. Although he came to rely on Savoy for help,[21] the rest of those powers mentioned above remained his implacable enemies.

: 11 :

The origins of his wars.

His wars drew their initial impulse from his desire to avenge the murder of his brother, as well as to insure his own safety from threats posed by his neighbors.[22] So as soon as he had Milan firmly under his control, he unleashed his war machine on Estorre and Giovanni Carlo, the murderers of his brother. He besieged Monza, where these two were hiding out, and occupied that town within a few days. Estorre was driven to seek refuge in the castle, where he was killed by cannon fire; Giovanni Carlo, meanwhile, managed to slip out of town in time.[23]

: 12 :

Bellum in Laudenses et Comenses.

Hac victoria elatus Philippus ad opprimendos ceteros hostes suos
vertitur. Capto itaque per insidias Iacobo Iohannis filio, qui Laudenses occuparat, patrem cepit ferarum more redactum in potestatem ob filii salutem. Deinde Lutherium Cumo praesidentem
ad se supplicem venire compulit, Luganensi valle ultro illi in prae-
mium data. Quibus ex rebus cum iam tutior esse cepisset, finibus
intra Ticinum Abduamque constitutis, recepta Placentia, Arcelis
expulsis, Tricii oppido expugnato, subinde ad maiora convertit
animum.

: 13 :

Bellum in Cremonenses, Brixiam et Pergamum.

Cremonam igitur vendicare cupiens, utpote Pado imminentem et
accomodam magnis rebus, Cabrino Fundulo bellum indixit. Fove-
batur autem is Pandulfi Malateste senioris opibus, Brixiae ea tempestate praesidentis ac Pergamo; quibus haud fisus, cum aliquan-
diu resistere illi posset, Cremonam tamen reddere instituit.
Recepta urbe, bellum ex bello quaeritans Philippus, quo paterni

: 12 :

War against Lodi and Como.

Elated by this victory, Filippo turned to deal with his other enemies. He used treachery to capture Giacomo, the son of Giovanni
Vignati, who had proclaimed himself lord of Lodi. He then captured Giovanni himself by luring him like a wild animal into a
vain effort to save his son.[24] Next he forced Loterio Rusca, the
ruler of Como, to come before him and beg for mercy, and then
gave him the valley of Lugano by way of compensation.[25] Having
accomplished these things, he began to feel more secure, with the
boundaries of his territories now established between the Ticino
and the Adda Rivers. So he occupied Piacenza, driving out the
Arcelli family,[26] took the town of Trezzo by storm, and then set
his mind on accomplishing still greater things.

: 13 :

War against Cremona, Brescia, and Bergamo.

He wanted to get hold of Cremona, since it was near the Po River
and would provide a suitable base for large-scale military operations, so he declared war on Cabrino Fondulo.[27] Fondulo had the
support of Pandolfo Malatesta the elder, at the time ruler of Brescia and Bergamo, but he was unsure how strongly Pandolfo supported him and therefore (even though he might have been able to
hold out for some time against Filippo Maria) he decided to surrender Cremona.[28] With Cremona in his grasp, Filippo Maria,
seeking to add war to war, and hoping to rebuild his father's vast

imperii opes vendicaret, Pandulfum aggreditur; nec multo post Pergamo per proditionem recepto, in Brixienses castra movit. Adventabat auxilio Ludovicus Firmanus, quo in itinere deleto, etiam Brixia ultro deditur.

: 14 :

Receptio Parmensis urbis.

Tanta fortunae felicitate ad deditionem conversi omnes sponte se illi subicere optabant. Itaque Nicolaus marchio Estensis Parmensem urbem, quam diu detinuerat, per legatos reddere amicitiamque eius petere coactus est, et ut lepidum Regium teneret, tributum illi pendere. Iam patrii nominis fama non Liguriam modo, sed Italiam omnem pervagabatur. Quam ob rem ne existimatione minor videretur, Tusciae urbes, quae in patris ditione olim fuerant, pollicitationibus ac blanditiis aggressus est, quo tutior sibi aditus esset in Tusciam, et Florentiae vires, cuius opibus semper inviderat, facile attereret.

empire, now attacked Pandolfo. He soon obtained Bergamo through betrayal, and moved his army into position around Brescia. Lodovico Migliorati, lord of Fermo, rushed to the aid of the besieged city, but his forces were destroyed before they could reach their destination.[29] So Brescia too finally surrendered.

: 14 :

The recovery of Parma.

In the light of such evident good fortune everyone turned to Filippo Maria with the idea of submitting to him voluntarily. Thus Marquis Niccolò III d'Este felt obliged to seek Filippo Maria's friendship by ceding to him Parma, a city he had held for some time.[30] Niccolò managed to keep Reggio Emilia by agreeing to pay tribute to Filippo Maria for the privilege. So the glory that had once belonged to Filippo Maria's father was again spreading its wings far and wide, not only across Lombardy but throughout Italy as a whole. Wherefore Filippo, not wanting to be held in less esteem, approached the cities of Tuscany that had once belonged to his father and showered them with allurements and promises. His plan was to gain a more secure entryway into Tuscany, a ploy that would then allow him to crush with ease the power of Florence, a city whose immense wealth he had always envied.

: 15 :

Bellum Genuense.

Primum igitur Genuam aggredi placuit, urbem maritimis in rebus Italiae inclitam, cuius vires paulo ante expertus fuerat; nam exules facilem eius urbis aditum pollicebantur. Delinitis itaque suavi oratione Florentinis, quasi non urbem sibi ascisseret, verum cives sede expulsos restituere optaret, bellum cepit. Praeerat urbi Thomas Feregosus, vir omnium aetatis suae longe prudentissimus, quem Alfonsi regis copiis adiutus urbe expulit, fortuna quadam usus ad proelium, cum Baptista Thomae frater ab regis ducibus maritimo proelio superatus esset.

: 16 :

Bellum in Helvecios.

Interea Germanorum manus Berincionam versus castra movens, ut oppido potiretur, ingentem Philippo cladem minabatur. Ea gens ab Helveciis quondam orta, ac nuper expulsa suis finibus, magnis copiis in nostros ferebatur. Electus itaque ad id bellum Franciscus Carmagnola cum ceteris ducibus, adventantes hostes haud longe ab oppido proelio excepit. Ad tria milia Germanorum in acie

: 15 :

War against Genoa.

But first he had designs on Genoa, a city renowned in Italy for its seafaring prowess, and whose powers of resistance he had recently experienced firsthand.[31] Now however Genoese exiles were promising him an easy entry into their city. He started by sending his orators to cajole the Florentines into thinking that he was not interested in occupying Genoa himself, but only wanted to restore the exiled citizens to their rightful home. Then he attacked. The doge at this time was Tommaso Fregoso, a man whose outstanding abilities placed him head and shoulders above all others of his day. Filippo Maria drove him out of the city with the aid of Alfonso of Aragon, though he had to rely on luck in the decisive battle. Meanwhile Tommaso's brother Battista was defeated in a naval engagement by the Aragonese.[32]

: 16 :

War against the Swiss.

At around this same time a company of Germans was moving toward Bellinzona, hoping to capture the town. They represented a clear threat to Filippo Maria. This foreign horde had its origins among the Swiss, but had recently been driven from its homeland and was now determined to invade Italy. Francesco Carmagnola had been selected along with other captains to lead our forces.[33] He met the enemy in battle as they were approaching Bellinzona. Tradition has it that up to three thousand Germans died fighting

cecidisse ea die fama est; reliqui salvis ordinibus abiere. Maximae
cladis lugubre signum videre plurimi solem iridis effigie circumda-
tum, quod Octavio olim Romam ingrediente visum fuisse Suetonius refert.

: 17 :

Bellum Florentinum.

Conversus deinde ad maiora, Florentinum inchoavit bellum, Nicolai Estensis consilio permotus; qui ut illum a Venetis averteret, vel
potius bellum differret, Tusciam in primis petere suasit. Quo in
bello cum fortuna usus esset, Carolum Malatestam virum inclitum
praesidentem Florentinorum copiis acie devicit apud Zagonariae
oppidum. Creditumque est hac victoria non Tusciam modo ab illo,
sed Italiam fere omnem proelio superatum iri.

: 18 :

Bellum Venetum primum.

Verum maior rerum secuta moles: quippe Florentini destituti suis
copiis, amisso duce, Venetorum opem implorarunt. Urgebat belli
vim Franciscus cognomento Carmagnola, olim Philippi dux, ad
Venetos delatus, et patrio expulsus lare. Eius igitur auspiciis,

on that day. The rest retreated in orderly fashion. Many people observed a doleful sign of this great slaughter, for they saw the sun surrounded by iridescent rings; Suetonius reports that Augustus once observed the same heavenly phenomenon as he was entering Rome.[34]

: 17 :

The Florentine War.

Turning now to even bigger things, Filippo Maria undertook a war against Florence. He was encouraged in this direction by Niccolò III d'Este who, in order to keep him from attacking Venice, or at least to delay such a move, advised him to focus on Tuscany as a first objective. In this war Filippo Maria had the good fortune to defeat Carlo Malatesta, the famed general in charge of the Florentine troops, in a battle fought at the town of Zagonara.[35] It was widely thought that with this victory Filippo Maria had opened the way not just to the conquest of Tuscany, but to that of virtually all of Italy.

: 18 :

The first Venetian war.

In fact still greater things were yet in store, for the Florentines, having lost their general and their army, turned to beg the Venetians for help. Francesco Carmagnola — formerly Filippo Maria's general commander, but now driven from his homeland and on

Brixia a Venetis oppressa. Receptae insuper pacis conditiones, Nicolao cardinale Sanctae Crucis suadente. Sed cum Philippus pacem distulisset, victae eius copiae ad Maclodium vicum, Pergamum in Venetorum devenit potestatem, cum utrinque terra pariter ac flumine pugnatum esset. Maximum cladis solatium non multo post liberatio Lucensis urbis, quam a Florentinis obsessam duce Nicolao nostri conservarunt.

: 19 :

Belli Gallici commemoratio.

Gallorum copiis ut offensus primo Veneto bello Philippus, ita secundo et tertio adiutus est. Nam Allobrogum[1] dux Amadeus priscae consanguinitatis haud immemor, Mariam filiam subinde uxorem illi dedit, tradita Amadeo Vercellarum urbs, quasi sequestris quaedam conciliandae pacis atque servandae. Fuere autem Philippi copiae superiore bello equitum duodecim, peditum septem milia, cum Venetorum et Florentinorum ampliores extitissent, classis utrinque Pado insisteret viris armisque referta.

the Venetian side—urged the Venetians to stand up and fight. Under Carmagnola's guidance the Venetians took Brescia. Peace conditions were then agreed upon, with Niccolò Albergati, the Cardinal of Santa Croce, acting as the chief mediator. But because Filippo Maria had shown reluctance to comply with the terms, his army was defeated at the village of Maclodio, bringing Bergamo under Venetian control, after both sides had fought hard on land and water. Some relief came to Filippo Maria a short while later with the liberation of Lucca. Florence had besieged this city, but our men kept Lucca safe under the command of Niccolò Piccinino.[36]

: 19 :

A note on the war with Savoy.

Filippo Maria had the Savoyards against him in his first war with Venice, but in the second and third wars he had them on his side. This came about because Duke Amedeo of Savoy, recognizing the ancient blood ties that linked the two families, gave his daughter Maria in marriage to Filippo, and received the city of Vercelli in return, as a sort of guarantee of lasting peace and harmony between the two houses.[37] Filippo's army in the first war with Venice numbered a mounted force of twelve thousand, with seven thousand foot soldiers. The Venetians and Florentines fielded an even greater number, and both sides stationed well armed and well manned fleets on the River Po.

: 20 :

Bellum Venetum secundum.

Inita cum Venetis ac Florentinis societate, haud multo post secundum bellum inchoavit, eodem duce Nicolao usus, viro optimo ad res gerendas. Pugnatum est flumine pariter ac terra. Veneti navali classe apud Cremonam devicti sunt. In Genuensium praeterea finibus varie certatum est. Marchionis Montisferati oppida paene tota oppressa sunt, secuti Venetorum partes. Memorabile etiam ea tempestate, quod belli auctor Franciscus Carmagnola, in suspicionem adductus, a Venetis supplicio affectus est. Finis belli atque discriminis Telina vallis, quo in loco cum maxime trepidatum foret, Georgius Cornarius Venetorum dux, devicto exercitu atque conciso, in Philippi devenit potestatem.

: 21 :

Bellum Venetum extraordinarium et victoria in Alfonsum regem.

Partae autem victoriae auspicia novum consecutum est bellum. Post pacis enim condiciones Venetorum et Florentinorum copiae devictae apud Imolam Nicolao duce. Verum altius impressum vulnus, et ut insperatum, ita difficilius ad medendum visum est:

: 20 :

The second Venetian war.

Not long after signing the peace treaty with Venice and Florence,[38] Filippo Maria undertook a second war with them. He appointed the same general commander of his forces as before: Niccolò Piccinino, a most capable military strategist. The war was fought on both land and water. The Venetian fleet was defeated in a naval engagement near Cremona.[39] Around Genoa however the fortunes of battle seesawed back and forth. Almost all the strongholds held by the Marquis of Monferrato were taken, for he had sided with Venice. It should be recorded too that it was at this time that the instigator of the war, Francesco Carmagnola, was accused of treachery and then executed by the Venetians.[40] The crucial and final episode of the war occurred in the Valtellina. Although for some time the outcome there was uncertain, Giorgio Corner, the Venetian commander, was finally captured, and his forces beaten and destroyed.[41]

: 21 :

A new war with Venice and victory over
King Alfonso of Aragon.

But no sooner had this victory been won than another war followed on. After peace terms had been agreed upon, Niccolò Piccinino defeated the combined Venetian and Florentine forces at Imola.[42] Then a new wound drove more deeply. And because it was so unexpected, it seemed much more difficult to heal. For

quippe cum Genuensium classis apud Gaietam Alfonsum regem
bello superasset, elati animis viribusque Genuenses Philippo rebellarunt. Sic preclarae victoriae finis extitit Genuensis urbis vulgata
defectio, quae etiam insequenti bello initium praestitit.

: 22 :

Bellum denuo in Genuenses.

Nam Genuenses, veriti Philippi impetum, totis se viribus ad arma
contulerunt, nihil pluris, ut fassi sunt, libertate facientes. Dux ad
id bellum Nicolaus Perusinus, qui superiori proelio contra Venetos
arma moverat. Sumptis igitur cum legione circiter viginti hominum milibus, ex Philippi principatu Pulciferam vallem ingressus
est, castrisque undique appositis per superiora montium duxit
exercitum. Iam urbi propinquabat, devictis civibus, iam arci prae-
sidium videbatur allaturus, qua nulla aetate nostra res unquam
gesta fuisset illustrior; si arcis praesidibus in sustinendo auxilio
eadem mens atque animus fuisset, quae illi in parando et mittendo
affuit. Desperata urbe, ad Albingam castra posita. Tandem Venetis Florentinisque obsistentibus, aliquantulum a bello temperatum
est.

when the Genoese fleet defeated King Alfonso near Gaeta, the Genoese got carried away by their success and revolted against the government of Filippo Maria.[43] So a great victory at sea resulted in a popular uprising in Genoa, thus setting the scene for the next war.

: 22 :

Another war against Genoa.

The Genoese in fact, fearing Filippo Maria's reaction, now allocated all their resources to the war effort, proclaiming that nothing was more sacred to them than their freedom. The leader of the Milanese forces was Niccolò Piccinino, the same commander who had defeated the Venetians at Imola. With an army of about twenty thousand men Piccinino moved from Milanese territory into the Polcevera Valley, established outposts practically everywhere, and led his main force along the heights of the mountains. On approaching the city of Genoa he defeated the citizen militia sent out to stop him. At this point he appeared to be on the verge of bringing relief to the Visconti loyalists holed up in the citadel, a feat that would have ranked as the most memorable of our age, if only those who were holding the fort had shown the same ardent desire to receive aid as Piccinino had shown in creating the opportunity to supply it.[44] With no hope of taking Genoa itself, Piccinino stationed his troops at Albenga. Finally, with the Venetians and the Florentines standing firm in their defense of Genoa, hostilities ceased.

: 23 :

Bellum Venetum quartum.

Bello Veneto quarto, quod cum Florentinis ac Genuensibus eodem tempore gestum est, acrius certatum est a Philippo. Nam Veneti, Iohanne Francisco ductore suo, qui Mantuae praeerat, primum repulso ab Abduae transitu, deinde Philippo adhaerente, cesserunt, additis ipsius copiis, quo tempore duce Nicolao Brixia obsessa, et quater bello lacessitis moenibus, cum fame simul pesteque laboraret, tanti oneris vim enixe pertulit, Francisco Barbaro praetore sustinente. Inde in Veronenses translata belli moles, copiae ultra Athesim insecutae Venetorum duces, cum fluvium ipsum vi traiecissent, haud mediocrem Philippo laudem praestitere. Expugnata etiam classis Benaco in lacu, Veronensis urbs primo impetu capta a nostris et praedari cepta. Verum cum tardius auxilia accessissent, Francisci Sfortiae praesidio firmata Philippum impulit, mutato consilio, exercitum in Flaminiam et inde in Tusciam mittere. Traiectae Apenini rupes hibernis tempestatibus; naves per ardua montium a Venetis Benaco immissae; nihil non arduum hoc proelio temptatum est. Tandem Nicolao ad Anglarium vicum bello concidente, cum copiae in Liguria amissae essent, pax denuo quaesita. Blancha Philippi filia, quam infantem paene Franciscus desponsaverat, illi tradita, Cremona in dotem cessit.

: 23 :

The fourth Venetian war.

Filippo Maria prosecuted the fourth Venetian war — fought against the Florentines and the Genoese as well — more vigorously. For the Venetians had to call off their attack after their general, Gianfrancesco Gonzaga, lord of Mantua, was first turned back while attempting to cross the Adda River, and then joined Filippo Maria's side. Gianfrancesco's troops reinforced those of Niccolò Piccinino, who at that time was besieging Brescia. That city, its walls battered four times by war, was holding its own against a massive force, enduring even the ills of famine and plague, thanks to the efforts of the Venetian officer in charge, Francesco Barbaro.[45] From there the focus of the war shifted to Veronese territory. The Milanese forces pursued the Venetians across the Adige, and having forced their way across that river they procured great glory for Filippo Maria. Then after defeating the Venetian fleet on Lake Garda, our men took the city of Verona by storm and began putting it to the sack. But because reinforcements were slow to arrive, and the city was heartened by the defensive action of Francesco Sforza, Filippo Maria was obliged to revise his plans and to send his forces on an expedition into Romagna and then on into Tuscany. Piccinino's troops crossed the Apennine passes in the dead of winter; the Venetians brought their ships over rugged mountains and launched them into Lake Garda; nothing was too much to attempt in this epic struggle. Finally, with Piccinino defeated in battle at the village of Anghiari, and our forces much depleted in Lombardy, it was time once again to sue for peace. Bianca Maria, Filippo's daughter, who had been betrothed when still a child to Francesco Sforza, now married him and Cremona became her dowry.[46]

: 24 :

Bellum Venetum quintum.

Bellum Venetum quod ultimum a Philippo incohatum est, desperatione quadam rerum et taedio potius quiescendi, quam iudicio et consilio ab eodem gestum constat. Cum enim haud facile pateretur Franciscum Sfortiam, adversantem conatibus suis, Venetorum partes fovere et parem quodammodo sibi esse cupere, praemissis legatis, qui Venetos placarent, mitioresque sibi efficerent, copias Cremonam versus movit, fisus populum pertesum dominatus eius, partes suas secuturum. Sic enim multi ac praeclari viri futurum pollicebantur. Negligentia autem ducum et inscitia fuso exercitu ad Casale oppidum, cum Veneti victoria elati, transmissa Abdua, Mediolanum accessissent, coactus est ultimo pacem quaerere, Franciscumque generum, alioquin sibi adversum, evocare ad subsidia sua. Accedebant ad haec auxilia Alfonsi regis, quorum adventu in spem ducebatur, vel honestae pacis, vel victoriae tandem bello consequendae; potitusque voto fuisset, Veronensibus secreto conspirantibus ad bellum, nisi inopina mors, veluti felicitatis eius invida, tantarum rerum eventum sustulisset.

: 24 :

The fifth Venetian war.

It is clear that Filippo Maria's final war against Venice was under-taken more out of desperation and a sense of frustration than as a result of any rational plan. He found it hard to bear that Fran-cesco Sforza opposed his will, favored the Venetians, and was de-termined to become his equal. So he dispatched legates on a mis-sion to placate the Venetians and make them more amenable to himself, then launched an offensive against Cremona, confident that the people there were thoroughly tired of Sforza rule and would be sure to come over to his side (so, at least, many leading citizens had promised was likely to happen). But the incompetent bungling of his military commanders led to the defeat of his army at Casalmaggiore, and when the Venetians advanced across the Adda in the full glory of their victory, threatening Milan itself, he was forced at last to seek peace, and to call Francesco Sforza — his son-in-law and erstwhile adversary — to his rescue. There was also help arriving from King Alfonso, and with such forces at his dis-posal Filippo hoped to win either favorable peace terms, or else a complete victory over his enemies. And he might have achieved this goal (for the Veronese were secretly plotting to enter the war) if death — as if begrudging him this final triumph — had not sud-denly and unexpectedly put an end to all his plans.[47]

: 25 :

Quae gesta sunt in omni principatu eius.

Haec sunt quae Philippus Mediolanensium dux per annos quinque ac triginta, tot enim illorum urbi praefuit, bello paceque gessit; cum omnium Vicecomitum qui a principio imperaverant, urbe exclusus ob fratris necem ac destitutus omni spe, coactus sit principatum sibi quaerere. Subegit autem Liguriam omnem, quae ab Alpibus ad Tyrenum usque mare pertinet, inclusa Genua, tum Aemiliam ac Flaminiam. Nam urbes Adriatico mari finitimas, praeterea Tusciam et Umbriam bellis excursionibusque vastavit.

: 26 :

Quibus proeliis interfuit Philippus.

Post adeptam urbem nulli bello praeter quam Genuensi et Veneto primo interfuit. Ita tamen ut nec acie certaret, nec strepitus castrorum sustineret; sed finitimis dumtaxat in locis opperiretur proelii eventum: ut Novas et Uvadae Genuensi bello primo, Veneto autem Cremam oppidum, vel cum longius Cremonam usque progressus ab urbe, quo Venetorum ac Florentinorum conatibus sese opponeret. Fuere quippe primo Veneto bello hostiles copiae equitum viginti, peditum decem milia: quibus haud facile obsisti

: 25 :

The deeds done during his reign.

These then are the things accomplished by Filippo Maria as duke of Milan in peace and in war during the thirty-five years he reigned over our city. Of all the Visconti who had ruled from the beginning, he alone, finding himself excluded from the city on account of the murder of his brother, and devoid of all hope, was forced to seek supreme power through his own efforts. Yet he subdued the whole of Lombardy, from the Alps to the Tyrrhenian Sea, including Genoa, and even Emilia and Romagna. And with his wars and campaigns he laid waste cities near the Adriatic coast, and Tuscany and Umbria as well.

: 26 :

The battles at which Filippo Maria was present.

After the taking of Milan, Filippo Maria no longer participated in person in his wars, the exceptions being the Genoese campaign and the first Venetian war.[48] And even in these latter instances he did not join in the fighting, or endure the confusion of the camp, but rather awaited the outcome of the battle nearby. In the first war against Genoa he stationed himself at Novi and at Vado; in the Venetian conflict he chose the town of Crema, but then went even further from his home base in Milan to Cremona, in order to throw himself personally against the onslaught of the Venetians and the Florentines. The enemy troops in this first Venetian war numbered twenty thousand cavalry and ten thousand foot soldiers.

potuisset, nisi sumptis ex omni potentatu suo viris armisque, eorum impetum praesentia sua repressisset. Eo in loco cum minus
fauste navali proelio pugnatum esset, conterritus rei eventu, belli
duces ad se ascivit, quaestusque propalam eorum imperitia desi-
diaque in deterius rem suam labi, Mediolanum rediit. Nec ulla
deinceps nisi per legatos suos atque duces bella administravit.

: 27 :

Quo in honore duces habiti sunt ab eo.

Non duces dumtaxat bello inclitos, verum milites proeliis expertos
passosque summam rerum inopiam, ut officiis assisterent, nec loco
cederent, adeo coluit, ut multi ex infimo gradu ab eodem ad summos magistratus evecti sint. Carmagnolam, vivente adhuc Facino,
sub quo militarat, sibi gratum ob armorum peritiam, demum inter
primarios viros habuit; neque foris tantum, sed domi et in consiliis
praeferre studuit, quo ceteris amorem gloriae iniiceret, obnoxiosque
sibi redderet. Franciscum Sfortiam peritissimum rei militaris
ascitum ad se, non honoribus dumtaxat, sed affinitate illustrem

Never could Filippo Maria have held his own against such a force without first calling forth the full measure of his capability in men and resources, and then checking the enemy's advance by lending his personal presence to the effort. In that campaign the naval engagement had produced indifferent results. Terrified that the outcome might be in doubt, Filippo Maria summoned his generals and openly complained to them that the war was being lost because of their incompetence and lack of initiative. Then he returned to Milan. From that time on he never again directed a campaign in person, but rather did so indirectly, through his civilian and military officials.[49]

: 27 :

The high regard in which he held his generals.

As for his fighting men, he took good care not only of the commanders famed for their exploits in war, but also of the common soldiers who had experienced the rigors of battle and extreme deprivation. He looked after such men in the hope that they would perform their duties and stand firm in combat. Indeed he looked after them to such a degree that he raised many of them from their lowly status to the highest levels of office in the realm. Carmagnola earned his admiration because of the abilities he displayed while still an officer under Facino Cane. So he had him take his place among the leading men of the duchy. He favored Carmagnola not only in public but in private as well, seeking his counsel, and thereby encouraging others to strive toward the same position of influence, and to become his loyal servants. He bound Francesco Sforza, that most skillful of generals, to himself not only by showering him with honors, but by favoring him with a

reddidit, generumque sibi effecit. Nicolaum Perusinum insignem bello ducem, a principio functum mediocri fortuna, suis demum praeesse voluit. Idem et de ceteris censuit. Quaerentibus nonnullis ex veteranis militibus, quendam Boniohannem Trotum sibi praeferri, cum ipsorum opera Mediolanum recepisset: 'Vere — inquit — dicitis, sed ut, urbe recepta, mihi obsequeremini cogitare debuistis'; nihilque amplius quam ut mandata exequerentur, admonuit. Longum esset enumerare eos qui ex infimo gradu ad supremum ab eodem elati sunt, existimatione dumtaxat rei militaris. Eo etenim opinionis accesserat, ut nihil non armis et viribus fieri posse existimaret; cetera vero, quae ingenio aut prudentia agerentur, si a militia abessent, haud multi faceret.

: 28 :

De astu eius in periclitandis ducum
et militum animis.

Rem militarem summa cura animadvertit. Neminem exercitui praefecit, cui non correctorem et veluti pedagogum quendam apponeret. Nicolao Perusino, cui prae ceteris in bello fidem dederat, scribas ex suis statuit, qui omnes actus eius ac progressus annotarent eumque continuo de omnibus certum facerent. Habebat praeterea nonnullos sibi fidos nec ignaros rei militaris, quibus privatim

marriage tie, and thus making him his own son-in-law. As for the famed captain in arms Niccolò Piccinino, whose early results were of a modest sort, Filippo Maria ended up appointing him supreme commander of all his forces. He made decisions regarding others in a similar way. A large group of veterans once petitioned him to make a certain Bongiovanni Trotti their captain, a request they felt was justified by their having helped Filippo Maria capture Milan.[50] "It may be true you helped me," he replied, "but you should remember that you also promised to obey me once the city was captured." He thereby warned these men to confine themselves to carrying out his orders. It would take a long time to list all of those whom he raised up, from the lowest depths to the highest rank, solely on account of their skill in arms. He had indeed reached the conclusion that nothing could be accomplished without the use of military force. It was his view that even the arts of negotiation and diplomacy were next to useless, unless they were backed up by a credible military machine.

: 28 :

His clever ways of testing the loyalty of his captains and soldiers.

His mind was focused to the highest degree on military matters. No one gained the supreme command of his forces without his appointing at the same time a special commissioner to watch over his every move. He stationed his most faithful secretaries beside Niccolò Piccinino, a man he trusted in the field above all others. Their duty was to take note of every single act and move he made, and to keep the duke fully informed of everything. He also had a number of men in his confidence, men knowledgeable about how

a ducibus multa imponeret bello peragenda: quo in numero Aras-
minus Triultius fuit, Georgius Anonus et Antonelus Arcemboldus.
Ducum praeterea scribas et secretarios, quos gratos illis aut fidos
cognovisset, muneribus alliciebat ac pecuniis, quo mentes eorum
exploraret. Nec ulli tantum credidit, cui non diffideret amplius.
Qua ex causa studiose lites inter omnes conserebat, variis etiam
modis suorum animos pertentare solitus, ne quid illum latere posset; quod multo solertius ac diligentius cum domesticis suis egit,
et his maxime quorum custodiae personam suam arcesve commi-
serat, sicuti plane suo loco referemus.

: 29 :

Qui duces praeclari sub vexillis
eius extiterunt.

1 Duces armorum rei militaris peritia doctissimos et expertos habuit, ex quibus primorem Carmagnolam plerique memorant.
Hunc ab armis sublatum Genuam transtulit. Habebat enim hoc
moris, ut si quempiam ab officio dimovere vellet, honoris spetie a
se dimitteret. Habuit et Angelum Pergulensem, virum acrem et
industrium. Item Aluisium Vermen, conspicuum nomine paterno.
Praeterea Franciscum Sfortiam ducem multis proeliis ac victoriis
illustrem, quem e Neapolis regno ascitum etiam generum sibi

a military campaign should be run. He was wont to inform these men in private about what was expected of the commanders. Among these trusted figures were Arasmino Trivulzio,[51] Giorgio Annoni,[52] and Antonello Arcimboldi.[53] As for the scribes and secretaries of his military commanders, if he learned that they had been taken into the confidence of their masters, he would ply them with gifts and money, hoping to probe their secrets. Never did he trust any of his people so completely that he forgot to distrust them even more. This is why he would deliberately stir up quarrels among his own men, in order to pry into their minds in every possible way and make it impossible for them to hide anything from him. He followed this practice even more diligently with his own servants, and particularly with his personal bodyguard and the wardens of his castles. We shall speak more about these practices of his in due course.

: 29 :

The famous military commanders who served under his banners.

He had in his service highly skilled military commanders, well versed in the art of war. Carmagnola is usually remembered as the first of these. Filippo relieved him of his military responsibilities and made him governor of Genoa. He was in fact in the habit, when relieving someone of their duties, of removing them by bestowing on them some sort of honorable position. He also had in his service Angelo della Pergola, a shrewd and energetic man. And he had Luigi dal Verme, whose name stands out because of his father.[54] And then there was Francesco Sforza, famed for his many victorious battles: Filippo recruited him from the kingdom of

fecit. Usus est autem vel in primis opera Nicolai Picenini fortis-
simi ducis atque obsequentissimi votis suis, de quo praescripsimus.

2   Nam Berardinum Ubaldinum multo post a se cognitum ob insignem prudentiam ac virtutem ad summos honores provehere
optavit. Meruere alii sub vexillis eius, inter quos Siccus Montagnana et Guido Torellus anumerandi sunt, alter consilio, alter
proelio utilior. Albericus etiam comes, ad eius stipendia delatus,
non minori comendatione celebrandus est. Meruit et sub eo Nicolaus Tolentinus, verum modico tempore; nam cum ab eo novissime abscessisset, bello Imolensi denuo interceptus, in potestatem
eius redactus est. Longum esset enumerare omnes, si Aluisium
Severinum, Gulielmum Montisferati,[2] Carolum Gonzagam, Ven-
ceslaum Lucensem, Petrum Iampaulum ex Ursinis, Ludovicum
Columnam, Talianum Furlanum reliquosque suo ordine referre
cupiam. Hoc unum dixisse sat est, nullum in Italia ducem bello
inclitum et notum extitisse, qui non ad stipendia sua moram dux-
erit, quique benivolentiam eius non ceteris principibus longe ante-
tulerit.

: 30 :

De vexillorum eius imaginibus.

Vexillo primum gentili ac bipartito aquilarum viperarumque discrimine, deinde paterno usus est, quod a Francisco Petrarca edi-
tum plerique prodidere: hoc in proeliis uti consuevit, turturis

Naples, and eventually made him his own son-in-law. But his main military commander was Niccolò Piccinino, the boldest of them all and the most obedient to his wishes. We have written about him extensively elsewhere.[55]

Filippo became acquainted with Bernardino Ubaldini only 2 much later, and wanted to raise him up to the highest honors on account of his outstanding ability.[56] Other commanders too served under his banners. Two of these should be listed here: Sicco Montagnana and Guido Torelli, the one more useful for his counsel, the other in battle.[57] Count Alberico is also deserving of honorable mention: he too was on Filippo's payroll.[58] And Niccolò da Tolentino also served under Filippo Maria, if only for a short time. In fact no sooner had Niccolò deserted Filippo's service than he was recaptured in action at Imola, and returned to Milan as a prisoner of war.[59] It would take forever if I were to try to list the names of all of Filippo's military commanders. The list would include Luigi da Sanseverino, Guglielmo di Monferrato, Carlo Gonzaga, Venceslao da Lucca, Pietro Giampaolo Orsini, Ludovico Colonna, Taliano Furlano, and others still.[60] Let it suffice to say only this: there was simply no famous commander in Italy who did not spend at least some time in Filippo's service, and who did not value his friendship far above that of all other princes.

: 30 :

The devices emblazoned on Filippo's standards.

He used the Visconti emblem at first, divided into two halves, with eagles in one and vipers in the other. Later he switched to his father's favorite, the one tradition says was designed by Francis Petrarch. He tended to use this latter device in battle. It bore the

figuram praeferente in solis iubare. Post diademate, palma et lauro illustri non vexilla modo, sed praeclara domus suae decoravit. Addidit et falchonis imaginem quarto in loco, ex Phoebi splendore terrentis aquaticas aves; commentus id, cum primum pecuniis militibusque stipatus Florentino inhiaret bello. Habuit et a me serpentis effigiem ex sole prodeuntis accensa face: quam ad fausta victoriasque paratam, morte preventus intactam reliquit, ut rinocerotis et volantis draconis insignia.

: 31 :

De clementia eius in bello.

1   Clementia cum ceteris in rebus, tum vel maxime in bello usus est. Ludovico Firmano suppetias ferenti Pandulfo Malatestae, cum Brixia obsideretur, et captivo ad se venienti libertatem praestitit summa liberalitate.

2   Carolum vero Malatestam, victis Florentinis, adductum ad se post captivitatem, ob famam nominis, et quod virum puer observaverat, singulari humanitate prosecutus est, demum muneribus adauctum atque exornatum suis reddidit.

3   Victus apud Gaietam maritimo proelio Alfonsus rex cum fratribus suis ad praesentiam eius accesserat. Hunc omnibus regni

image of a dove in the rays of the sun.[61] Later still he adorned not only his standards, but also the most magnificent parts of his palace with a design that incorporated a crown, a palm branch, and a stately bough of laurel. He then added a fourth image, featuring a falcon shining like the sun, to frighten waterfowl. He contrived the idea for this one when he was flush with money and troops and eagerly pursuing war with Florence. He also had from my own hands the device of a serpent emerging from the sun with a fiery torch. This particular one had been prepared for celebrating successes and victories, but he did not live long enough to use it. The same fate befell the devices painted with a rhinoceros and a winged dragon.

: 31 :

His clemency in war.

He showed clemency in many areas, but most especially in war. 1
Lodovico Migliorati was captured while bringing aid to Pandolfo Malatesta during the siege of Brescia.[62] When Lodovico was then brought before him, Filippo demonstrated great generosity by ordering him to be freed.

Carlo Malatesta is another case in point: after the Florentine 2
defeat at Zagonara he was taken prisoner and delivered to Milan.[63] Filippo was mindful of this man's fame. He had admired him from childhood. He accordingly treated him with special kindness, then loaded him up with gifts and had him returned to his people with honor.

King Alfonso too, defeated in a naval battle near Gaeta, ended 3
up a prisoner in Milan, along with his brothers. Filippo treated Alfonso — surrounded as he was by the leading men of his

principibus eadem calamitate afflictis circumseptum ita pie
humaneque tractavit, ut nihil ipsis deesse videretur, nisi quod in
patria non essent. Regnum quippe Neapolis ditioni regis subicere
tentavit; idque effecisset, ni Genuenses, victoria elati, praemiorum
spe rectores suos expulissent.

: 32 :

De fama nominis eius.

1 Ea ex re tantum laudis et splendoris assecutus est, ut non solum a
Christianis principibus coleretur, amaretur, verum etiam apud in-
fideles nomen eius celebre esset atque vulgatum.

2 Ladislaus Poloniae rex, qui praeclaro illo in proelio contra Teu-
cros pro fide pugnans in Graecia periit, contracta cum illo arctiori
amicitia, quam pater habuisset, legatis muneribusque praemissis,
benivolentiam erga illum multis documentis testatus est. Idem Li-
tuaniae et Daciae reges, idem et Prusiae fecere. Iohannes Bizantii
imperator, Philippei nominis fama permotus, plusculis diebus ad
eum visendum Mediolani substitit. Asiae insuper et Affricae reges
Mediolanum legatos cum muneribus misere, amicitiam ultro ef-
flagitantes.

3 Sigismondus Romanorum rex, invitatus ad Italiae regnum exor-
nandum sumendumque diadema, cum paucis ad eum venit ste-
titque Mediolani, quamvis praesentiam suam non adisset. Nullus
denique toto orbe princeps fuit, cui non acceptissima esset memoria sui nominis, rerumque ab illo gestarum gloriam in honore non
haberet.

kingdom, all afflicted by the same catastrophe — with such respect and kindness that they could complain of nothing, unless it were that they were not in their homeland. Filippo even tried hard to get the Kingdom of Naples to submit to Alfonso's rule.[64] And he might have succeeded, were it not that the Genoese, carried away by their success and hoping for further rewards, drove the Visconti governors out of their city.

: 32 :

His fame.

Filippo's clemency earned him such praise and renown that the love and adoration he enjoyed was not limited to Christian princes: even among the infidels his name was widely known and celebrated. 1

Ladislas, king of Poland, who died in Greece while fighting for the faith in that famous battle against the Turks,[65] was Filippo's close friend and revered him like a father. He sent him gifts and emissaries, and made his goodwill known in other ways as well. The same goes for the kings of Lithuania, Dacia, and Prussia. John Paleologus, emperor of Byzantium, having heard tell of Filippo's fame, stayed in Milan for several days in order to visit with him.[66] The kings of Asia and Africa too sent their gift-laden envoys to Milan, begging to be included among Filippo's allies. 2

Sigismund, king of the Romans, when invited to be crowned king of Italy, came to Milan with a small retinue to see Filippo, although he was never admitted to his presence.[67] There was simply no prince in the whole world who was not well disposed toward Filippo, and who did not honor the glory of his deeds. 3

: 33 :

De diligentia eius circa rem publicam.

Rem publicam varie administravit, modo remissius se gerens, modo asperius. In qua re si cui forte videatur errasse, non tam culpae suae imputet, quam suorum pravitati: nam in delinquentes saepe animadvertit. Thodeschinum Federicum antiquiorem ex cubicularibus suis audientiae publicae praefecit; mox ex libito multa molientem sumovit e dignitate. Oldradum vero Lampugnanum ex primoribus aulae suae, quod minus temperantem ire cognovisset, deposuit e gradu, quamquam in ceteris obsequentem sciret. Civilia officia nisi bello fatigatus et egens vendidit, ita tamen ut nemini parceret. Memini me adolescentulum, cum in aula eius obversarer, vix obtinuisse, ut patri meo magistratus servaretur, quem ipse statuisset. Matrimonia nisi se conscio cum suis fieri edicto prohibuit. Beneficia quoque ecclesiastica a nullo impetrari voluit, nisi ipse mandasset, in qua re Thodeschinum, de quo scripsimus, veluti pontificem constituit in urbe. Legatos ac nuncios per universum fere orbem assidue tenuit. Nemini gratiam petenti annuit, nisi per interpositam alterius precem. Nulli tamen verbo renuit; si qui improbiores essent, ut per alios memoriae subicerent, admonuit. Itaque benignitatis et naturae suae conscius, cum statuta per se

: 33 :

His care in managing the affairs of state.

His conduct in government varied: sometimes he ruled with gentle hand, while at other times he could act harshly. Any errors he made however should be attributed not to him, but to the perversity of his officials, for he frequently punished these latter for their misbehavior. He appointed Todeschino de'Federici, one of the most senior members of his household, to preside over public hearings.[68] But he soon removed him from office when he discovered that his new appointee was acting in an arbitrary manner. He demoted Oldrado Lampugnani, a high-ranking official at court, once he learned that Oldrado was exceeding his brief.[69] He did this even though he knew that in other areas Oldrado was behaving correctly. Filippo would put offices up for sale only when he found himself under extreme financial pressure, in times of war, and then his policy was to spare no one. I myself remember how as a young man at court I was barely able to make sure that my father kept his office,[70] whereas it was Filippo Maria who had appointed him to it in the first place! Filippo also issued a decree forbidding those in his service to marry without his prior consent.[71] And he allowed no one to seek ecclesiastical benefices without his approval. For this purpose he set up the aforementioned Todeschino as a kind of pope in Milan. He kept his envoys and ambassadors busy throughout practically the whole world. He granted no favors to anyone unless their requests were channeled through a third party. He nevertheless would refuse no one verbally. If he found fault with petitioners, he would advise them to resubmit their requests to him through another administrative channel. He was fully aware of his kindly nature: whenever he found himself reluctant to modify a previous decision he would withdraw into complete

mutare nollet, cedebat e turba, in secessumque delatus, nulli
vacabat, non tam elatione aut superbia motus, quam facilitate
ingenii sui, quam quis benignitatem rite diceret.

: 34 :

De astutia eiusdem in deligendis consultoribus.

In deligendis consultoribus, quos consiliarios vocant, mira astutia
utebatur. Nam viros probos et scientia praeclaros eligebat, hisque
impuros quosdam et vita turpes collegas dabat, ut nec illi iustitia
initi, nec hi perfidia crassari possent, sed continua inter eos dissensione praesciret omnia; eratque ergastulum quodam, ut sic dixerim, cicurum ac silvestrium ferarum. Franchino Castelioneo,
cuius fama apud omnes nota erat, Iohannem Franciscum Gallinam
adiunxit, hominem vitae levioris. Idem inter ius dicentes factitavit:
nam dissimiles natura viros Nicolaum Arcemboldum et Iohannem
Ferufinum, quorum alter astutissimus, alter sincerissimus vir fuit,
una copulavit. Legatos etiam si quos emitteret, contrariis moribus
inter se deligebat. Eadem series ad secretarios usque defluxit,
quippe cum optimis saepenumero pessimos, et indoctis peritos

seclusion. At such times he would see no one. But this behavior was caused not by haughtiness or pride, but rather by his naturally lenient disposition, a character trait some have rightly said stemmed from genuine kindness.

: 34 :

His cleverness in choosing his advisors.

He showed remarkable shrewdness in the way he selected his counselors, the ones who bore the title *consiliarii*. His technique was to appoint honest men of great learning and then give them vile and morally corrupt colleagues. He did this in order to prevent the former from gaining influence by exploiting their righteousness, and the latter from doing so by resorting to treachery. Rather, the constant struggle between the two sides would mean that the duke would be amply informed as to everything that was going on. The result was that his administration became a kind of prison farm, stocked (if I may say so) with both tame and wild animals. So the duke chose Giovanni Francesco Gallina, a man of dubious character, to be paired with Franchino Castiglioni, whose good name was known to everyone.[72] And he applied the same policy when making judicial appointments, for in that area he joined together two men of distinctly different caliber, Nicolò Arcimboldi and Giovanni Feruffini, the one a devilishly clever customer, the other entirely trustworthy.[73] So too, if the duke chanced to send envoys on a diplomatic mission, he chose men whose characters were diametrically opposed. And he used the same tactic with his secretaries, for he liked to pair up the best men with the worst, and the competent with the incompetent, even showing that he preferred the latter to the former, in complete disregard of

adiungeret, hisque illos preferret, nullo meritorum habito respectu, quo interiores cuiusque sordes ac virtutes eliceret, et veluti inter se collisas anteponeret oculis, et quae quisque non faceret modo, sed cogitaret, agnosceret.

: 35 :

De urbium administratione.

Urbes non aeque in cura habuit. Mediolanensem tamen quoad licuit servavit immunem, nec nisi Veneto bello oppressus oneribus affecit. In exornanda vero urbe negligentior a nonnullis habitus est, cum moenia partim incuria partim vetustate corruerent. Id autem accidisse crediderim, quod raro aut fere numquam eam inviseret. Nam a principio dominatus sui vias publice sternendas mandavit; deinde post annum aetatis quadragesimum nusquam urbem ingressus est, aut cuipiam ex carioribus id licere voluit, cum ipse ex arce plerumque excederet, et ad oppida vicina usque migraret. Urbem certe toto tempore principatus sui ab omni contagione servavit inlesam, dispositis magna diligentia custodibus et locis, in quibus peste aliqua infecti ducerentur curarenturque a medicis, quos ad huiusmodi custodiam etiam salubriori tempore paratos habuit.

their actual merits. What really mattered to him was that the secret vices and virtues of each and every one of his employees
would be fully revealed, and would, so to speak, clash before his
very eyes, so that he would come to know not just what each man
was doing, but even what he was thinking.

ː 35 ː

How he governed the cities of his realm.

He did not treat all of his cities in the same manner. Milan for
example he exempted from taxation for as long as he could, and
only imposed taxes on it when he came under pressure in the Venetian war. As for the embellishment of Milan, many feel he was
quite neglectful, for the very walls of the city were going to ruin
partly out of negligence, and partly because they were so ancient. I
am personally inclined to think that he allowed this to happen
because he rarely if ever visited Milan. For at the beginning of his
reign he ordered the streets to be paved in the public interest. But
then, after he turned forty, he ceased coming into the city altogether, or to allow any of his close associates to come in. His wont
was to leave the Castle of Porta Giovia and to travel directly to his
other nearby residences. It is nevertheless true that he kept Milan
free of plague for the entire duration of his reign. He did this by
ordering a careful watch to be kept, and by establishing places
where plague victims could be isolated and treated by doctors.
These doctors were kept on alert even in times when plague was
not an immediate threat.

: 36 :

De aedificiis per eum conditis.

In aedificando sumptuosus et elegans. Extant pleraque aedificia ab eo condita, maioris tamen impensae quam firmitatis; nam quae per ipsum avitis arcibus adiecta sunt, ad necessitatem magis quam ad ornatum confecta videntur. Sola moenia ad occiduam partem arcis Mediolanensis interiecta veteri muro, quae ab sinistra monumenta dividunt, miraculo prope similia fuere. Aedificavit et in oppido avito arcem Cusagi ad septimum lapidem ab urbe satis luculentam inter nemora, conscitasque manu latebras ferarum, per quas studio venandi a curis levaretur. Amplioris praeterea iucunditatis domum in Viglevani oppido erexit, ex cuius speculariis per ampla aularum spatia devectus, circumspiceret undique subiectas et patentes camporum amenitates. Illud autem praecipuum ex omnibus aedificium ipsius opera erectum constat, oppidum scilicet Piceleonis, cuius moles circumacta moenibus tanta latitudine aequatur, ut nullis machinis aut tormentis labefactari queat.

: 36 :

His building projects.

In building his tastes ran to both extravagance and elegance. A number of the buildings he constructed still stand, though they testify more to lavish expenditure than to solidity of structure. Where he made additions to his ancestral castles, he did so more out of necessity than for aesthetic reasons. There is one exception: the walls on the western side of the Castle of Porta Giovia. These are interlaid into the old wall, and separate the fortifications on the left. They were truly a miracle of architecture. In his ancestral heartland Filippo also built the Castle of Cusago, seven miles from Milan and rather splendid in its forest setting. This place included suitable coverts for wild beasts and here he could come to enjoy the excitement of the hunt and forget his cares. In addition to this he built an even more pleasant abode in Vigevano: from its windows, as he passed through the vast salons, Filippo could gaze out in all directions at the beauties of the fields spread out below. But by far the most important of all the buildings he erected was the fortress of Pizzighettone. Its massive bulk was contained within walls so thick that no artillery or cannon fire could ever hope to smash it to the ground.[74]

: 37 :

De cura et restitutione sacrarum aedium.

Aedes sacras pluribus in locis aut disiectas restituit, aut ex integro aedificavit. Mediolanense templum, quo nullum aetate nostra architectura et marmore illustrius visitur, ut in dies erigeretur, diligentissime curavit. Nam spectaculis publicis, quibus oblatio annua fiebat, aliquando interfuit, et absens omni pomparum ordine celebrari iussit a suis; exteros etiam legatos, si qui accessissent, adesse voluit. Cum Bernabovis avi sui curiam solo aequasset, disiectis peristilis, columnas omnes ecclesiae contulit, quae Petri Martiris nomini inscribitur, hisque sacerdotum atria ornavit, structis bifariam candidis nigrisque lapidibus. Omnibus praeterea in oppidis, ad quae peregrinationis causa veheretur, templa construxit; nec Mediolani dumtaxat, sed exteris in locis, ut Genuae videmus, solemnia suo nomine erectis sacris celebrari voluit.

: 38 :

De matrimoniis et prole eiusdem.

1 Expositis his quae ad res bello paceque gestas spectare videbantur, deinceps interiores eius mores domesticamque vitam ex ordine dicemus.

: 37 :

How he cared for and restored sacred buildings.

In quite a few locations he either restored churches that had fallen into serious disrepair, or built entirely new ones. He made sure that work continued apace on the Duomo of Milan, a building that must be regarded as the most outstanding piece of stonework and architecture constructed in our time. In addition he had funds set aside annually to support public entertainments. He some-times attended these in person, but if he were absent he ordered that they be held with all due pomp and circumstance by his reti-nue. And he also wanted foreign dignitaries to attend, should any be in Milan at the time. When he tore down the house of his great-uncle Bernabò, and the courtyard was lying in ruins, he had all of its columns brought to the Church dedicated to Saint Peter Martyr. He then used these columns to beautify the cloister there with a double peristyle of black and white stone. He also built churches in all of the strongholds where he was accustomed to spend time. He wanted masses to be celebrated in his name not only in Milan, but abroad as well, in places like Genoa, wherever he had erected sacred buildings.[75]

: 38 :

His marriages and children.

Having thus far related what pertains to Filippo's actions in peace and war, I will next proceed to tell of the inner man and to detail his private life.[76]

2   Sponsam pepigit adolescens Sophiam marchionis Montisferati filiam, quam certis deinde ex causis omisit. Interfecto vero fratre, cum egens omnium de vita dubitaret, suadentibus amicis, Beatricem antea Facino nuptam duxit uxorem, auctore vel in primis Bartholomaeo de la Capra Mediolanensi archiepiscopo, ut eius opibus non exercitus modo, sed urbes a Facino captas obtineret. Fuerat autem Facinus ex ducibus Iohannis Galeaz Philippi patris, post cuius obitum, dessidentibus inter se urbibus atque militibus, Alexandriam, Terdonam aliaque oppida vi ceperat, demum Mediolano per factionem intercepto, Papiam occuparat. Defuncto igitur Facino in arce Papiensi diutino ex morbo, nactus temporum comoditatem, eam sibi uxorem desumpsit. Bello autem Veneto primo, pari fere necessitate coactus est Mariam Allobrogum ducis filiam uxorem ducere.

3   Ex utraque nihil liberorum tulit. Ex Agnete vero concubina modico intervallo filias duas genuit, Blancham scilicet et Luciam. Blancha Francisco Sfortiae denupta liberos tulit Iohannem Galeaz et Ippolitem. Lucia cum infans adhuc esset, modicis exactis diebus excessit e vita.

While still quite young he was engaged to marry Sofia, the   2
daughter of the Marquis of Monferrato, but for various reasons
the marriage never took place. Then when his brother had been
murdered, and he was in dire need and even feared for his own
life, his friends persuaded him to marry Beatrice, the widow of
Facino Cane.[77] The man advocating this scheme was the archbishop of Milan, Bartolomeo della Capra. The idea was that such
a marriage would provide Filippo with both an army and the immediate possession of the cities that had once been under Facino's
control. Facino had in fact been one of the captains hired by
Filippo Maria's father, Duke Gian Galeazzo. When Gian Galeazzo
died, and a state of confusion ensued, Facino had seized Alessandria, Tortona, and other places by force of arms. He eventually
gained Milan through political intrigue, and then occupied Pavia.
So when Facino died in Pavia after a long illness, Filippo Maria
seized his chance and married the widowed Beatrice. During his
first war with Venice, however, similar circumstances forced him
to marry Maria, daughter of the Duke of Savoy.[78]

He had no children from either of these two marriages. But his   3
concubine Agnese del Maino gave him two daughters in quick succession: Bianca and Lucia. Bianca later married Francesco Sforza
and had two children by him: Gian Galeazzo[79] and Ippolita. Lucia
died in infancy, having lived for only a few days.

: 39 :

Quemadmodum erga uxores se habuerit.

1   Beatricem uxorem a natura procacem et avaram per aliquod tempus patienter tulit, ita ut eodem cubiculo admitteret cibariisque ab
ea confectis uteretur assistentemque mensae suae, veluti pedotri-
vam, facile perferret; mox adulterio convictam capite mulctavit,
extorta prius veritate per tormenta.

2   Cum Maria Allobroga seperatim vixit: nam domum illi privatim
aedificavit in arce Portae Iovis. Prioris praeterea suspicione adeo
semovit ab omni virorum congressu, ut solae mulieres domesticis
illi ministeriis assisterent, nec quispiam ad eam accederet nisi mo-
nitus ab eo. Hanc Antonio pantomimo agnomento Bechariae
custodiendam tradidit. Plerumque etiam accersitam in priori thalamo expectare iussit, deinde remisit intactam, quamquam adeo
cupidam sui, ut si forte dextram eius tetigisset, abluere recusaret.
Ferunt novum quodam incidisse, quod illum a contubernio eius
deterreret: nam cum ad se evocatam illustri die comprimere optaret, canem custodiae electum, percepto strepitu, in illum prosi-
luisse, eaque ex re pavefactum a concubitu eius abstinuisse. Huius
ut interiorem mentem scrutaretur secretioraque praesciret, sacer-
dotem quendam confessorem eius ordinavit, qui delicta quaeque
exquisitissime perquireret intellectaque, si periculum inspiceret,

: 39 :

How he behaved toward his wives.

With his wife Beatrice, by nature a bold and grasping woman, he   1
showed remarkable submissiveness at first, even admitting her to
his sleeping quarters, eating the food she prepared, and allowing
her to be present at his meals, as a kind of supervisor. Soon however, when she had been convicted of adultery, he had her be-
headed, after first getting her to confess under torture.[80]

With Maria of Savoy he lived apart, for he built her private   2
quarters within the walls of the Castle of Porta Giovia. Suspicion
engendered by what had happened with his first wife prompted
him to make sure this second one would have no contact whatsoever with men; so only women were allowed to enter her service,
and no one could approach her without obtaining his prior approval. He placed her under the guardianship of the pantomime
Antonio Beccaria. He frequently summoned her to the marriage
bed he had shared with his first wife, ordered her to stay there
awhile, then dismissed her untouched, although she for her part
was so eager for physical intimacy with him that if she so much as
managed to brush his hand she would later refuse to be washed.
It is said that a strange occurrence caused him to avoid sleeping
with his wife, for it transpired that once, having had her called
into his bedroom at dawn with the intention of making love to
her, one of his most alert watch dogs, hearing a noise, suddenly
leaped upon him, giving him such a fright that he henceforth
shunned the marriage bed. In order to probe into his wife's inner-
most thoughts, and to find out her deepest secrets, he appointed a
certain priest to be her confessor. This man's job was to examine as
thoroughly as possible any transgressions she might confess to,
then to report immediately if he discovered anything suspicious.

subito referret. Agnetem concubinam pari modo observari voluit in oppido Abiatis. Blancham praeterea filiam una cum matre educari iussit, nec nisi viro maturam traduxit in urbem.

: 40 :

De pietate eiusdem in parentes et fratres.

1 Patris memoriam religiosissime coluit, nec nisi seriis in rebus, quae ab eo gesta essent, referri voluit. Matrem vero adeo dilexit, ut nemini ex his, qui necis eius conscii fuerant, indulserit. Cabrinum Fundulum post receptam Cremonae urbem haud multo deinde ad necem compulit, quod matri suae insidias una cum reliquis struxisse noverat. Speronum etiam Petrasanctam veluti participem eius sceleris, non dignitate modo submovisse contentus, supplicio affecit.

2 Cum Iohanne Maria natu maiore, quem unicum fratrem legitimum habuit, primo concorditer et amice vixit, cum seperatim hic Papiae, ille Mediolani moram duceret; mox sugerentibus aemulis ad bellicas contentiones usque descendit, quae res non mediocrem calamitatem utrique attulit. Quippe Facinus, de quo praescripsimus, temporum comoditate percepta, cum Mediolani urbem per factionem recepisset, conversis signis Papiam occupavit. Captus est ea tempestate et bonis omnibus exutus Ubertus December genitor meus, Iohannis Mariae secundi Mediolanensium ducis secretarius;

The duke wanted his concubine Agnese del Maino subjected to the same level of surveillance within the Castle of Abbiategrasso. He ordered in addition that his daughter Bianca was to remain there and be raised by her mother. He would not allow Bianca to come to Milan until she was of marriageable age.

: 40 :

His devotion to his parents and brothers.

He was most assiduous in cultivating the memory of his father, 1 and would not tolerate his being remembered for anything other than for his greatest deeds. His love for his mother was such that he was unwilling to pardon any of those who were responsible for her death. He had Cabrino Fondulo executed not long after the taking of Cremona, because he learned that he had been one of those who had plotted treachery against her. He was not content to have another participant in the same plot, Sperone da Pietrasanta, removed from his high office, but had him put to death.[81]

With his elder and only legitimate brother Giovanni Maria he 2 at first lived harmoniously and in peace, for they maintained separate residences, the one in Pavia and the other in Milan. But soon the rivalry between factions led to open conflict, a move that severely damaged both parties. For Facino Cane, whom we have already mentioned, exploited the tumult to seize Milan, then unleashed his forces to occupy Pavia as well. My own father Uberto Decembrio, secretary to Giovanni Maria, second Duke of Milan, was taken prisoner at this time and stripped of all his property. The reason was that he had tried to negotiate a settlement between

nam cum herum suum cum Philippo fratre conciliare cuperet, litteris a Facino interceptis, custodiae iniicitur.[3]

3   Sed ut ad Philippum redeam, quamquam fratri adversaretur,
eum tamen unice dilexit, quippe cum imaginem eius a Michelino
depictam, cuius fama inter ceteros aetatis suae illustris fuit, in deliciis habuit. Idem cum fratres duos diversis e matribus genitos et
nothos haberet, Gabrielem scilicet et Antonium, iuniorem ex his
Antonium penes se continue habere voluit, et veluti filium in eadem aula innutritum erudivit, ornavit; quinetiam cum Mediolani
ducatum suscepisset, Novariensis urbis dominum instituit; reliquit etiam heredem; demum ob intemperantiam procacitatemque
vivendi alienavit a se; nec nisi Nicolai marchionis Estensis verbis
exhortatus, denuo restituit. Iacobum praeterea Gabrielis filium
evocatum ad se, quamvis nothum et ambiguae stirpis, non solum
consilio praeesse voluit, verum etiam Terdonensis urbis dominio
praefecit reliquitque pariformiter heredem, cum Antonii vitam
omnino reprobaret; cuius demum protervos mores temeraritatem-
que loquendi quam patienter tulerit, notum est. Habebat enim
hoc vel in primis a natura praecipuum, ut suorum errata diutissime perferret, nec nisi delictorum turba fatigatus a clementia de-
sisteret.

his master and his master's brother Filippo Maria. When Facino intercepted the letters pertaining to this matter, he had my father arrested and thrown into jail.[82]

But to return now to Filippo, although it is true that he op-   3
posed his brother, he loved him dearly nonetheless, for he kept a picture of him, painted by the most famous of the artists of those times, Michelino da Besozzo, among his most treasured posses-sions. Filippo was equally devoted to his two brothers born of different mothers and both illegitimate, Gabriele and Antonio.[83] He wanted the younger of these, Antonio, to be constantly at his side, and he had him brought up and properly educated at court, treating him like a son. When he had taken over the Duchy of Milan, he made Antonio lord of Novara. He even made him his heir, but later changed his mind on account of the man's lack of discipline and immoderate conduct. It was only when Niccolò d'Este lodged a special appeal on Antonio's behalf that Filippo re-stored him to favor. He also summoned to his court Giacomo,[84] Gabriele's son, even though he was illegitimate and of uncertain stock. Not only did he appoint Giacomo to preside over his coun-cil, he even made him lord of Tortona and his heir, since he disap-proved entirely of Antonio's lifestyle. The patience he showed in bearing Antonio's reckless behavior and wild tongue is well known. For Filippo had one quality inscribed in his character above all others: he could put up with the faults of his family members for a very long time, and would only act against them when they had truly worn him down with a long list of crimes.

: 41 :

Quemadmodum suorum animos experiebatur.

1 Nullus princeps adeo callidus in pertentandis suorum animis fuisse legitur, qui non huius astu et calliditate superatus sit. Utebatur enim inexquisitissimis artibus et fere immeditatis. Praeterea ut cuiusque mores cognovisset, astus anectebat; dicere enim solebat neminem ex suis sic secrete degere, cuius mentem, cum libuisset, non excuteret; et ut verbis suis utar, cui non bollum evomere compelleret.

2 Modus autem pertentandi suorum mentes hic fere fuit: cum domesticis non fideret, certa lege cubiculares astrinxerat, ut sine interprete thalamum exire nemo auderet, aut cum ullo colloqui; in cubiculum recepti non nisi quibusdam versarentur nihilque secreto dicerent. In qua re delinquentes annotabat. Remisiores vero, aut si quos continentiores animadverteret, alia et quidem diriori via experiebatur. Nam solitos ad se accedere plerumque excludebat, exclususque observabat an forte quaererentur, aut quippiam temere de se dicerent; qua ex causa hoc dicto utebatur: 'Credidissem, si tacuisses.' Cum errore aliquo devictos deprehendisset, modo

: 41 :

The methods he used to probe the minds of his men.

We know of no prince in history so skilled in assessing the loyalty   1
of his dependents that he could outrank Filippo Maria in shrewdness and cunning. In this area the duke truly perfected techniques
of the most exquisite and refined kind imaginable. He was quite
capable, in order to get to the bottom of someone's character, of
thinking up some clever plan appropriate to the case. He used to
say that there was no one in his entourage who could keep a secret
from him, for anytime he wanted he could shake it out of them,
or, to use his own words, he could force them "to cough up what
was eating them."

Here is how he would put his men to the test. Since he did not   2
trust anyone in his household, he bound those closest to him to a
strict set of rules. No one was to dare leave the duke's private
chambers unaccompanied, and there was to be no talking as they
exited. People were to be admitted to his presence only in groups,
and while in attendance were not allowed to whisper in low tones
among themselves. The duke himself took note of anyone who
disobeyed these rules. For those who obeyed, including even the
most obedient of the obedient, he devised ever more rigorous
tests. He might for example single out a group of men who were
used to having frequent access to his person, and suddenly refuse
to see them. He would then observe how they reacted, whether for
example they complained of ill treatment, or whether they unad-
visedly said anything bad about him. In such cases, the duke
would say to the men concerned: "You would have won my trust,
if only you had been able to keep your mouths shut." When he
caught anyone in flagrant violation of the rules, he would sometimes shower them with gifts, while at other times he might just

augebat donis, modo spoliabat, nunc ad honores pervehebat, nunc ad infima quaeque detrudens vexabat animo.

3   Quosdam novo inquisitionis genere tentavit: nam modestiam professis voluptates subiciebat, et an continentes vere essent, scrutabatur. Fuere etiam, quos exoletorum suorum contubernio admoveret, quasi litteris erudituros quempiam ex his lasciviorem, quibus loca secretiora et opportuna tradebantur: demum per rimas observabantur a suis an quidquam attentarent, aut lascive molirentur.

4   Nullus denique in aula eius observatus est, ut Ianus Feregosus Genuensium dux dicere solebat, qui non aliquo calliditatis genere vexatus sit, et ad intemperantiam demum ob fragilitatem iramque compulsus.

: 42 :

De patientia in delinquentes et modo puniendi.

1   Delinquentes patienter tulit, hactenus tamen ut ulcisceretur in tempore. Neminem ex suis, quamvis iratus, contumelia affecit, aut asperioribus verbis verberibusve insectatus est. Solebat enim tacitus persistere, et quae quisque aut diceret aut faceret quietus annotare; deinde alio loco, alio tempore, prout libuisset, ulcisci. Iratum

as easily strip them of everything they owned. He could lift such offenders up to the highest honors, or cast them down to the lowest depths, and utterly crush their spirits.

There was one category of men for whom he devised a test with   3
an entirely new twist, for he would take those who preached moderation and dangle the prospect of pleasure before their eyes, just to see whether they were really able to resist temptation. He might bring a man of this kind into contact with his harem of young boys, for example, on the pretext of getting him to educate one of the more lascivious among the bunch. The preceptor would be hived off with his pupil in some very private place, one most propitious for mischief. Then the two of them would be observed through peepholes by some of the duke's men, to see whether they tried any funny business, or made any nasty moves.

In short, no one who came under surveillance in the duke's   4
court — and we have the words of the Doge of Genoa Giano Fregoso to back this up — ever escaped without being harassed by some trick or another. The tendency was to crack under such pressure and eventually to betray one's feelings of anger and helplessness.

: 42 :

His patience with wrongdoers and his way of punishing them.

With those who did wrong he showed patience, until the time fi-   1
nally came to punish them. He never subjected any of his own people to abuse, or attacked them verbally or physically, even when they made him angry. His method was rather to remain silent, and to take note quietly of what each offender said or did; then at some future time and place of his own choosing, he would take his

deprehendere haud facile fuit: nam ridere consueverat; unico ex signo venae infra frontem tumefactae prodebat animum.

2   Cum aliquando litteras illi recitarem, praesente quodam ex suis, interrogassetque illum nescio quid, is vero vel timiditate vel ignorantia sileret, indignatus sagittae astam, quam manu tenebat, perfregit in caput; mox facti pertaesum saepius ad astantes dixisse constat: 'At hic nihil respondit coegitque me hac sua obstinatione delinquere.' Fuit is Paulus ex antiquioribus lixis in inicio sui principatus.

3   Ceterum ut nemo ad iram tardior illo fuit, sic ad conciliandum difficilior. Nam immeditatis temporibus in excogitatis artibus unumquemque secundum gradus detorquebat, vel consiliis ingredi solitos privabat honore, vel regia excludebat, vel per insolitos modos spoliabat officiis, aut alio quopiam turbationis genere vexabat, ut quisque se plecti prius sciret, quam reatum intelligeret.

4   Neminem ab ullo suorum verberari passus est. Si qui ausi essent, puniebat; nihil tamen magis quam linguae intemperantiam cohercuit, in qua re longinquitate temporis metiebatur delicta.

5   Saepe etiam sortem suam conquerentes verbis afflixit, inquiens eos pati oportere, quae multi deinceps passuri essent, neminem quippe apud se diuturnum habere locum. Quosdam etiam per

revenge. It was indeed difficult to catch him in an angry mood, for he was habitually merry; the one thing that betrayed his inner wrath was a vein that would swell up on his lower forehead.

Once when I was reading him a letter, with one of his people present, he happened to ask that person a question. Whether out of fear or ignorance, the poor man remained silent, whereupon Filippo Maria flew into such a rage that he broke the shaft of an arrow he held in his hand over the man's head. Then, horrified by what he had just done, he kept repeating to those who had witnessed the incident: "The fellow refused to answer me; it was his stubbornness that caused me to do wrong." The man in question was one Paolo, an old camp follower from the early days of Filippo's reign.[85]

On the other hand, just as Filippo was the slowest of the slow to be moved to anger, so no one was more difficult to win over. For just when you were least expecting it he would unleash some long-meditated plan, dishing it out to each according to his station. He would take someone who belonged to the inner circle of his counselors and strip them of their privileges, or maybe cut off their access to his palace, or deprive them in some other way of their position; or he might think up some other means of unsettling them, so that they were basically struck down by the punishment before they even knew they had committed an offense.

He would not allow any of his own people to be beaten. If someone dared raise a hand against one of them he would be punished. One thing above all others, however, he could not stand, and that was incessant tongue wagging. Here he measured the gravity of the offense by the length of time it had gone on.

He often upbraided those of his men who complained of their lot, saying they had best get used to hardship, as many of them were destined to undergo further suffering, seeing as how no one stayed for long in his favor. There were indeed those who found themselves banished from the court for ten years, nor were they in

decenium exclusit ab aula, neque aliis tamen officiis interim am-
movit. Quibusdam carceres perpetuos indixit, nonnullos pro de-
functis habitos custodiri iussit. Quo in numero fuit Georgius
Cornarius Venetorum dux, quem captum in Telina valle, quod asperius in eum invectus esset, hoc supplicio affecit: clausus enim
Modiciae per decenium et amplius, elato funere, pro defuncto
conclamatus est.

6   Nonnullos praeterea sibi invisos exteris in locis clam detineri
fecit; deinde ad se perductos cum tormentis affecisset, ad eadem
loca transferri iussit, ita ut nec a quo capti aut quibus in partibus
deducti et affecti poena essent, facile cognoscerent. Pluribus annis
nonnullos teterrimo carcere inclusos tenuit, ut Iohannis Caroli
iunioris filium ac Cabrini Funduli, quem sponte desipientem iussit
liberari.

: 43 :

De dissimulatione ingenii sui.

1   Dissimulandi ingenio neminem illi parem fuisse legimus: adeo
enim astutissimus et sagax fuit, ut iuxta vetus proverbium per-
petuo regnare posset. Itaque raro quid vellet fatebatur, sed novo
quodam dicendi genere celabat omnia. Cum quempiam ex suis

the meantime offered any alternative appointment. Still others were sentenced to imprisonment for life, and of those he ordered quite a few to be pronounced dead, even though they were still being held as prisoners. One of these latter was Giorgio Corner, the Venetian military commander.[86] When captured by our forces in the Valtellina, this man railed a bit too violently against Duke Filippo, who accordingly devised the following punishment: the gentleman was shut up in the prison at Monza for ten years and more, while in the meantime his funeral was celebrated and he was pronounced dead.

Filippo ordered quite a few of his enemies to be held secretly in remote locations. He then had them brought before him, and when they had been tortured he had them returned to these same outlying places. In this way people were prevented from ever knowing who had captured them, or where they had been taken and punished. He had a number of people shut up in the darkest dungeons for many years. Such was the case with the son of Giovanni Carlo the younger,[87] as well as with the son of Cabrino Fondulo.[88] When the latter had finally gone completely and utterly mad Filippo had him freed.

6

: 43 :

His genius for dissimulating.

We have read of no one who ever matched his skill in the art of dissimulation. Here he was truly so incredibly astute and accomplished that, to quote an old saw, he might well have ruled forever. He would for example rarely reveal his intentions, preferring instead to hide everything in deliberately convoluted language. He might for example pick out someone at court who had an out-

1

virtute aliqua celebrem et notum minus in honore haberet penes
se, non cessabat identidem praeconiis et laudibus eum tollere, ut
plerique mirarentur, aliter sentire eum, aliter facere, torquebatque
audientem, veluti incertum sortis suae.

2   Quibus autem honores opesque tribuisset, verbis insectabatur,
nunc saevitiae arguens, nunc stulticiae, quasi felicitate illa indignos
et inutiles eadem censura prosequebatur omnes. Cum a curis aliquando vacaret, de suorum conditionibus loqui consueverat, et ut
libuisset, alios laudare, alios reprehendere, ut a circumstantibus
deferretur sermo, et vel spe illos aleret, vel torqueret metu.

3   Cum aliquem inter suos habere cuperet, multo ante accersebat
implebatque spe, deinde cum oblitus videretur, revocabat. Bene-
meritis etiam de se opes collaturus, miro astu per alios errogabat,
quasi inscius collati beneficii. Eo modo in bonis et malis inopine
aggrediebatur omnes; quin imo aliud ab eo quod quisque expete-
ret, et alia quidem via conferebat.

4   Illud profecto admiratione dignum, quod experti nonnumquam
sumus: cum cuipiam ex suis opes aut honores impartiri cuperet,
multis ante diebus levissimis de rebus interpellare, vel quaestione
praeposita, vel ambigua interpretatione admonere solitum, ut

standing reputation in some field of endeavor and demote them. He would then go around singing the fallen man's praises to the skies, leaving people to wonder at his saying one thing and doing its opposite. But in fact the whole show was calculated to torment his listeners into thinking that they might be next in line to lose his favor.

If he had showered someone with riches and honors, he would then criticize them, calling them a boor or a fool. The point of the exercise was to make anyone who had been honored feel unworthy and inadequate, and to show everyone else that they too were subject to the same strictures. When the duke was not too busy, he might sometimes chance to talk about the people at his court. In so doing he would casually praise some individuals and complain about others, the idea being that his hearers would report what he had said to the interested parties, raising hopes in some quarters, and spreading fear in others.

If he wanted to enlist someone in his service, he would start off by summoning them and filling them with high hopes. Then after a long while, just when he seemed to have completely forgotten about the matter, he would suddenly call the person in question back to the court. If he needed to reward one of his people for outstanding performance, he would very cleverly arrange to have the reward presented by someone other than himself. That way he could pretend to know nothing of the business. This tactic left him free to treat everyone in the same unpredictable way, for better or for worse, so that you might receive something from him that you least expected, and it would be conveyed to you through some unusual channel.

And here is something really odd, that I myself experienced on many occasions: when he wanted to honor or reward someone at court, he would begin the process days in advance by pestering them with strange and ambiguous questions on irrelevant and vaguely menacing topics. This naturally led the person subjected

admiraretur ille, nec satis discernere posset insolitam loquendi formam et inextricabiles ambages incertae mentis. Quin imo ut interiorem eius animum nulli patefaceret, saepenumero beneficia in eos delata conquestus est, quibus ipse contulisset, eosque supplicio affectos esse, quos sponte condemnasset.

: 44 :

De irrisione in plurimos facetissima.

1 Neminem praeterea adeo probatum apud omnes animadvertit, cui non facete irrideret. Scripsit aliquando ad Eugenium quartum summum pontificem, veluti de salute sua desperaret, scire se peccatorum turba circumsaeptum vereri, ne in exitu poena plecteretur, paratum se pati omnia, dummodo salvus esse posset, rogare eum ac precari, ut animae suae tutelam sumeret. Respondente deinde illo ac benigne suadente quid agendum esset, et oppida quaedam, ut culpae satisfaceret, ab eodem deposcente, in hunc modum rescripsit: corpus suum se minus carum habere quam animam, statum vero dominatus sui saluti corporis et animae anteferre.

2 Confessorem habuit Petrum Alzatum Ordinis Praedicatorum, virum insigni religione ac doctrina, quem ad se plerumque frustra

to such treatment to wonder what was up, it being impossible to plumb the depths of talk so strange and twisted that it seemed to issue from a deranged mind. The fact that Filippo Maria revealed his deepest thoughts to no one meant that often he would complain about someone receiving favors, when it was he himself who had conferred them, or he would express regret that certain people had been put to death, when he himself had ordered their execution.

: 44 :

His taste for a good joke.

He spared no one — not even the most exalted of personages — the barbs of his sharp wit. Once he wrote to Pope Eugenius IV, pretending to be at death's door. He knew — so he wrote — that he was surrounded by a pack of sinners, and he feared that at his death he would be condemned to the fires of Hell. He was ready, he said, to make any sacrifice, so long as it would guarantee his eternal salvation. He concluded by pleading with the pope to show him how he could save his soul. The pope answered by advising him most kindly as to what was to be done: the best way for him to make amends would be to cede to the papacy a certain number of his fortified towns. To this Filippo wrote back as follows: well might he value his body less than his soul, but he held the security of his state to be far more important than the salvation of either body or soul.[89]

His confessor was the Dominican friar Pietro da Alzate, a most devout and learned man. Filippo would often needlessly call him in and then, after keeping the poor fellow waiting for hours on

accersiret, deinde diutius expectantem demitteret, praemonitum
operiri commodiores confitendi horas.

3   Venerat aliquando ad eum Amadeus Pedemontium princeps,
cuius sororem conubio duxerat: contemplatus itaque habitum eius,
quo idem ceterique sui utebantur, exilem admodum atque inep-
tum, Gallorum more, canes venaticos adduci iussit, contectos eo
vestis genere, quo in silvis uti solent, ut ab apris tuti sint, simi-
lesque eorum ornamentis per irrisionem esse dixit.

4   Obsequentes sibi etiam plerumque delusit. Francisco Sfortiae
genero suo offerenti subsidia sua, cum Brixiam obsideret, asseren-
tique se magno precio a Venetis requiri, nil aliud respondit, quam
ut ad eos cito pergeret, nec quousque Brixia a suis caperetur expectaret, magnum subinde sibi dedecus et damnum affuturum.

: 45 :

*Qua industria etiam hostes ad
benivolentiam alliciebat.*

1   Miro praeterea ingenio non subditos modo, sed hostes ad benivolentiam alliciebat, nec per Italiam solum, sed universum fere terrarum orbem multorum votis obsecutus est, quo plurimos sibi ob-
noxios faceret. Bello Veneto primo Mediolanenses in regiam cogi

end, he would dismiss him, telling him that a more convenient time for confession would have to be found.

It happened once that his brother-in-law Amedeo, Prince of 3 Piedmont, paid a visit to his court.[90] Filippo noted the way this prince was dressed, and saw too that his retainers were wearing the same outfit: all of them were attired in the Savoyard fashion, which was outlandish and primitive by Milanese standards. So Filippo had his hunting dogs brought in, each one draped with those protective coverings that are used on the hunt to keep them safe from the tusks of wild boars. Then he circulated the joke that the Savoyards were dressed like his dogs.

Filippo was often capable of mocking even those who humbly 4 sought his favor. His son-in-law Francesco Sforza for example offered to help him subdue the town of Brescia, adding that his services were also being requested by the Venetians, who were ready to pay him quite a handsome sum. But Filippo's only answer was to advise his son-in-law to join the Venetians as quickly as possible, before Brescia fell to the Milanese forces. That way Francesco would be on the losing side and suffer the full consequences of defeat.[91]

: 45 :

With what skill he could win friendship
even from his enemies.

He possessed a truly remarkable gift for winning the support not 1 only of his subjects, but even of his enemies, so that throughout Italy, and indeed practically the whole world, he gratified the wishes of many, gaining ever more converts to his cause. In regard to the first Venetian war for example, he had Milanese citizens

iussit, consulturos an pacem potius bellumve sequeretur; qua ex re promptiores eos ad exponendas facultates suas reddidit. Eo modo ut Senenses propicios sibi efficeret, aras in eorum urbe struere tentavit sanctorum suorum sacra continentes, quibus affici se diceret magna pietate.

2   Cum Nicolaum Perusinum ad stipendia sua habere cuperet, novo quodam honoris genere Franciscum eius filium demereri studuit; nam astiludio inductum solemni pompa, quamquam multis imparem, victoria donavit. Ludovicum etiam Mantuani marchionis filium, ex simultate quadam exclusum a patre, denuo illi conciliavit, eoque modo parentem eius benivolum sibi fecit, cum antea hostis esset.

3   Ugucionem Contrarium Venetorum partes foventem ultro Mediolanum ad regimen accivit, meditatus ea ex re Venetos facilius sibi credituros. Francisco Sfortiae genero suo, adversanti conatibus suis, mira quadam calliditate illusit, ut a Venetis averteret; nam filiam eius Blancham, quam illi desponsaverat, Ferrariam misit, velut ultro concessurus, quod pridem recusarat, et simul suspicionem illaturus amanti et cupido, ne Leonello marchionis filio in uxorem eam traderet.

4   Cum cuipiam sublandiri cuperet, admitti in regiam statim iubebat, eoque modo mitiorem ac promptiorem efficere solebat.

brought into the palace so that he could consult with them as to whether he should pursue war or peace. In this way he made his subjects more willing to foot the bill for war.[92] He used a similar technique with the Sienese: in order to win them over to his side he undertook to build a number of altars in their city. These were meant to house the relics of certain Sienese saints, to whom Filippo professed to have the profoundest devotion.[93]

When he wanted to enlist Niccolò Piccinino to serve in his 2 army, he thought up quite a clever way of honoring Niccolò's son, Francesco: having invited the young man to participate in a tournament, he then had him solemnly crowned as the victor, despite his mediocre performance. Filippo also managed to bring about reconciliation between Ludovico, son of the marquis of Mantua, and his father Gianfrancesco; for Ludovico had become estranged from his father due to family rivalries. In achieving this, Filippo even won the friendship of the marquis himself, whereas prior to this time the man had been his sworn enemy.[94]

Filippo convinced the Venetian partisan Uguccione de' Contrari 3 to join his government, thinking that by such a move he might make himself a more trustworthy figure in the eyes of the Venetians.[95] He devised an extremely clever trick to lure his future son-in-law Francesco Sforza, who was opposing his plans, into leaving the service of the Venetians. This involved sending his daughter Bianca, who was betrothed to marry Francesco, to Ferrara, making it look as if he were about to do something he had refused to do before, that is to give Bianca over to become the wife of Leonello, son and heir of the ruler of Ferrara. Such a prospect was bound to worry Sforza, who was wracked by desire and eager to marry Bianca himself.[96]

Whenever Filippo wanted to win over someone's affections, he 4 would order that they be given access to his court. This was a sure way of making them his pliable creatures. In the end it was by using such means that he turned so many of his enemies into

Postremo huiusmodi ex rebus plurimos ex hostibus amicos reddidit, praelata pietate, quamquam id a natura insitum haberet, ut victis semper faveret, victoribus obsisteret.

: 46 :

De adolescentibus institutis ad custodiam corporis sui.[4]

1   Adolescentes egregia forma praeditos et ornatu insignes penes se constituit. His regia tota patebat, cum his domestica colloquia, secreta, seria iocosque comunicabat; quocumque ipse diverteret, una proficescebantur. Iidem per vices dispositi continuo illi aderant, sive mensae, sive thoro,[5] sive alibi consisteret, una versabantur; his denique corporis sui non custodiam modo, sed curam dederat, quod alii licebat nemini. Hos per biennium et amplius, quam personae suae admoveret, sub pedotrivi[6] alicuius custodia inclusos paulatim exercebat, et an solitudinem, taciturnitatem ceteraque illi solita patienter ferrent, experiebatur. His non parentibus, non fratribus loqui fas erat, deinde probatos ad se accersebat; quibus continui custodes aderant, ne cum quopiam temere loqui aut congredi auderent.

2   Horum cum patientiam diutius expertus esset, aetate provectos, vel militiae admovebat, vel dignioribus officiis aulae praeferebat. Ab his praeterea responsa nobilibus dabantur, et quicquid

friends. The whole thing involved an outward show of kindness, though it was also true that he had engraved into his character one constant: he always extended his favor to the defeated and took a stand against the victorious.

: 46 :

The young men to whom he entrusted the care of his person.

He surrounded himself with well-endowed young men of great 1 beauty.[97] He gave them free run of the palace, and shared with them his private conversations, his secret dealings, his business and his pleasures. Wherever he went, they followed. They took turns being constantly by his side; whether he was at table, in bed,[98] or anywhere else, they would congregate around him. Their job was not only to keep watch over him, but also to minister to his bodily needs, something he would entrust to no one else. Before bringing these boys into direct contact with himself, he would have them trained in isolation under the supervision of a preceptor for a period of two years or more. The point of this exercise was to see whether the boy could bear the loneliness, the silence, and other quirks that were typical of the duke's personality. During this trial period the boy was not allowed to speak with his parents or siblings. Only when he had passed the test would he then be called to join the duke's circle. But once in service the boy would still be carefully watched, lest he dare meet or speak with anyone on the sly.

When such a boy had thoroughly proved himself through years 2 of service, and grown into adulthood, the duke would make him an officer in the army, or appoint him to some high position at court. It was through trusted men of this kind that he would

secretiori cognitione dignum esset, ad eum referebant. Nonnulli igitur ex ipsis praeclaro ingenio singularique prudentia noti evasere: quorum e numero Rainerius Vancalven fuit, natione Germanus adolescens, non solum magnitudine animi, sed dexteritate corporis longe praecellens; e nostris Andreas Biragus naturae mitioris atque illo dignitate longe superior, Iohannes Antonius Brixiensis civis, cui ob eximiam apud eum gratiam atque auctoritatem non familiares modo, sed senatus assurgere eumque principis vice colere ac venerari consueverat. His agros, pecunias, oppida elargiebatur, et quicquid lucrari illis libuisset, ultro permittebat. Hi denique erant, in quibus consisteret maiestas status sui, quos populus tamquam deos aliquos coleret, fuere et alii apud ipsum illustres, sed nequaquam his de quibus scripsimus ulla ex parte comparandi.

: 47 :

De custodia domus eius
et ingrediendi ordine.

1   Regiam eius nemo nisi solitus notusve ingrediebatur. Habitabat autem Mediolanensem arcem. Nulli itaque ad illum adcessus patebat, nisi praemonito eo atque praeviso. Custodibus enim adhibitis,

communicate with the Milanese nobility, and he also charged them with referring to him any matters requiring the utmost confidentiality. In this way quite a few of these favorites of his became famous for their skill and dexterity in handling delicate business. One example was the German lad Rainer Van Calven, who possessed not only superior mental gifts, but great physical prowess as well.[99] As for the Italians, there was Andrea Birago, a man of rather mild temperament and far superior in rank to the German fellow. Then too there was Giovanni Antonio, who hailed from the city of Brescia. He enjoyed such power and prestige at court that not only servants but even senators would rise up as he passed, venerating him as the duke's alter ego and courting his favor. Men such as these were rewarded with landed estates, monetary gifts, castles, and whatever else they might desire;[100] there were no limits to Filippo Maria's generosity with them, for he felt that they represented the majesty and power of his state, and should be worshipped like gods. There were of course other people of influence at court, but none who could even come close to matching those about whom I have just written.

: 47 :

*The watch kept over his residence
and how entry was regulated.*

Only those who were frequent and well-known visitors were allowed access to his place of residence, which he had established in the Castle of Porta Giovia in Milan. No one could gain entry here without his prior knowledge, for he had guards stationed throughout the palace, and their duty was to keep track of all movements in and out of the building. Entry was granted to those listed in the

qui introeuntes exeuntesque annotarent, diligentissime observabat omnes. Ingrediebantur vero in scriptis dediti praefinito servorum ordine, prout quisque maiore minoreve dignitate frueretur, quod quidem nulli nisi iusso licebat. Legatos vero, si quos eum adire oporteret, qua familia stipati essent, quo ordine servorum inquirebat; deinde prout libuisset, vel admittebat ad se, vel excludebat. Aulam priorem nobiles frequentabant, in his consiliares ac primores viri, nec aliud quam sedentes opperiebantur abeundi horas, nonnunquam consilio vacabant. Quidam mensae eius ministrantes in ulteriorem recipiebantur, pauci in cubiculum, et hi quidem vel servilibus officiis intenti, vel exoletorum suorum numero delecti. Nemini transgresso finitima urbi flumina, quamquam iussu eius, redire in regiam licuit, nisi denuo petita licentia. Nulli ad specularia accedere nisi constituto, paucis sedere concessum.

2   Hanc vitae solitudinem, quam primum Pergami urbem recepit, instituit. Cum ad se venientes audire nollet, simulata occasione unum ex domesticis evocabat, quasi cum eo locuturus, qua in re saepenumero Michaelem Comensem postulavit. Quoque magis ab omni suorum contubernio se amoveret, edicto prohibuit quempiam per pestifera transvectum loca ante quadragesimum ad se diem ire posse aulamve introire. Qua excusatione plurimos etiam e saluberrimis locis venientes exclusit a se; nec ullum valitudine aut morbo laborantem intra regiam extingui passus est, Iohanne Antonio, de quo praescripsimus, dumtaxat excepto.

day's protocol, together with the members of their retinue, each in order of their rank, all of which of course was subject to the duke's approval. If he was scheduled to receive the envoys of a foreign power for example, he wanted information on their dependents and their servants. He would then decide whether or not they would be admitted to see him. His antechamber was packed with Milanese nobles, including members of his councils and other leading figures. They would have to sit there for hours, waiting for permission to leave. Occasionally they would transact the business of government. Those who served him at table would be admitted to the inner sanctum. Very few were allowed to enter his bedroom, and these were either housekeepers, or they were selected from among his stock of wanton young boys. No one who had crossed the rivers that surround the city was allowed to return to the palace without obtaining fresh authorization, and this rule applied even to those who were summoned back by the duke himself. It was forbidden to appear before a window, unless by express permission. Few had the right to sit down.

He began to cultivate this solitary lifestyle shortly after con- 2 quering Bergamo.[101] When he was tired of listening to petitioners, he would feign some reason why he had to summon one of his courtiers, pretending he needed to have a word with him. The man he usually called for in these circumstances was Michele da Como. In order to remove himself as far as possible from physical contact with others, Filippo issued an edict prohibiting anyone who had been in plague-infested lands to come anywhere near him or his court for forty days. Using this excuse, he was able to keep away from himself even people who were coming to see him from quite healthy places. And another thing: he would not tolerate having anyone who was suffering from ill-health or sickness die within the walls of his court. The one exception here was the aforementioned Giovanni Antonio.

: 48 :

Quo ordine magistratus et digniores
admittebantur ab eo.

1 Solemnibus ac festis diebus neminem pullo indutum ad se accedere permisit; si qui accessissent, aditu prohibuit. Delectabatur vel
in primis purpureis candidisque coloribus; qua ex causa non magistratus modo, sed inferiores hoc vestis genere utebantur. Consiliares plerumque post cibum admittebat, nec tamen omnes, sed
eos dumtaxat, quos ad epistolas adesse oporteret, audiebatque
percursim, deinde ocio vacabat. Ceteris non idem habebatur ho-
nos: pauci in priorem aulam recipiebantur, paucissimi in secundam, demum, magistratibus egressis, una abibant.

2 Accedentibus ad eum principibus, nulli obviam profectus est
extra urbem, praeterquam Nicolao marchioni Estensi, quem unice
post reconciliationem dilexisse creditur; praeterea Iohanni Francisco Mantuae praefecto, cui in portis dumtaxat ultro affuit. Sigismondo Romanorum regi Canturium usque immeditatus occurrit
allocutusque illum est, fluvio utriusque acies dividente, armatus ob
praesentiam percussorum fratris, quos ille dominio aspirans una
duxerat. Ceteros, inter quos et reges extitere, recepit in curiam,

: 48 :

*The rules whereby officials and dignitaries
were admitted to see him.*

On festive or holy days he allowed no one dressed in dark colors to 1
enter his palace; if anyone tried to do so, they were denied access.
His preference was for purple and white colors, which is why not
only the officers of his court but also the less important people
there were required to dress as they did. He usually received the
members of his councils after meals. But not all were admitted:
only those whose presence was needed to assist with the day's correspondence. He would give his counselors short shrift, then turn
his attention to leisurely pursuits. But not everyone was so honored: few were admitted to his waiting room, and fewer still
moved on from here to the inner sanctum. When these fortunate
few finally emerged, everyone departed together.

When ruling princes came to visit the duke, he never went out 2
beyond the city walls to meet them. The one exception was Niccolò III d'Este, the Marquis of Ferrara. Niccolò was thought to be
the only person for whom Filippo Maria had conceived a true af-
fection, after the two were reconciled. There was also the case of
Gianfrancesco Gonzaga, lord of Mantua, but Filippo only went
out as far as the city gates to meet him. As for Sigismund, king of
the Romans, Filippo rashly rode out as far as Cantù to hold talks
with him. There the river constituted the only dividing line between two hostile armies. Filippo himself was decked out in full
battle array, given that Sigismund's forces included those who had
murdered his brother.[102] Sigismund had in fact brought these
people on purpose, as his intention was to reclaim Milan for the
empire. With all of the other rulers who came to visit him,
some of whom were kings, Filippo Maria stuck to his practice of

praemissa nobilium cohorte, quae illos idoneis in locis solita dignatione exciperet.

: 49 :

De secessibus finitimis ab urbe
et aquaeductibus per eum conditis.

1   E secessibus finitima urbi frequentavit, ut Cusagi arcem inter nemora virentesque lucos ac manu consitos sitam, in qua se oblectabat venandi studio; deinde haud longe Abiatis oppidum, vel cum longius Viglevanum usque proficiscebatur, frequenti populo et insigni arce domoque conspicuum, divertit et plerumque Galliate aucupio ductus, cum egresso domum campi longe lateque patescerent. Raro Modiciam, rarissime Papiam invisit, quamquam loci amoenitate traheretur; nam praeter urbis pulchritudinem, adlabente fluvio, inclitam et iucunditatem domus, cui nulla in Italia par est, agros circumsaeptos muro habuit, in quis lacus ac nemora inerant omni ferarum genere referta. Haec loca ab avo eius quondam incohata pater perfecerat.

2   Incepit et aquaeductus ab urbe, per quos ad omnia fere loca, in quibus assueverat, navi veheretur, sic compacta classe, ut cubiculi et aulae forma remaneret idemque servorum esset ordo. Eo modo

receiving them in his court, though he would send out a delegation of nobles to greet them in a suitable place, and according to the usages associated with their rank.

: 49 :

His places of residence near Milan and the waterways he built.

Among his country retreats he favored those located nearest to Milan.[103] An example was the Castle of Cusago, with its carefully tended groves and leafy forests. Here he loved to revel in the joys of the hunt. From here too he could proceed to the nearby town of Abbiategrasso, or even further afield to Vigevano, the latter place being famous for its thriving populace and its magnificent castle and residence. And often he would be lured on to Galliate by its promise of fowling, for when he went outdoors the fields stretched out before him in all directions. It was rare for him to visit Monza, and even rarer were his stays in Pavia, even though he felt quite drawn to the latter place on account of its many attractions. For besides the outstanding beauty of the city, with its gently gliding river, and the splendid castle, absolutely unequaled in Italy, there was the enclosed park, with its lakes and forests full of every possible kind of game. The building of this complex had been initiated by his grandfather, and completed by his father.[104]

Filippo developed a network of waterways radiating out from Milan, whereby he could be conveyed by boat to practically all of the places he was accustomed to visit. And the fleet that carried him was designed so as to replicate the layout of his private quarters and court, and to preserve the usual distribution of roles assigned to those who attended him. In this way he was borne along

Cusagum primo, deinde Abiate, post Belreguardum Papiamque ferebatur. Cum iam pinguior equo gravaretur, aliquando eo instrumento vectus est, quod legiam appellant, equis machinam per terram trahentibus. Egredientem urbem insignes currus, mulorum turba atque equorum conspicuo ornatu sequebatur. Meditatus est et aquae rivum, per quem ab Abiate Viglevanum usque sursum veheretur, aquis altiora scandentibus machinarum arte, quas concas appellant.

3   Egrediebatur autem potissime, cum quid laetum expectaret, morae impatiens. Eoque tempore modo hostia cubiculorum permutari, modo ipocausta ac fenestras in aliam transferri partem iubebat, ut regresso domum novitas ipsa solamen afferret.

4   Ex urbibus Cremonam Veneto bello primo, quo propius hostibus occurreret, ac Novariam tempore pestis invisit; verum paucissimis in eis commoratus est diebus.

: 50 :

De forma et figura corporis eius.

Forma fuit a principio non ineleganti, corpore eximio, et quod iustam staturam excederet, nulla deformitate addita, capite tereti et oblongo, quale manufactum plerumque aspicimus, capillo nigro ac demisso pone cervicem, oculis vegetis croceo suffusis, naso

first to Cusago, then to Abbiategrasso, and afterward to Bereguardo and to Pavia. Later on, when he became too fat to ride a
horse, he would sometimes be conveyed to his destination in what
was called his "skiff," with horses pulling the contraption overland.
As the duke issued forth from Milan he would be followed by a
cortege of triumphal cars, drawn by richly adorned mules and
horses. He also planned to have a canal built, whereby he might be
brought from Abbiategrasso up as far as Vigevano. This was to be
achieved by mechanically lifting the waters through a series of
what are called "locks."[105]

Whenever he would leave Milan in search of the pleasures of   3
the country Filippo was extremely impatient of any delays. In leaving too he would sometimes order that the doors to his rooms be
changed. Or he might have the fireplaces and windows switched
around, so that when he returned there would be something new
in place to bring him solace.

As for his cities, he visited Cremona during the first war with   4
Venice, in order to be nearer to the action, and he also went to
Novara during a time of pestilence. But his stays in these two cit-
ies lasted only a very few days.[106]

: 50 :

His physical appearance and attributes.

In the beginning his physical appearance was by no means dis-
pleasing.[107] He was an imposing figure of more than normal
height, but without other defects. His head was well proportioned
and longish, somewhat like those we are accustomed to admire in
sculpture. His hair was black, and he wore it long in the back. His
eyes were lively and tinged with a golden saffron color. He had a

brevi, productis superciliis, ore lato, mento resupino, maxilla ampla, mediocribus auribus, collo vero pinguiore; in ceteris corporis
partibus equalis, nisi quod manu breviore, et restrictioribus erat
digitis; pedibus vero adeo incurvis, ut vel stanti baculus plantae
subiceretur; facie obfusca, licet reliquo corpori candor inesset,
aspectu autem cogitanti adsimilis. Cuius effigiem, quamquam a
nullo depingi vellet, Pisanus insignis ille artifex miro ingenio spi-
ranti parilem effinxit.

: 51 :

De vestitu et reliqua supellectile domus eius.

1 Vestitu ac reliquo corporis ornatu etiam ab ineunte adolescentia
perinsignis fuit. Induebatur autem sericis purpura intinctis, vel
cum vilius, lana confectis vestibus eodem colore, vel amethestino,
ut a puericia assueverat; procedente mox tempore etiam ab eo se
continuit, cum nonnullos funereis in rebus prohibitos in regiam
venire pullo indutos, eo vestis genere abusos cognovisset. Delectatus est ea potissimum veste, quae honestissima haberetur, infra
poplitem demissa, clausis manicis, et ab utraque parte consutis
tunicis, ut etiam ensis per scisuras vestis truderetur, zona a tergo
reiuncta.

2 Kalendis vero Maiis, in quibus laeto omine urbem egredi et
primicias arborum deferre mos erat, viridi amiciebatur; cum aestas

94

small nose, thick eyebrows, and a wide mouth. He had a weak chin, large jaws, and ears of average size. His neck however was rather thick. The other parts of his body were of fairly standard size, except for his quite small hands and short fingers. His feet too were so crooked that he sometimes needed the support of a cane to stand on them. The skin of his face was dark in color, but the rest of his body was lily white. The general impression he made was that of a man lost in thought. He never wanted to let anyone paint his portrait, but that great artist Pisanello nevertheless created by a stroke of genius a living, breathing image of him.[108]

: 51 :

His clothes and the furnishings of his palace.

Even when still quite young he was renowned for his distinctive 1 dress and for the finery of his attire. He usually wore clothes made of silk with a purple dye. When dressing more informally however, he would switch to woolens of the same hue, or perhaps of dark violet, a color he had been accustomed to wear since childhood. But he soon gave up wearing this color altogether, for he noticed that people were using it to get around the ban on coming to the palace dressed in the dark hues of mourning.[109] He preferred above all else a type of garment considered to be most dignified: it fell to below the knee, with closed sleeves and lining sewn into either side so that you could whip out your sword through a secret opening. A belt fastened the garment in the back.

In the springtime, when it was the custom to issue joyfully 2 forth from the city and to gather the first fruits of May, the duke would deck himself out in green. When summer brought on the

incalesceret, nonnunquam sagulo eoque militari modo fimbriato,
in omnes partes subsuta purpura ac renitente; hieme sibilinis pel-
libus e Dacia usque devectis; medio tempore variis et armelinis,
aliquando argento intexta veste usus est; caligis duplici colore
destinctis, quarum dextera candido, sinistra amethestino fulgebat.
Postremo deposito omni ornatu, cum iam gravior esse cepisset,
nihil amplius quam cubicularibus indutus est tunicis, quas forma
strictiores et ad pedes usque demissas, turciscas appellant.

3   Capitis nullum onus pertulit. Levibus amictus infulis et ante
pendentibus, collum assidue vitta circumligabat, nec nisi estatis
temporibus huiusmodi velamenti genere carebat. In tondendo et
comendo tam incuriosus, ut saepe barbam negligeret.

4   Cum supellectile ornatissima et splendidissima habundaret, vix
modicis auleis et his quidem solemnibus diebus regiam ornari
passus est. Raro peristromatibus cubicula induit. Argento vero
modico, nec nisi ad quotidianas dapes necessario usus est.

: 52 :

Quibus cibariis potissimum utebatur.

1   Cibariis admodum communibus delectatum eum ferunt, praecipue autem usus est rapis, quod radicis genus a Comensi urbe
saepenumero iussit afferri; delectabatur et eo ferculi genere,
quod ex panico contuso, deinde decocto fit. Item pane ex milio

hot weather, he would usually wear a short cloak fringed in the military style and trimmed all around in shiny purple. In winter he wrapped himself up in sable furs that he had specially brought in from Dacia. Between seasons he would wear clothes lined with vair and ermine, sometimes with a silver trim. The leather shoes he wore were of two different colors: the one on the right foot was white, the one on the left foot of dark violet. Later on in life, when he began to put on so much weight, he gave up all this finery and took to wearing nothing more than dressing gowns of the long and rather tight-fitting variety that are known as "Turkish robes."

He could not bear to have anything heavy on his head. He 3 would wear a light woolen kerchief that hung down in front, fastening it in place with a fillet that he would wind several times around his neck. It was only in summer that he would abandon this protective headgear. As for cutting and caring for his hair, he was so negligent that he often went about unshaven.

Although he possessed the most splendid and stunning furni- 4 ture, he allowed only a very few tapestries to be hung in the palace, and these only on festive occasions. Rarely would he tolerate having any carpets in his bedrooms. He used very little silver at table, only what was strictly necessary to serve the daily meals.

: 52 :

His favorite foods.

They say he liked to eat simple foods,[110] especially turnips of the 1 kind he would often have brought to his table from Como. He also enjoyed a dish made from millet, ground up and then boiled. From childhood he had become accustomed to eating bread made from millet mixed with wheat, although he wanted it to be baked

frumentoque confecto a puericia assuetus, quamquam in confi-
ciendis panibus multiplici ex forma pistorem fatigaret. Pisces fere
omnes respuebat, thimalis exceptis. Vinum primo dilutius, deinde
meratius affectavit. Ex carnibus potissime in mensa vitulo, aedo
pulloque utebatur; vel cum voluptas exposceret, perdice aut fa-
siano aut coturnice, nullo condimento adhibito, quae tamen maxime appetebat, cum tempus prohiberet, nihil tamen pinguioris cibi
perferre poterat; qua ex causa etiam coturnicibus adipem iussit
auferri.

2   Plurimum quoque eo cibo oblectatus est, qui ex ovo caseoque
confectus farcitum viscer dicitur; vel qui ex farina aquaque com-
pactus eodem condimento repleri solet. Iocinera praeterea pullo-
rum et avium, aut epar apri, cum e venatione rediret, aut vituli,
cum pinguesceret, appetebat; haec autem nulla pompa ferebantur
in mensam. Ex fructibus nihil praeter fragra aut persica magnificet,
aut in bellariis pira aut poma paradisia caseo decocta. Cetera vero,
quae a pigmentariis summa industria parari solent, adeo asperna-
tus est, ut ne aeger quidem ac cubans huiusmodi cibariorum quicquam attingeret.

and served in constantly varying shapes and sizes. He refused to eat most fish, the one exception being the grayling. In the beginning he mixed his wine with water, but later began to drink it undiluted. As for the meat dishes, his favorites were veal, kid, and chicken. If he wanted to indulge himself with a special treat, he would opt for partridge, pheasant, or quail, served without seasoning. His desire for these delicacies increased when he could no longer have them: he was in fact unable to digest fatty foods and for this reason ordered that the fat be removed even from the quail he ate.

He was particularly fond as well of a dish that is made from egg 2 and cheese and is commonly called the "stuffed gut." He also liked another dish based on a mixture of flour and water and filled with the same ingredients. When returning from the hunt he would enjoy eating liver too: chicken or fowl liver, or perhaps the liver of a wild boar. Later, when he had grown fat, he preferred to eat calf liver. But such dishes were served to him without any special ceremony. As for fruit, he had high praise only for strawberries and peaches, or, if it was desserts you were talking about, for pears or paradise apples cooked with cheese. He spurned all those delicate dishes that the purveyors of such things prepare with so much care. Even when he was not well or confined to his bed he would absolutely refuse to touch food of this latter kind.

: 53 :

De modo incedendi et loquendi.

1 Toto tempore principatus sui nemo eum nisi inhaerentem alteri, cum deambularet, aspexit. Initebatur vero quam maxime uni ex cubicularibus suis, cui Scaramuciae nomen fuit, olim Iohannis Mariae germani sui lixae vulgatissimi, quem deinde a puero ad cubiculum evexit assidueque in mensa secum habuit. Hunc autem adeo dilexit, ut cum aliquando in silvis aprum vi canum retinere non posset, venabulo accurreret ac paene titubantem liberaret ab impetu ferae.

2 Deambulabat autem matutinis temporibus ante cibum, cum frigesceret, in aula hipocausto et igne assiduo; cum aestas in hipetro, vel locis arci finitimis, arborum fontiumque amoenitate conspicuis, vel directis ippodromi in formam, nonnunquam vite contectis. Post cibum cum aliquantum quievisset, equo vehebatur; itidem ante coenam factitabat. Cum ambularet, nihil aliud quam sensim perorabat, demissa voce, aut laudes Deo referebat, mira quadam digitorum gesticulatione annumerans quot ymnos, psalmos laudesve retulisset; quae etiam ab astante aliquo annotabantur, ita, ut interrogante eo, referret numerum, quem honorem paucis tribuit.

: 53 :

His manner of walking and talking.

Throughout his entire reign he was never to be seen otherwise   1
than clinging to some fellow or other as he ambled along. To tell
the truth the person he liked best to lean on in this way was one
of his valets, Scaramuccia by name. This Scaramuccia was notorious for having served in his boyhood under Filippo's brother
Giovanni Maria. Filippo then made him his personal attendant
and constant companion at meals.[111] Filippo was indeed so at-
tached to Scaramuccia that on one occasion during the hunt, when
his pack of dogs were unable to stop a wild boar, Filippo came
running up with a spear and freed Scaramuccia in the nick of
time, just as the poor man was about to succumb to the ferocity of
the beast.

Filippo's habit was to take his strolls in the morning before hav-   2
ing his meal. In cold weather he would stay indoors, walking in
the well-heated rooms of the palace. In warm weather he would
walk outdoors, either in places bordering the castle, where there
were most pleasant trees and fountains, or on the paths laid out in
the form of a racetrack, where he could shelter from the heat in
shady vineyards. When he had eaten his meal he would rest for a
while, then go riding. He also liked to ride before dinner. When
walking he would be mumbling his prayers softly, in a low voice, or
muttering praises to the Lord God. With strange movements of
his fingers he would count up how many hymns, psalms, and
lauds he had reeled off. There would also be a person nearby
whose job was to keep a tally, so that if Filippo asked, he could be
told the exact number. The honor of keeping the count fell to only
a select few.

3   Subinde vero aut epistolas audiebat, si quae incidissent nota digne, aut cum aliquo assidue vadens loquebatur. Erat autem eius sermo de rebus potissimum bellicis, aut canum, aut avium naturis et equorum, aut rebus ioco dignis; circumferebatque ad audientes caput, nonnumquam retro aspiciebat, quod usitatissimum illi fuit, voce raucidiore plerumque increpans, aliquando cachinans iactabundo similis. Cum ad aulae finem pervenisset, ita subsistebat, ut se volvens pedis plantam parieti incuteret, a tergo cane aliquo comitante herilem gressum.

: 54 :

De modo comestionis et dormitionis eiusdem.

1   Cibum quocumque loco quocumque tempore, prout libuisset, solebat assumere. Cum impatiens sitis esset, et a bile vexaretur, aestivis maxime temporibus, pincernam continue post se habuit, qui vase argenteo altera manu ciatos ferret, altera vinum, ut sitienti vel minima praeberetur operiendi causa. Saepe intempesta nocte cocum iussit accersiri, aviditate ductus vitulini epatis, eodemque tempore animal iussit interfici. Ad haec ministeria viros apprime doctos habuit: Iohanninum camerarium institutum cibariorum

Next Filippo would attend to his correspondence, if there was   3
anything that required his attention, or he would grab someone to
babble to, walking and talking at the same time. His conversation
was mostly about war, or about his dogs, or about the qualities of
various birds and horses, or it veered into light banter. He had the
habit of twisting his head around from one of his listeners to another. Often he would turn and look at what was happening behind his back: that movement was really typical of his behavior.
Sometimes his rather harsh voice would explode like a clap of
thunder, while at other times it would subside into cackling like
that of a man possessed. When he reached the end of the room he
was walking in he would come right up to the wall, put his foot
against it and give a little shove as he spun around and started
back. Behind him would be one of his dogs, following in the foot-
steps of his master.

: 54 :

His eating and sleeping habits.

He was used to taking his food whenever he desired it, irrespective   1
of the time or place. As he was always thirsty, and suffered from
the bile, he had a cupbearer follow him around everywhere, especially in summer. This man bore a silver tray with a ladle on one
side and wine on the other, so that if the duke grew thirsty he
could be served immediately with a minimum of fuss. Quite often
too the duke might call for his cook in the middle of the night
because he had a sudden urge to eat calf liver. When that happened he would order the animal to be slaughtered then and there.
He wanted the men in charge of his food and drink to be highly
skilled professionals. One such was Giovannino, the man in charge

condimentis, per quem altilia, antequam decoquerentur, adlata ante se ac deplumata conspiceret contemplareturque; nec illo inferiorem Antonium Cruciferum, qui solo odoratu, dicam an visu, vina dignosceret, ac nonnunquam in conspectu suo de eorum varietate ac bonitate iudicaret. Venena veritus, etiam custodes custodibus adhibuit, ut altero propinante aut hauriente vinum observaret alter.

2   Cum ad lectum diverteret somnum petiturus, induebatur quodam vestis genere, amictu ac calceatu dispari ab diurno habitu; variabatque per vices thoros, sic ut eadem nocte ter lectum mutaret, transversus cubans, quod a nemine hucusque factum legimus. Aestate vero, si quando ocio indulgeret, palam iacebat, diploide indutus, demissaque ad oculos infula circumvolvebat se, curioso adsimilis ac meditanti, cubicularibus suis ludo vacantibus, quorum motus haud multi faciebat. Ardentiore vero caelo saepenumero nudus iacuit, nullo opertus tegmine, inspectantibus suis.

of seasoning his foods. He required this Giovannino to bring before him the birds he was about to eat, plucked clean and as yet uncooked, so that he could inspect and examine them with care. Then there was Antonio della Croce, who was not a whit inferior to Giovannino in status. This man specialized in wines: he could identify them just by their color or their bouquet. It was he who frequently advised the duke in person as to which wines were to be preferred for their particular qualities and virtues. The duke was especially fearful of being poisoned, so he had his servants carefully monitor one another's actions: while one poured out and offered the wine, another would be stationed there as an observer.

When he went to bed, the duke would be dressed in a different 2 style of clothing and footwear from that he wore during the daytime. It was also his custom to keep changing beds, so that he was quite capable of using three different beds in a single night. He was in the habit of lying across his bed as he slept, and this is something we have never read of anyone else ever doing. In the summertime on the other hand, if he felt like resting, he would lie down in full view, wrapped up in a cloak, with a bandana to shade his eyes, and would turn himself to one side, looking for all the world like someone who was indulging in a moment of blissful meditation. In the meantime his servants would be playing games nearby, but the racket they were making did not disturb him in the slightest. When the weather turned really hot he would often lie thus completely naked, with nothing to cover him whatsoever, while his servants looked on.

: 55 :

De vi memoriae eius et
quemadmodum suorum mores notos habuit.

1   Memoriae vi superavit omnes; quod maximum principis decus et
ornamentum esse Plato existimat. Reminiscebatur enim quaecumque vel audivisset, vel dixisset; et quamquam magno temporis
spatio repetita memoriter tenebat: cum alicui quamvis extero semel convenisset, aut cum illo contulisset, plurimis deinde elapsis
annis visum repetebat. Nemo licet ignotus sic clam ac latenter in
maxima suorum turba sese immiscuit, quem non statim deflexa
cervice, ut mos illi fuit, oculo deprehenderet, quisve esset inter-
rogaret.

2   Illa leviora, sed tamen nota digna, quod familiares omnes, ar-
cium custodes, aucupes, curae solus habuit. Canum soboles semel
visas ab origine prima referebat. Equorum frena, quamquam varia,
memor repetebat. Suorum praeterea virtutes ac vitia referre solitus, quae quisque, quo loco, quove tempore, quid turpiter aut secus egisset, praedicabat. Habebat enim nonnullos infimae conditi-
onis homines, qui urbem peragrantes, quae dicerentur aut fierent
sensim scrutarentur, deinde ad suos referrent, ab his postremo ad
eum deferebantur omnia.

: 55 :

The power of his memory and
how he kept track of everyone's doings.

He surpassed everyone in the powers of memory, a faculty that   1
Plato regards as being the highest accomplishment of the ideal
prince.[112] He had the ability to recall everything he had ever heard
or said, and these things remained lodged in his memory for a very
long time afterward. Having once met someone, or conversed with
them, he could recall their features years later, even if they had
come to him as complete strangers. There was no one, no matter
how obscure or insignificant, who could hide himself away in the
huge crowd of his court attendants. If anyone tried, Filippo would
immediately crane his neck in the usual way, spot the man and cry
out: "Who's that over there?"

Even relatively minor details deserve to be mentioned here, for   2
he alone kept track of the members of his household, the wardens
of his castles, and his bird catchers. He could recognize the offspring of his dogs, having seen them only once, at their birth. He
knew from memory the bridles of his horses, though they were of
various shapes and sizes. Because he took careful note of the virtues and vices of those surrounding him, he could list the crimes
and good deeds of each man, and tell you when and where the
actions took place. He had in his employ in fact quite a few men
of the lowest social extraction, whose job was to fan out across the
city and to observe as discreetly as possible whatever was being
said or done. They then relayed this information to the duke's
men, who in turn passed it on to the duke himself.

: 56 :

De habitudine corporis eius ab adolescentia.

1   Ab ineunte adolescentia adeo tenui valitudine usus est, ut mater,
quae illum prae ceteris natis suis observabat, pulmentis contusis
aleret; solebat enim illum, materno quodam dicendi more, non
Philippum, sed Penicum appellare. Haec autem et ipse multis post
annis, cum princeps esset, referre solitus: aiebat enim usque adeo
se affectum taedio pulmenti huius, ut saepenumero equorum sta-
bulum ingressus epulum evomeret ac subinde panem a lixis erep-
tum clanculum assummeret. Iohannes Franciscus agnomine Bal-
bus, insignis phisicus, qui illum a principio aetatis suae, ab omni
valitudine incolumem sanumque praestiterat, dicere solebat eundem longis ex febribus a principio correptum adeo elanguisse, ut
ex macie ossa patescerent videreturque spina pectori coniuncta,
deinde ad pinguedinem summam evasisse.

2   Multis quippe post annis collum ceroto illitum tulit, imbecilita-
tis causa; mox cum valuisset, abiecit. Cum narium praeterea oppi-
latione teneretur, ita ut in summa hanelitus sui parte laboraret
sordesque in unum collectae morarentur, vix magno expulsi halitus
impetu se ipsum vendicabat; quem morbum studiose occuluit, nec
nisi a cubicularibus quibusdam fidis sciri voluit. Haec enim intervallo repetita lues reliquam eius incolumitatem maxime afflixit, sic
ut plerique existiment oculorum caecitatem, quae subinde secuta
est, ab hoc morbo cepisse initium; vomitum etiam, quo saepissime

: 56 :

His physical condition from adolescence onward.

From early childhood his health was so poor that his mother, pay-   1
ing more attention to him than to her other children, would feed
him on a special diet of gruel. She liked to call him, in her moth-
erly sort of language, not Filippo, but Penico. Here however is
what he himself used to say many years later when he had become
duke of Milan: he used to say that the gruel he was fed as a child
made him so sick to the stomach that quite often he would go into
the stables and vomit it up, after which he would seize bread
from the stable attendants and devour it in secret. Giovanni Francesco de Balbis, the illustrious physician who had pronounced him
healthy and without defects at birth, used to remark that in childhood his health was undermined by long bouts of fever, and that
these produced in him such excessive thinness that his bones
stood out through the flesh and one could see the spot where
the spine joined the thorax, whereas in later life he suffered from
obesity.

Many years later a physical weakness obliged him to wear a   2
kind of wax plaster smeared over his neck. He threw the stuff
away as soon as his health was restored. He also suffered from
nasal obstruction. In fact, he suffered from it so badly that he had
trouble breathing: the mucus would build up to a point where he
could barely free himself from its grip by blowing his nose most
noisily. He was very careful to keep this particular affliction of his
from public view. He made sure that only a select few of his most
trusted valets knew about it. This nasal condition would recur
regularly, and probably had serious consequences for his general
health. Many believe it was the cause of his loss of eyesight, a development of his later years, and it probably explains his frequent

utebatur, eiusdem mali fuisse causam. Evomebat autem quam fa-
cillime, antequam e lecto surgeret, modico assumpto mero, et cum
bile iterum eiecto; mox ex ulcere tibiae impresso, cum dietim cura-
retur, vomitum omisit.

3   Per biennium, antequam e vita excederet, sensim captus est
oculo dextro, deinde post sequentes sex menses alterum amisit;
caecitatem vero sic erubuit, ut visum simularet, cubicularibus clanculum eum admonentibus. Magnam vitae suae partem sanus inte-
gerque peregit, demum ex ocio consenuit, pinguis et gravis, nec
equo vacans, nec labori. Caloris impatiens fuit, aestivis maxime
temporibus; canicula oriente, non enim aceto et aqua cubiculum
dietim aspersisse contentus in hypogeum descendebat, cathedra
insidens, per quam machinae in formam modo demittebatur,
modo ad summa scandebat, fune delatus. Hieme etiam plerumque
adopertis speculariis iacuit sine igne et hypocausto, frigescentibus
ceteris.

: 57 :

De consilio medicorum et quantum
illis crediderit.

1   Medicos circa se continue habuit, qui per vices dispositi nunc
mensae, nunc cubiculo, nunc aucupio vacantem circumsisterent
consilioque admonerent. Ex his gratissimus illi fuit Matheus Vitu-
donus, quem a ministerio ad consilium evexit; post illum vero
Stephanus Spala phisicae peritus; deinde huic proximus Iohannes

attacks of vomiting as well. He would in fact vomit quite easily, just before rising in the morning: a little sip of wine was all it required, and his vomit would contain traces of bile. Later on however he developed a festering sore on his shinbone and once he had undergone treatment for it, the vomiting stopped.

Two years before his death he gradually lost sight in his right eye, and after another six months he lost sight in his left one. He was so ashamed of his blindness that he pretended to see what was going on around him, using his attendants as secret informants. He lived the greater part of his life in good health and free from disease. But in later life he began to deteriorate through lack of exercise: he grew fat and sluggish; he no longer went riding or attended to work. He could not bear the heat, especially in summertime. When a heat wave came on he was not content simply to have his room doused down daily with water and vinegar. He would descend into the cellar seated in an armchair in which he could be mechanically lowered down and then brought back up again by the use of ropes. In winter he mostly slept with the windows closed, without a fire or heating of any kind, while everyone else in the house froze to death.

∴ 57 ∴

His circle of doctors and the extent to which
he trusted their advice.

He kept his doctors around him at all times. Whether he was eating, sleeping, or fowling, they attended him in turns and offered constant advice. His favorite doctor was Matteo Vittudoni, whom he promoted to the rank of counselor. After him came Stefano Spalla, a most learned physician. Next came Giovanni Francesco

Franciscus, de quo praescripsimus, et Ioseph Castronovatus audacia praeclarus; ceteri non eadem dignatione habiti sunt.

2   Horum consilio ita utebatur, ut nihil ex consuetudine sua im-
mutaret; quin imo plerumque acerbius instantes repelleret a se ac
contemneret. Cum minima ex motiuncula aliquando trepidaret,
aucupio intentus, medicum accersebat rogabatque, qua ex causa
quid capite pectoreve aut quavis alia corporis parte sensisset,
incognitumve doluisset; itidem vel cubans, vel incedens percunc-
tabatur, in ceteris vero negligebat. Potiones eorum quasi sumptu-
rus, circumferri iubebat; deinde prandio accersito, negabat adesse
horam.

3   Delectatus est autem vel maxime simplicitate, dicam an puri-
tate, Luchini Belogii, antiquissimi phisici, adhibebatque nonnunquam vel consilio, vel mensae, captus festivitate quadam ineptis-
simi sermonis. Philippum autem Pillicionum, quem ultimo apud
se habuit, ad iocos incitabat, cum ille nullis conviciis aut salibus
parceret, sed quaecumque ei libuissent, propalam diceret.

4   His nec fidem adhibuit magnis in rebus, nec honoribus aut
divitiis ullis impartivit, sed, quod paucis aliquando concesserat,
veniendi facultatem ad se praestitit.

de Balbis, about whom we wrote in the previous chapter, and Giuseppe Castronovate, a man famous for his courage. The duke's other doctors did not enjoy the same level of privilege and prestige as these men.

Filippo followed the advice of his doctors only insofar as it did 2 not interfere with his established patterns of behavior. Indeed if his doctors grew overly solicitous he would often chase them away in contempt. If he felt a slight attack of fever coming on, while fowling for example, he might summon one of them and ask why he was experiencing a certain sensation in his head, or in his chest, or in some other part of his body, or why he was feeling a pain he had never felt before. He might ask the same questions when he was lying in bed, or out on a walk. But otherwise he paid no attention to his doctors. If they prescribed some potion or other for him to drink, he would order that it be carried about the palace aimlessly. He would then call for luncheon to be served and declare that the time for taking medicines had passed.

He derived immense pleasure from the simple, unassuming 3 ways of the elderly physician Luchino Bellocchi, and often invited him to attend meetings of his counselors, or to share a meal. He was quite captivated by the way the old man would prattle on in complete and utter ineptitude. With Filippo Pellizzone, who was his attending physician late in life, he liked to share a good joke, for the man literally sparkled with wit and would speak his mind freely on any topic he thought pleasing.[113]

The duke made sure his medical men exercised no influence 4 over his political decisions; nor would he bestow on them any recognition or riches. On the other hand, he allowed them free access to his person, a privilege he had been wont to concede only to a chosen few.

: 58 :

De exercitatione armorum et equitandi a principio.

1 Armorum et equitandi cupidus a principio fuisse dicitur. Memini me adolescentulum eumdem vidisse Kalendis Maiis, vivente adhuc Facino, cum haud longe ab Ticino veteri urbe primicias arborum ex more quaereret militibus immixtus; quorum consuetudine adeo afficiebatur, ut amorem, quem antea illis ostenderat, effectu comprobaret. Quippe post adeptum principatum nihil pluris, quam illos fecit, multis quoque et praeclaris bonis exornavit; nam villas, agros, oppida concessit, felicitatemque suam militari opere firmavit.

2 Cum autem gravior esse cepisset, nec equo veheretur, nec castrensibus interesset ludis, non destitit tamen a contractatione armorum; nam modo equos perspectabat: adolescentibus ad id munus electissimis eos regentibus modo arma, modo equorum faleras ac frena requirebat, quae privatis in locis summa industria paraverat recognoscebatque singula miro studio. Saepe etiam thoracem suum veluti e conditorio erutum ostendit, inspectantibus multis. Nec usquam gratius quicquam egit, quam illustribus viris et ad se venientibus visendam praebere arcem, in qua omnia armorum genera, bellicarum rerum machinamenta congesta habuit.

: 58 :

His lifelong passion for weapons and horsemanship.

It is said that from the very beginning he loved to handle weapons   1
and ride horses.[114] I myself can remember seeing him on a May
Day when I was still a child and Facino Cane had not yet passed
from the scene: he was with a band of soldiers and was gathering
the first fruits of spring (as is customary on that day) not far from
the ancient city of Pavia. He grew so used to being with his soldiers that he later gave proof of the deep attachment he had always
felt for them. For having once seized power in Milan he held these
men in the highest esteem, showering them with many valuable
gifts. He gave them farms, fields and towns, and regarded military
might as the very foundation of his power.[115]

Even when he had begun to put on weight, and could no longer   2
ride and take part in military exercises, he still could not keep his
hands off the weapons and instruments of war. He would inspect
the horses and oblige the leading stable boys to let him handle first
the weapons, then the trappings and bridles worn by the horses.
He took the greatest care to have these items stored in chosen
places, and was passionate about his ability to recognize each and
every implement. Often he would even have his personal suit of
armor hauled out of storage so that he could show it off to admiring crowds of onlookers. There was nothing he enjoyed more than
taking a group of eminent visitors on a tour of his castle, where he
had collected every possible kind of weapon and machine of war.

: 59 :

De equorum, canum, pardorum et volucrum
cura et oblectatione.

1 Summam praeterea voluptatem ex equorum usu et inspectione
percepit, nec minore disciplina huic ministerio deditos admonuit.
Erat itaque insigne spectaculum stabula eius, praeclaro iumento-
rum genere referta, intueri, et instratos ostro alipedes, pictisque
tapetis, ut poeta inquit; qua in re neminem illi parem fuisse crediderim. Tanto igitur studio ac diligentia, tam magno pretio non
equos modo, sed quae ad equorum usum necessaria sunt, compa-
rabat, ut omnium aliarum rerum videretur oblitus; habebat quoque disposita suo ordine cuiusque opportuna frena, quibus uteretur; habebat et qui selariam facerent eruditos, quo quisque statura
foret equus, quibusve lupatis aut frenis indigeret, quos assidue
exercebat. Ex his prior Bernardus Fossatus a Sellis cognominatus,
et Antonius eius filius, quibus se adeundi licentiam praestitit consuetudine artis, qua summe oblectabatur.

2 Non minore insuper voluptate generosorum canum industriam
ac probitatem admiratus est, ut qui non inferiore pretio canes
quam equos plerumque compararit; nam cum equum forma et
virtute praecipuum quingentis aureis, nonnunquam talento per-
solverit, canum soboles a Britania et longinquioribus quoque

: 59 :

The delight he took in caring for his horses, dogs, panthers, and birds.

He also derived the greatest pleasure from handling and inspecting   1
his horses, and he made sure that those whose responsibility it
was to look after them were well versed in their craft. His stables
were an amazing sight: they were full of horses of the finest breed,
"fleet of foot and caparisoned with purple and embroidered hous-
ings," as the poet says.[116] I myself am quite ready to believe that
there has never been anyone who could match our prince for the
finery on display in his stables. He would purchase with the utmost care and personal attention not only the horses, but everything required for their use, spending such lavish sums as to seem
oblivious to all else. He made sure that each horse was properly
equipped with the appropriate trappings, and that these were kept
in an orderly manner and ready for use. He made sure his grooms
were highly trained, and that they knew how to fit out each horse
according to its size and weight, and which animals required the
sharp bit and which the smooth. Among the grooms his favorites
were Bernardo Fossati, who earned the nickname "the Saddler,"
and his son Antonio. He accorded to these two men the privilege
of free access to his person, on account of their vast knowledge in
the equestrian arts, a passion he shared completely.

He took no less pleasure however in admiring the faithful devo-   2
tion of well-bred dogs. He would often buy dogs at prices not inferior to those he might spend for a horse; so whereas he might be
willing to pay out five hundred pieces of gold, and sometimes even
a talent, for a particularly fine specimen of a horse, he was also
quite capable of having the offspring of dogs brought in from
Great Britain, and from provinces even further afield, spending

provinciis summa impensa magnisque ad reges praemissis muneribus accivit. Ex his gratissimos caseo manu sua exhibito sequi assuescebat; nec in aliquod animalium genus iratus sic cupide desevit, ut saepe equum descenderet, minus parentes ipsemet verberaturus. Sic equos intempestivius hinientes vel linguae vel testiculorum incisione compescuit; pari modo frena dedignantes, sublatis dentibus, ferre compellebat.

3   Pardos etiam ab Soldano Arabum rege et Oriente toto repetebat. Eadem illustrium avium penes illum cura fuit, asturum maxime, quae ex Dacia usque et Panonia et Ripheis, ut ita dicam, montibus ferebantur; quorum copia adeo affluebat, ut in his alendis trium milium aureorum singulo mense impensam tulerit, essetque uniuscuiusque precium decem aureorum, quos persolveret, afferentibus aves.

: 60 :

De aucupio et venatu.

1   Cum venatu aut aucupio vacaret, aut quietus feras expectabat, aut equo sensim vehebatur; et cum maxime venationi videretur intentus, cogitabat volvebatque animo, quid in seriis rebus ageret. Hoc ipse plerumque professus est nullam ex huiusmodi exercitio voluptatem maiorem percepisse, quam meditationem praevisionemque rerum agendarum.

huge sums of money in the process and sending generous gifts in advance to the kings of these places. He trained his favorite dogs to follow him around by showing them a lump of cheese he would hold in his hand. There was no other animal he would get so angry with: often he would jump off his horse so that he could personally whip dogs that had disobeyed him. In the same spirit he disciplined horses that neighed too much (and at the wrong times) by having their tongues or their testicles cut off. And as for those horses that refused the bit, he compelled them to wear it by removing their teeth.

He eagerly sought panthers from the Sultan, king of the Arabs, and from the Orient in general. And he was just as eager to import rare birds, especially hawks, from as far away as Dacia, Pannonia, and even (dare I say) from the Rhipaean Mountains.[117] The number of birds he owned grew so huge that just feeding them cost him three thousand pieces of gold per month. And to anyone who brought him these birds he would pay ten pieces of gold for each specimen.

: 60 :

Fowling and hunting.

Whenever he went fowling or hunting, whether he was lying in wait for the prey or ambling along on his horse, he might well look as if his attention was focused entirely on the chase, whereas in reality his mind was occupied in thinking over the far weightier matters of state. He himself used to say that there was nothing that pleased him more about the hunt than its way of providing him with an opportunity to meditate on what his next political move would be.

2   Venabatur autem cupidissime in silvis, ut Cusagi, apros, vel lata camporum planicie ad cervos et damas, et ubique ad aves locis amenissimis opportuna habitatione, ut Belreguardi oppido et Viglevani, Modiciae ad coturnices, palustribus autem in locis ad aereas aves; sic enim appellant festivissimum aucupii genus, cum ad altiora scandentes paene visu consequamur; harum causa lacunas aquis uberes pluribus in locis fodi iussit. Piscatus est et rete nonnunquam; verum maior in aucupio voluptas illi ac venatu fuit. Habuit et capreolorum greges lucis muro circumseptis, quos hieme aleret pabulo advecto. Glandiferas etiam arbores a nullo concuti passus est, quo suibus suppeterent. Proposuit et poenas his, qui lepores aut aves aut quodvis genus ferarum agitassent. Distinxit et locorum regiones, in quibus venari liceret; prohibitis autem in locis vicarios habuit terrarum custodes, qui neminem mandatis eius adversantem paterentur, aut indemnem esse sinerent.

: 61 :

De variis ludendi modis.

1   Variis etiam ludendi modis ab adolescentia usus est: nam modo pila se exercebat, nunc foliculo, plerumque eo ludi genere, qui ex imaginibus depictis fit, in quo praecipue oblectatus est, adeo ut integrum eorum ludum mille et quingentis aureis emerit, auctore vel in primis Martiano Terdonensi eius secretario, qui deorum

He was especially fond of hunting the wild boar in woods such 2
as those situated around Cusago, or of racing after deer in the
fields stretching across the wide plains thereabouts. And he would
go fowling in the pleasant surroundings of his country estates, at
Bereguardo, for example, and Vigevano. At Monza he sought
quail. In marshy places he went "stirring up airy birds," which is
our way of describing a most pleasant sort of fowling where the
eye can hardly follow the birds as they soar rapidly skywards. To
foster this particular sport he ordered ponds to be dug in various
places and filled with water. Sometimes he went fishing with a net,
but he took greater pleasure in fowling and hunting. He kept
flocks of roebucks in a wooded enclosure, and would feed them in
winter with fodder brought there for that purpose. He would not
allow acorn-bearing trees to be shaken down, so as to make sure
that the wild pigs had something to eat. He set punishments for
anyone caught disturbing hares, birds, or any other wild animal.
He also established areas where hunting was allowed. Where it
was forbidden he stationed wardens to keep a close watch. Their
job was to make sure the rules were respected, and if not, that the
transgressor paid the full penalty.

: 61 :

The games he enjoyed playing.

From childhood onward he enjoyed playing all sorts of games. He 1
took a special fancy to pass-ball and balloon-ball,[118] but his favorite
was a game played with images painted on cards. So thrilled was he
with these cards that he spent one thousand five hundred pieces of
gold to purchase a full set of them. The man primarily responsible
for their creation was his secretary Marziano da Tortona, who

imagines subiectasque his animalium figuras et avium miro ingenio summaque industria perfecit.

2 Oblectatus est et astragalis, quod ludi genus ab Homero repeti-
tum noviores celebrant. Solemnibus quoque diebus nonnumquam
alea lusit. Saepenumero schacorum exercitio, sic enim vulgares
nuncupant, interfuit, magis quam lusit. Hibernis etiam tempestatibus nive contendit. Cetera vero alendi ingenii recreandaeque
mentis artificia sic neglexit, ut nec histriones visere, nec mimos
perspectare, nec musicos audire curaverit; stultos omnes contemp-
serit, Donato ex Petri Basilica dumtaxat excepto, a quo a pueritia
altus innutritus fuerat; hunc aliquando garulantem, Scaramucia
Balbo ex aulicis suis irritante, mira attentione audire consueverat.

3 Affuit etiam geminis e Cypro advectis pueris regio munere,
stupenda membrorum levitudine, modo caput inserentibus lum-
bis, modo inflexa spina circulari laxitate contortis brevi in spatio.
Illud gentile ac patrium, quod angues resectis dentibus, certo anni
tempore manibus detectis tenuit, eorum contactu timidioribus
pavorem illaturus, ceteris vero risum.

: 62 :

De studio litterarum a pueritia et
scribendi astu.

1 Litterarum studiis a pueritia edoctus fuit sub Iohanne Thienio
praeceptore suo, qui non litteris, sed moribus eius praesens astitit
ac veluti paedagogus quidam erudivit, nec quicquam indecorum

elaborated a stunning work of genius depicting the gods of my-
thology and beneath them an array of exotic birds and animals.[119]

The duke also enjoyed rolling knucklebones, a game mentioned   2
by Homer and now fashionable once again because of that.[120] On
holidays too he would often play at dice. As for the game they call
chess, he was more often a spectator than a player. In wintertime
he liked to throw snowballs. But he was so immune to other forms
of entertainment and recreation that he showed no interest at all
in theatrical or musical spectacles and had only contempt for court
buffoons, with the sole exception of Donato Basilicapetri, a man
who had nourished and raised him in childhood. He could listen
with total concentration to this man's endless prattle, much to the
irritation of his other favorite, Scaramuccia Balbo.[121]

He also attended the performances of the child twins brought   3
to him as a royal gift from Cyprus: the flexibility of their bodies
was such that they could insert their heads in their loins, or bend
their spines to form a kind of loose circle, all with truly amazing
speed and dexterity. At a certain time of year he liked to play a
trick that was emblematic of family and fatherland: he would hold
in his bare hands live serpents (whose teeth however had been
dulled). The point was to frighten squeamish spectators, and to
make others laugh.

: 62 :

His literary studies from childhood and
his cunning turns of phrase.

As a child he was educated by his private tutor Giovanni da   1
Thiene, whose chief concerns were moral rather than literary, and
who consequently taught like a true pedagogue, making sure his

fieri ab eo permisit. Eruditus est autem praecipue ex Petrarcae so-
nitiis, confectis materno carmine, quorum lectione adeo afficiebatur, ut princeps etiam aliquo assidente annotari faceret prae-
poneretque quae prius, quaeve posterius legi cuperet. Audivit et
Martianum Terdonensem summa attentione explicantem vulgares
libros, quos Dantis appellant. Audivit et Livii historias, verum
nullo ordine, sed ut quaeque memoratu digna subicerentur, excer-
pens quod gratius sibi foret. Epistolas omnes, cum legerentur,
agnovit nullo edocente, quamquam Latinae linguae haud apprime
doctus; sic orationes edentibus in conspectu suo respondit, nihil a
proposito distans, nisi Latino sermone. Delectatus est et Gallorum
libris mira vanitate referentibus illustrium vitas. Historias etiam ab
antiquis editas vulgari eloquio aut a doctis traductas e Latino,
continentes gesta clarorum virorum, cupidissime audivit.

2   Postremo cum epistolis vacaret, per alios edebat quid dicendum
respondendumve esset. Hoc solum proprium et veluti peculiare
ingenii sui specimen fuit, nec quid clarum aut sincerum scriberet,
sed praeposita dicendi forma, aliquid in fine adderet, quod ambi-
guitate ipsa confunderet priorum scriptionem.[7]

pupil stayed on the straight and narrow path. Filippo's core curriculum in literature consisted in the sonnets of Petrarch, written in Italian verse. The young man was so affected by his reading of these poems that when he became duke he insisted that someone in his entourage be designated to comment on and elucidate them. And it was he himself who established the order in which he wanted the sonnets to be read.[122] He also listened with the greatest attention to Marziano da Tortona, whose lectures focused on the vernacular works of Dante. He listened to readings from Livy as well, but in no particular order, preferring rather to select the highlights, and to home in on the passages he found to be most instructive. When the diplomatic correspondence was being read, he could understand it without the aid of a translation, even though his grasp of Latin was not the best. Moreover he responded to formal orations that were delivered in his presence, and his responses were fairly on the mark, except for his poor command of Latin. He also enjoyed reading the French *chansons de gestes* that spin such tall tales regarding the heroes of old. He listened with great delight as well to histories relating the deeds of famous men, whether in their established vernacular versions, or as translated by humanists from the Latin.[123]

Toward the end of his reign, when attending to the correspondence, he would give instructions through an intermediary as to what was to be said or answered. There was just one thing that was truly peculiar to him alone and quite typical of his style, and this was his never wanting to write anything that was clear and transparent. Rather, having laid out beforehand what was to be said, he would add an observation at the end that would strike a note of ambiguity, throwing into confusion everything that had come before.

2

: 63 :

Quo in honore litterati habiti sunt ab eo.

Humanitatis ac litterarum studiis imbutos neque contempsit, neque in honore penes se praecipuo habuit; magisque admiratus est eorum doctrinam, quam coluit. Antonium Raudensem Ordinis Minorum, virum praeclari ingenii magnaeque virtutis, et a quo pleraque in maternum sermonem traducta habuit, nulla ferme gratia dignatus est. Histriones ac poesim turpiter professos non secus ac stultos reiecit a se. Fuit ad eum Franciscus Barbula poeta Graeculus,[8] multaque pollicitus se scripturum ad laudes eius ac historiam rerum ab eo gestarum relaturum: cum nihil perfecisset, seu vanitate eius territus, seu diffidentia suarum rerum, haud multi fecit contempsitque viaticum petentem, quem salario iuvisset. Pari modo Chiriacum Anconitanum multo plura pollicentem respuit et regia interdixit. Ceteros simili fiducia ad se venientes ac pauculis diebus expertos neglexit posthabuitque, ut Thomam Ferentinum,[9] eximiam quandam memoriae edocentem artem, ac Ferdinandum Beticum, sic fidentem disciplinae suae, ut Tagis in morem e sulco erutus, divinandi scientiam cum anima videretur assumpsisse.

: 63 :

How he treated men of letters.

As for humanists and men of learning, he neither held them in contempt, nor accorded them any particular place of honor at this court. He was more an admirer of their accomplishments than a patron or supporter of their work. He showed no special favor to the Franciscan friar Antonio da Rho, a man of great genius and singular abilities who translated quite a number of works into the vernacular for him.[124] He would have absolutely nothing to do with the clowns and buffoons of literature. The Greekling poet Franciscus Barbula came to him with promises that he would sing his praises and write a history of his deeds. But when Barbula failed to deliver the goods—whether through want of inspiration, or lack of faith in his own powers—Filippo dismissed him without further ado, and even refused a travel allowance to the man he had previously put on a salary.[125] He reserved the same treatment for Cyriac of Ancona,[126] who promised him even more than Barbula had dared promise: he drove Cyriac from his court and forbade him ever to return. There were others too who came to him with various schemes: after a trial period lasting a few days Filippo would forget their very existence. One example was Tommaso Morroni, the teacher of a highly refined version of the art of memory.[127] Another was Ferdinando Betico, whose confidence in his ability was such that he seemed to have taken on the art of divination at birth, and to have sprung Tages-like from the plowed earth.[128]

: 64 :

Qui clariores ex familia eius extiterunt.

1   Familiam omni ex ordine fidam honestamque possedit, quam diligentissime referrem, nisi pluribus in locis, ut casus attulit, recensuissem digniorum nomina. In consilio Guarnerius Casteleoneus praeclarus fuit, et Guido Torelus, ac prius Gaspar Vicecomes equestri ex ordine, ac illo posterior, verum dignitate prior, Iacobus Isolanus, quem ob cardinalatus dignitatem Genuam transtulit rectoremque constituit. Fuit et illo ex ordine Marsilius Cararius ex principibus olim Patavinae urbis, et Antonius Bossius propria ex virtute elatus ad dignitatis gradum. In secretis Iohannes Aretinus, et Conradinus Vicomercatus. Habuit et apud illum gratiam Zaninus Ritius, deinde Lancelotus et Aluisius Crottus.

2   Ex domesticis qui mensae eius assisterent, Franciscus Siriatus et Oldradus Lampugnanus, a quibus gubernaretur, amiceretur omni fere tempore principatus sui. Ex cubicularibus Brunorum Brixiensem potissimum in deliciis habuit; nam Franciscum Landrianum non nisi ad colloquia iocosque servavit, ut facilius falleret, adepta auctoritate. Domesticis autem in rebus plurimum Iohannis Balbi et Iohannis Mathei nec non Thomae Bononiensis opera[10] usus est.

: 64 :

The most outstanding men of his court.

He had in his employ respected and loyal men at every level of   1
his administration. I would list them all one by one if I had not
already mentioned the names of the worthier among them here
and there in my work as I touched on various topics. In his privy
council there were excellent men such as Guarnerio Castiglioni
and Guido Torelli;[129] and even before their time there had been
Gaspare Visconti, of the knightly order, and then the somewhat
later but still greater Iacopo Isolani.[130] When the latter had become a cardinal of the Church, Filippo moved him over to Genoa
and set him up as governor of that city. Other men of similar rank
included Marsilio da Carrara, descendant of the former rulers
of Padua, and Antonio Bossi, who earned his exalted position
through his own merits.[131] Giovanni d'Arezzo and Corradino Vimercati were members of Filippo's privy council,[132] while others
who enjoyed the prince's favor were Zanino Riccio, and then
Lanzalotto and Luigi Crotti.[133]

As for those who were admitted to his table at mealtimes, let   2
me mention Francesco Siriato and Oldrado Lampugnani: these
two were his minders and protectors pretty much throughout his
entire reign.[134] Among those in his immediate entourage his absolute favorite was Brunoro da Brescia, while he kept Francesco
Landriani in his service only for jokes and light banter, tricking
him the more easily thereby into thinking that he still had influence.[135] In household matters he relied most heavily on Giovanni
Balbi and Giovanni Matteo Bottigella, as well as on Tommaso da
Bologna.[136]

3   Nobiliores praeterea et exteri regiam eius frequentabant, e quibus primorem Octavianum Ubaldinum fuisse crediderim, quo in
iuvene gravitas senilis quaedam fuit; nec illo multo inferiorem
Christoforum Torellum, et quem prius recensere oportuit, Enicum
Hispanum, iuvenem singulari ingenio virtuteque praestantem. Militari autem in re locus probitati fuit Ottolini Zoppi, praeterea
Moreti Sanazarii et Iacobi Lonati. Reliquorum autem famam et
claritatem obruit superiorum documentis et exemplis diutissime
comprobata virtus.

: 65 :

De cura religionis et modo orandi.

1 Non ab re dixerim fuisse in eo quandam orandi et religionis dili-
gentiam persimilemque divinitati placandi numinis curam. Cum
dies certos voto dedicasset, si quid praetermisisset, orabat erogabat-
que pecunias, ac notula a se addita pronunciabat his verbis: 'Dominus erravit'; aequabatque pretio peccatum.

2   Nullum diem sine orationis officio transmisit; quin etiam cum
deambularet, aut equum ascenderet aut veheretur, orabat. Saepenumero e thalamo egressus, cum caelum intueretur, adoperto capite secretas Deo laudes referebat. Ex quo coniectari licet mentem
eius non expertem fuisse divinitatis; nam hipocresim omnino contempsit, optimum sinceri principis iudicium. Si quid adversum

He also had exalted personages from outside Milan in atten- 3
dance at his court. Foremost among these I would list Ottaviano
Ubaldini, a young man truly wise beyond his years. Not far behind Ottaviano I would place Cristoforo Torelli.[137] And yet another person I should have mentioned sooner was the Spaniard
Iñigo d'Avalos, an outstanding young man of amazing gifts and
ability.[138] The duke's most tried and trusted military advisors were
Ottolino Zoppi, then Moretto da Sannazzaro and Giacomo
Lonati.[139] There were others at his court whose merits and fame
might well warrant a mention, but the proven ability, in words and
deeds, of those we have named above outshines all the rest.

: 65 :

His observance of religious duties and his way of praying.

I do not think I would err in saying that he was a prayerful and 1
devout person, consumed by a desire to please God that was almost divine in inspiration. He had certain days set aside for devotions, and if he ever forgot to observe any of these he would pray,
give alms, and add a special reproach to himself by saying these
words: "The master did wrong." And he would make sure that the
alms he gave were in proportion to the gravity of his offense.

He never let a day pass without reciting his prayers; he prayed 2
constantly, even while on a walk, or riding, or being driven somewhere. Often on rising from his bed in the morning he would lift
his eyes to the heavens, cover his head, and mumble secret prayers
to the Lord God. From this habit of his one can infer that his
mind was not without a spark of divinity, for he shunned all hy-
pocrisy, behavior worthy of a true prince. If during the night he

somno praevidisset, experrectus procurabat: quippe unico dumtaxat comitatus, ad Orientis partes supplicabat submissa voce, quod genus orandi secretum dicebatur, deinde ad Occidentem se volvebat, demum ad reliquas caeli partes, iugi silentio operientibus suis.

3   Ea ex re summos pontifices semper excoluit, et quamquam bello coactus Ecclesiae videretur infensus, utilitatem propriam religioni submisit; nam cum civitates Ecclesiae spectantes bello excepisset, ac Flaminiam fere omnem sibi subegisset, ultro omnia Martino quinto pontifici reddidit. Sic cum Eugenium quartum pontificem ad concilium evocasset, quod ipse constituerat, et dignitatem eius labefactari cognovisset, in integrum restituit, posthabita soceri auctoritate, quem in spem pontificatus solus evexerat.

: 66 :

De pavore nocturno et
custodiarum ordine.

Solitudinis ac quietis nocturnae timidissimus fuit, ita ut nisi aliquo excubante quiesceret. Cum adolescens adhuc esset, cubiculares omnes circa se iacens collocabat, ut nulla pars thori vacaret a suis, veritus lemures ac nocturna phantasmata. Princeps amplius

had had a dream foreshadowing some disaster, his one concern on waking would be to ward off the impending evil: so assisted by a single attendant and turning himself to the East he would pray in a low voice (he used to say that this was his own secret method of praying); he would then turn to the West, and then finally to the other parts of the heavens, while all this time his servants stood by watching in absolute silence.

It was because of this religious nature of his that he always 3 cultivated the favor of the popes. And although the logic of war forced him into a posture of hostility toward the Church, he placed personal advantage second behind his devotion to religious principle. So although he conquered cities that belonged to the Church, and seized control of practically the whole of Romagna, in the end he surrendered all of these conquests to Pope Martin V. And the same goes for Eugenius IV, for having summoned this pope to appear before the Council that he himself had instigated, and having then seen how the papal prestige began to totter, he restored Eugenius to his position of supremacy, dashing thereby the claims of his own father-in-law, whose hopes to be elevated to the papacy he alone had originally championed.[140]

: 66 :

The fears that beset him during the night and the mounting of the guard.

He was extremely fearful of the stillness and quiet that came on at nighttime, so much so that he could sleep only if someone stood watch. While he was still young, he used to station his valets all around where he slept, so that no portion of his bed would be unprotected, for he feared the ghosts and phantoms of the night.

insidias pertimescebat; qua ex causa vigiliarum seriem disposuit tam rato ordine, ut prima vigilia constituta cohors excubaret, deinde singule suo loco ac tempore, nunquam interposito ordine. Pari modo noctem dies sequebatur, non absimile his, qui in castris degunt. Nam supra cubiculum quidam pernoctabant, nonnulli a lateribus, plerique in cubiculo; requirebatque ab his horas somno excitus: hi autem vel referebant, vel ab attentioribus percunctabantur. Eo modo noctes fere omnes insomnes agebat, persimilisque erat suorum color lucubratae nocti. Aves praeterea a natura vigiles et voce referentes auditos strepitus in arce tenuit. Saepenumero etiam vigilia fessus cubiculum perambulabat somnum expetens comitantibus suis.

: 67 :

De superstitione in omnibus et fulgurum timore.

1 Non immerito quis superstitiosissimum eum principem dixerit, qui Octavii aliorumque imperatorum vitam moresque ignorarit. Sorbarum arbores quocumque in loco recidi iussit, motus ratione, ut aiebat, quod pestiferam earum umbram esse didicisset perpessis rabidos morsus. Sic corvos omnes proposito pretio necari iussit,

Once he assumed power he grew even more frightened that he might be attacked in his sleeping quarters, so he had his guards posted in such a way that the first vigil of the night was assigned to one detail, and they were relieved by another, and so forth without interruption through the night and into the daytime as well. The system was not unlike that which prevails in a military camp, for there were guards stationed immediately above his bedroom, others on each side, and quite a few too in the bedroom itself. Whenever he woke from his sleep he would ask those in the room what time it was, and they would either answer him or ask someone who was more awake than themselves. This is how he would pass almost every one of his sleepless nights, and the pallor of those who attended him showed that they had not slept either. In addition to all this he kept birds in the palace that were naturally watchful at night and would screech their lungs out on hearing any noise. Often he would pace up and down in his bedroom, worn out with fatigue, desperately seeking sleep, as his attendants followed him to and fro.

: 67 :

His superstitious nature and his fear of lightning.

People unfamiliar with the private lives of Augustus and other Roman emperors might well be forgiven for thinking that Filippo Maria was the most superstitious prince that ever lived.[141] He ordered service trees to be chopped down wherever they grew, his reason being (as he said) that he had heard how noxious the shade cast by this kind of tree could be, inflicting sharp pains on its victims. And he offered a reward to anyone who obeyed his standing order to kill all crows, paying up once their dead bodies were

adlatos prius ad se. Locum habuit in cubiculo signo seiunctum a ceteris, in quo Silvester, olim cubicularis suus, ante obitum decubuit; itaque in eum nemini ingredi fas fuit. Per hunc cum aliquando Todeschinus ex praefectis mensae eius epulas ferens, licet improvidus, pedem posuisset, adlata iussit auferri, prandiumque ex novo instaurari.

2   Erat in regiae medio pirus antiquissima arbos, ad quam ferae oblectationis causa deligarentur irritarenturque a canibus: huius interitum adeo indoluit, ut quinque simili ex stirpe eodem in loco pangi iuberet. Nespilorum arbores adultas custodiri fecit, memoria fructus inter insignia delati.

3   Quotannis etiam Kalendis Ianuariis equum candore notabilem et insigni apparatu conspicuum ad se duci iussit, veluti monumentum secuturae felicitatis. Si calceum sinistrum pro dextro inscius aliquando induisset, ut nefastum abhorrebat. Si aves insolita voce tempore noctis praesertim concinentes audiret, formidabat. Impium etiam apud eum fuit Veneris in die abraso cuipiam occurrere; aut avem, potissimum coturnicem, in campis advolantem manu capere; aut sacro Iohannis Baptiste Decolationis die equum ascendere; aut deinceps per annum simili in luce idem facere; aut Beatae Mariae solemnibus impium quicquam agere. Horum enim imagines religiosissime coluit, tum Beatorum Antonii, Christophori, Sebastiani, Guinifortis, Petri Martiris, praeterea Magdalenae et Helisabet, ut in devotionibus eius constat.

brought to him. He had a special place marked off in his sleeping quarters where his former valet Silvester had lain, prior to his death. This space was sacred and no one was allowed to enter it. So when once it happened that the chief steward Todeschino, while serving the prince's meal, accidentally put his foot in the forbidden zone, Filippo Maria ordered that the food be carried back to the kitchen, and that the meal be started all over again from scratch.

In the very center of his palace there stood an ancient pear tree. 2 It was customary to tie wild animals to this tree for sport, and to let the dogs of the house torment them. The demise of this tree saddened Filippo Maria to such an extent that he ordered five trees of a similar kind to be planted in exactly the same spot. He wanted full grown loquat trees to be especially well cared for, out of respect for the fruit that appeared emblazoned on the Visconti coat of arms.

Every year on the first of January he would order that a horse of 3 whitest white be finely arrayed and brought before him, a ritual that was supposed to bring him good luck. If it happened that he accidentally slipped his left shoe onto his right foot, he took this as a bad omen.[142] If he heard birds crying out with strange sounds, especially in the middle of the night, he immediately took fright. He regarded it as unlucky to encounter on a Friday anyone who had just shaved, or to go catching birds, especially quail, in the fields on that day; it was equally wrong to mount a horse on the day set aside to commemorate the beheading of Saint John the Baptist, or to do likewise thereafter throughout the year on similar holy days, just as it was absolutely forbidden to do anything improper on the feast days devoted to the Virgin Mary. He was also most assiduous in worshipping the images of these two holy figures, as well as those of Saints Anthony, Christopher, Sebastian, Guiniforte, Peter Martyr, and Mary Magdalene and Elizabeth, as shown by his prayerful devotions.

4   Nihil tamen aeque ac fulgurum motus expavit. Cum e celo tacta esset arx Mediolanensis urbis, ac flamae longe lateque saevirent, per suos prohibuit incendia, quae praesens videre noluit, abhorrens fulminales ignes. Ea ex causa cubiculum in quo assueverat, duplici murorum fornice munivit contra repentinos et inexpectatos ictus fulgurum. Ad subita etiam caeli tonitrua in cubiculi angulo suis circumsaeptus delituit. Imaginem quoque Beatae Barbarae eam ob rem veneratus est. Numisma praeterea ex auro cudi iussit sub astrorum virtute propulsans aethereos motus.

: 68 :

De observatione astronomorum et diligentia
ad lunaris motus.

1   Astronomorum iudicio et disciplinae adeo credidit, ut peritiores eius artis ad se accersiret eorumque consilio universa paene ageret. Habuit in primis Petrum Senensem et Stephanum Faventinum, utrumque edoctum artis eius. Ultimis vero diebus principatus sui opera ac consilio Antonii Bernadigii, nonnunquam et Aluisii Terzagi, saepenumero Lanfranchi Parmensis usus est. Habuit et inter phisicos Heliam Hebraeum, professum divinandi artem. Ab his institutus dies ad bellum ac pacem eligebat, quique optimus peregrinationi aut quieti foret, requirebat. Regredienti in urbem nulla lux contraria fuit unquam.

There was however nothing he feared more than lightning.[143]   4
When once lightening bolts struck the Castle of Porta Giovia,
causing a fire to spread out in all directions, he ordered his men to
fight off the conflagration; he himself could not bear to look upon
the flames, such was his horror of fiery lightning. After that incident he ordered the room where he slept to be reinforced with
double-vaulted walls, to protect it against sudden and unexpected
lightning strikes. As soon as he heard thunder in the sky he would
hide himself away in a corner of this room, surrounded by his
retinue of servants. He venerated the image of Saint Barbara for
this very reason. In addition to which he had a gold medal cast
that drew upon the power of the stars to drive away storm clouds.

: 68 :

His respect for astrologers and his observance
of the lunar cycles.

So strong was his belief in the teachings and pronouncements of   1
the astrologers that he summoned to his court the most skilled
practitioners of the art, and followed their advice in virtually everything he undertook to do. He had the highest regard for Pietro
Lapini da Montalcino and for Stefano Fantucci da Faenza, each of
them masters of his craft. In the latter days of his reign however,
he often drew upon the expertise and advice of Antonio Bernareggi, as well as on that of Luigi Terzaghi, and even more often
on that of Lanfranco of Parma. Among his physicians he kept one
Elia Ebreo, who professed the art of divination.[144] Relying on
people like these Filippo would choose which days were more suitable for peace or war, and which best for travel or staying at home.
There was never any unfavorable sign when it came to deciding on
a return to Milan.

2   Cum quidpiam severum aut magnum agitaret, consultores eos
adhibebat, nec deerat in minimis etiam fides; quod nescio an vanitate dicam, an opinione potius faceret, aut alia quavis ratione ad
huiusmodi credulitatem adductus sit; certo enim dicitur eundem
opinione fatalis necessitatis credidisse omnia ex destinato fieri. Ea
ex causa plerumque dictitabat res ad cogitatum non succedere.
Cum navem ingressurus esset, per plusculos dies differebat iter;
mox veluti concertatione mentis abiecta, prodibat ad navem atto-
nito similis ac stupenti. Itidem et equum ascensurus faciebat. Luna
in coniunctione solis existente, intra penetralia domus se recondere
solebat ac miro silentio magistratus excludebat a se, nec ulli interim responsa per suos praebebantur. Simile in oppositione eius
observabat, verum multo minus, ut ad instantius petentes hoc solum rescriberet: 'Expecta modicum, respondebo tibi.'

3   Horilogium habuit in Papiensi bibliotecha, omnium aetatis
nostrae memorabile ac paene divinum, confectum a Iohanne Pata-
vino insigni astronomo, in quo septem errantium stellarum motus
cernerentur, quod ad huiusmodi servitia paratum continue habuit.

Whenever Filippo Maria was meditating some great or weighty 2
plan he would call in these consultants. He trusted their views
entirely, down to the smallest details. I am not sure what drove
him to such credulity, whether it was desperation, or actual belief,
or some other cause. But what can be said for certain is that he
was of the view that a sort of fatal necessity predetermined everything that happened. And for this reason he often repeated that
things never turned out according to one's plans. If he were about
to take a journey by boat, he would delay his departure for several
days, and when he finally made up his mind he would board with
a chastened heart, as if in a kind of trance. The same was true of
his behavior if he were about to mount a horse. When the moon
was in conjunction with the sun, he would hide himself away in
the deepest recesses of his castle, shunning the officers of his court
and maintaining total silence. During such times it was impossible
to obtain replies to any queries, even through intermediaries. It
was a similar story when the moon was in opposition to the sun,
but in a much lesser way, so that after much insistence one might
hope to get a written response of the kind "Wait a bit, and I will
answer you."

He had a clock in the library in Pavia that was a memorable 3
and almost divine wonder of our age. Its inventor was the famed
astronomer Giovanni Dondi of Padua, and it showed the orbits of
the seven planets.[145] Filippo Maria kept this clock ever at the service of his interest in the planetary motions.

: 69 :

De signis infelicitatis exercituum suorum.

1 Mirabile profecto ac stupendum omnes exercituum suorum clades die rato previsas et demum intellectas extitisse. Quo tempore exercitus in Liguria et Tuscia simul habuit, paulo ante tacta e caelo Mediolanensis arcis moenia pinaeque disiectae, demum igne per stabula demisso, tota regia fumo oppleta, equi a praesepibus erepti et hinc inde discurrentes horridum quodam secuturae cladis praebuere spectaculum; nam paulo post utriusque exercitus interitus auditus est.

2 Simili modo cum adversus Cremonam copias movisset, paulo ante fortuitus ignis in eam curiam delatus est, quae Mediolanensi ecclesiae magna ex parte coniuncta est, vixque accurrentibus multis extinctus. Itidem bello Veneto primo domus Belreguardi inopino incendio paene assumpta, qua ex causa coactus est etiam solemni die, quod insolitum illi fuit, domum permutare.

3 Antequam Brixie urbem amitteret, omnis columbarum multitudo, qua oblectabatur, interiit. Notatum est etiam huiusmodi praenostica aeque sex mensium spatio praecessisse insequentes clades diemque Mercurii maiori ex parte hac in re tristem fuisse ac lugubrem.

: 69 :

The signs that predicted the defeat of his armies.

It is a truly marvelous and amazing thing to record that every one 1
of his military reverses occurred exactly as had been foretold,
down to the very day. Take the time he had two armies in the field,
one in Lombardy and one in Tuscany. It happened that not long
before, the walls surrounding the Castle of Porta Giovia were
struck by lightning and the battlements were torn asunder. The
stables then caught fire and the entire palace was filled with smoke,
while the horses broke loose and ran amok, all of which was
clearly a sign that some great military disaster was looming. And
in fact shortly after this came the news that both of the Milanese
armies had been completely destroyed.

Something similar occurred when his forces were advancing on 2
Cremona, for not long before, a fire broke out in the court located
adjacent to the Cathedral of Milan and it was brought under control only with great difficulty.[146] Much the same thing happened
during the first war with Venice: his residence at Bereguardo was
suddenly all but consumed by fire, forcing him to relocate, even
though the move had to be made on a feast day, something he
rarely undertook to do.

Just before he lost the city of Brescia, an entire flock of doves — 3
birds in which he took great delight — perished to the last one. It
was noted too that each of these signs preceded the foretold disas-
ters by a period of six months, and that Wednesdays tended to
bring particularly bad luck.

: 70 :

De signis mortis eius et quo tempore cessit e vita.

1   Per trienium antequam vita excederet, imminentis obitus signa
praevisa sunt. Praecipua totius regiae avitae aula in Mediolanensi
urbe uno die, animadvertente nullo, corruit. Mortarii oppidum
eodem fere tempore fortuito igne concrematum et absumptum
paene funditus. Eiusdem regiae ianuae, paulo antequam obiret,
nocte intempesta, nullo impellente, cecidere. Maiora tamen ac cla-
riora in morte patris sui Iohannis Galeaz signa extitere: nam
priusquam extrema valitudine corriperetur, stella crinita, quam
cometem vocant, per continuos tres menses fulxit circa occasum
solis exoriens, subindeque aegrotante eo perseveravit ac mox defuncto videri desiit.

2   Paucis ante obitum diebus quendam ex vernaculis suis Ves-
continum nomine accersitum ad se iussit finitimum arci templum
Beatae Mariae invisere scrutarique, an sepulcrum ad modulum
corporis sui alicubi sciret; velle enim se eo loci humari, in quo ab
omnibus calcari posset. Quibus ex verbis non tam fortuito id a se
prolatum credimus, quam per divinationem quandam significasse
locum sepulcro suo destinatum. Eadem vocis divinitate interitum
domus suae facile detexit, cum eidem Vescontino per iocum diceret, ne se amplius e Vicecomitum familia appellari sineret, finem
quippe evenisse eorum stirpi.

3   Octavo Idus Augusti cum gravari cepisset, per sex sequentes
dies nec venas medico praebuit, nec quicquam ex consuetudine

: 70 :

The signs foretelling his end and the hour of his death.

For three years prior to his death there were signs that his life 1
was nearing its end.[147] The great hall in the ancestral seat of the
Visconti government in Milan[148] suddenly collapsed in a single
day, without warning. At about the same time the town of Mortara accidentally caught fire and burned nearly to the ground. And
the doors of his own palace were mysteriously blown open in the
middle of the night, just before he died. Even greater and less
ambiguous signs had preceded the passing of his father Gian Galeazzo Visconti: for prior to his being seized by a mortal illness, a
tailed star, known as a comet, shone continuously in the sky for
three months, rising with the setting of the sun.[149] This phenomenon persisted throughout Gian Galeazzo's illness and ceased as
soon as he had passed away.

Not many days before his own death Filippo Maria summoned 2
one of his servants, who bore the name Viscontino. He ordered
this man to visit the nearby Church of the Virgin Mary and to see
whether any of the tombs there would be of a size to accommo-
date his body, for he wanted to be buried in a place where everyone would be able to trample over him. It is my belief that such
words did not issue from his lips without design, and that he
meant to allude somewhat mysteriously to his choice of a final
resting place. In the same mysterious way he revealed that the end
of the House of Visconti was at hand, for he told this Viscontino
jokingly that he should cease allowing people to call him by that
name, since the Visconti line was about to be extinguished.

When he finally fell seriously ill on August 6 he refused over 3
the following six days to allow his doctors to bleed him, nor would
he tolerate any changes to his usual routine. Indeed when his

pristina immutavit; quin imo Philippo eius medico exhortanti, ut ommisso epulo, quod ex ovis vinoque sumebat, pulmentis contusis uteretur, respondit se neutro usurum, si alterum adimeret; ita ut nemini dubium sit eum sponte appetiisse mortem, quam, oculorum caecitate bellorumque taedio defessus, potiorem vita duceret, cum paulo ante vulnus, quod in crure sustinebat, a Francisco medico constringi iussit.

4   Decessit autem Idibus Augustis, in die solemni paulo ante secundam horam noctis in Mediolanensi urbe, ea arcis parte, quae ad Cumanam portam pertinet, anno aetatis quinquagesimo quinto, diebus quadraginta minus; tam constanti animo, ut taedio nonnullorum imbeciliora quaedam suadentium se in contrariam partem averti iusserit, dextra uni ex cubicularibus porrecta. Qua ex re magnitudinem ac generositatem animi sui contemplari licet, qui cum mortem tantopere formidari visus sit, ut etiam eius memoria angi se diceret, quod aliquando non esse necesse esset, omniaque eius monumenta, omnes de ea disserentes averteret ac vitaret, tam cupide obierit fatalem diem.

personal physician, Filippo Pellizzone, warned him to stop taking his regular meals, which included eggs and wine, and to eat gruel instead, he replied that he would eat neither the one or the other, if ever his regular food were taken away. From this reply everyone deduced that he wished to die, and that, now that he was worn down by his blindness and weary of war, he actually preferred death to life, although not long before he had had Francesco, his doctor, tend to a wound he had sustained in the leg.

He died on the thirteenth of August, a Sunday, just before the   4 second hour of the night, in the city of Milan, in that part of the castle that looks toward the Porta Comacina. He was in his fifty-fifth year, forty days short of his fifty-fifth birthday. He showed such admirable fortitude in facing death that, annoyed with the fuss those at his bedside were making, he ordered them to turn him around to face away from them, only holding his right hand out to one of his page boys. In these last moments we can recognize Filippo's true greatness and generosity of spirit, for here was a man who had feared death to such an extent that he used to say that the very thought of it — the thought that one must inevitably cease to be — struck him with terror. Here was a man who had tried throughout his entire life to banish every reminder of death, who could not stand even hearing talk of death, now actually hastening along to meet his final hour.

: 71 :

*De testamento per eum condito et adeptione
libertatis per Mediolanenses.*

1   Primis diebus principatus sui Antonium germanum heredem
suum instituit. Mox defessus perversitate morum eius, Iacobum
nepotem, Gabrielis filium, praeferri iussit. Sunt qui Blancham eius
filiam ab eo legitime inscriptam ac heredem institutam referant.
Verum seu consulto, seu temere, paulo antequam excederet e vita,
Alfonsum Aragonum nominavit regem heredemque a se relictum
protulit solemni testamento.

2   Tota nocte cum corpus in cubiculo eius iacuisset, sequenti die
circa vesperas per cubiculares elatum et inter utrumque arcis
pontem situm, inde a primoribus aulae sublatum, comitante populo, maiori ecclesiae illatum est, ac tumultuario funere erectum in
eam partem, quae altari maiori imminet, illustri loco; mox aestatis
temporibus stilante tabe depositum ac inferius humatum.

3   Mediolanenses erectis animis cum primum principem sublatum
conspexere, in forum convenerunt, ibi coactis magistratibus, sta-
tuto ordine, quid a quoque agendum esset, felici omine libertatem
assumpserunt.

: 71 :

His last will and testament and how the Milanese regained their freedom.

In the early stages of his rule he made his half brother Antonio his 1
heir. But he soon became discouraged by Antonio's bad character
and ordered that his nephew Giacomo — the son of Gabriele — be
given preference. There are some who allege that he had his natural daughter Bianca Maria legitimized and that he made her his
heir. But the truth is that just before he died, whether by design or
not, he evoked the name of King Alfonso of Aragon and appointed him heir to the duchy in his last will and testament.[150]

Filippo's body lay throughout the night in his bedchamber. On 2
the following day toward evening it was lifted up by his servants
and placed between the two bridges of the castle. From there it
was carried by the leading men of the court in a procession to the
Duomo, with the people of the city following behind. The funeral
itself was witness to tumultuous scenes, as the body was hauled up
to a prominent place overlooking the high altar. But soon the body
began to dissolve and decompose due to the summer heat, so it
was taken down and buried deep in the ground.

The citizens of Milan meanwhile felt their spirits rise as soon as 3
they saw their prince was gone. They called a meeting in the public square, summoned their magistrates, and established a new
constitution with clear lines of responsibility. Thus did they reas-
sert their freedom in a manner that seemed to augur well.

ANNOTATIO RERUM GESTARUM
IN VITA ILLUSTRISSIMI
FRANCISCI SFORTIAE
QUARTI MEDIOLANENSIS DUCIS

Actorum militarium victoriosissimi principis
Francisci Sfortiae epitoma feliciter incipit

Quae in vita Francisci Sfortiae victoriosissimi ducis militaribus auspiciis a principio aetatis suae usque ad civitatis Mediolanensium adeptionem et pacem cum Venetis ultimo factam res gestae continentur, brevissime hoc opusculo descriptae sunt, servato ordine annorum eius, in quibus res fama et laude dignas fecisse noscitur, additis etiam illustrium monumentis, si quae eodem tempore obvenerunt. Ex his ostenditur per historiae annotationem quemadmodum virtute propria superior ceteris ducibus aetatis suae fuerit, cum primum Francisco Carmagnolae, cuius fama perinsignis fuit, proelio congressus nulla ex parte peritiae armorum eius cesserit; Nicolaum Piceninum magnanimum ductorem in re militari longe superarit; Philippum denique Mariam clarissimum principem voluntati suae obsequi coegerit; vicerit postremo Venetos, et Mediolanensium principatum adeptus sublimior inter omnes Italos evaserit, facilitate et clementia nulli cedens. Ex quo ab illustribus principibus eius affinitas appetita est, et pax Italiae praebita.

A RECORD OF THE DEEDS OF THE MOST ILLUSTRIOUS FRANCESCO SFORZA FOURTH DUKE OF MILAN

Here begins a brief account of the deeds in arms
of that most victorious of princes, Francesco Sforza.

The military deeds of that most victorious captain-at-arms Francesco Sforza—starting from his earliest beginnings, down to his taking of the city of Milan and the peace he at last concluded with the Venetians[1]—are the subject I shall very briefly treat in this short work. I shall observe the chronological order in which deeds worthy of glory and renown are known to have been performed, and I shall include other notable matters as well, should there be any that deserve to be mentioned as we proceed. The point of the exercise will be to demonstrate, by reviewing the history, how vastly superior Francesco Sforza was in ability to the other military captains of his day. For first of all, he more than held his own on the field of battle against the extraordinarily famous Francesco Carmagnola; he far surpassed in military skill that magnanimous captain Niccolò Piccinino; and he managed in the end to impose his will on that most illustrious of princes, Filippo Maria Visconti. More recently he defeated the Venetians, established his rule over Milan, and has become the leading figure in Italy, inferior to no other prince in his exercise of generosity and clemency. For this reason, illustrious rulers have eagerly sought to forge marriage alliances with him,[2] and peace has returned to Italy.

: I :

Praefatio Petri Candidi.

Francisci Sfortiae rerum gestarum gloriam si stilo aut verbis ae-
quare voluerimus et meritis haud imparem laudem reddere, non
Ciceronis eloquentia, ut Firmianus inquit, sed longe beatiore atque
ampliore a nobis utendum erit; et quae non virtutem modo atque
auctoritatem reique militaris peritiam, quae in summo duce praecipue exoptari solent, sed felicitatem huius principis ac clementiam
in primis referat. Quamobrem abunde a nobis satisfactum fuerit,
si privatam dumtaxat vitam relinquentes, res bello paceque partas
quodam veluti compendio scripserimus.

: 2 :

De origine eius et parentis sui laude.

Fuit huic parens nomine Sfortia, vir bellicis artibus maxime illustris atque memorandus, qui ex Cutignola opido provintiae Flaminiae satis celebri ortum duxit. Ceterum, ut de Alexandro scriptum
legimus Philippo gloria clariorem evasisse, sic huius famam filii
splendor et virtus superavit: nam indolem eius ac prima militiae
rudimenta contemplanti, quaeve subinde ab eodem confecta sunt,
tantam laudem prae se ferunt, ut non modo parentem suum
anteisse, sed priscorum ducum nomen obumbrasse videatur.

: 1 :

The preface of Pier Candido.

Were we to strive to find the words equal to the glory of the deeds of Francesco Sforza, and praise him according to his merits, we would require not the eloquence of Cicero (as Lactantius says[3]), but a style even more elevated and sublime, a style capable of expressing not only the man's power, his might, and his skill in the arts of war — all qualities that one expects to find in a military leader — but a style that would also convey the kindness and clemency of the man who now rules Milan. And for this reason we will have to consider ourselves satisfied if, leaving aside his private life, we are able to succeed in writing a brief account of the deeds he performed in war and in peace.

: 2 :

The origins of Francesco Sforza and the fame of his father.

His father bore the name "Sforza," and was a renowned captain of war who hailed from Cotignola, a well-known town located in the province of Romagna.[4] However just as we read that Alexander the Great overshadowed Philip of Macedon by becoming far more famous,[5] so the shining glory of Francesco Sforza has obscured the fame of his own father. For anyone who gazes upon Francesco's abilities as they began to take shape early on, and were then confirmed later in his career, will admit they were so worthy of praise that the man not only outstripped his father in excellence but even outdid the famed military captains of antiquity.

: 3 :

De scriptorum ignorantia.[1]

Non immerito itaque eorum ignorantiam dicam, an temeritatem, cogor admirari, qui res tam illustres tamque praeclaras versiculis quibusdam perscribere et posteritati mandare posse existimarint, cum eosdem minime latere debeat nullam esse mediocrium poetarum auctoritatem apud doctos, qui non hominum modo ac deorum sentencia, ut Oratius scribit, sed scholarum insuper iudicio et rhetorum reiecti sunt et explosi. Nos autem, ratione stiloque suffulti, sic acta splendidissimi ducis complectemur, ut famam veritas, diuturnitatem brevitas ipsa tueatur.

: 4 :

De nativitate Francisci Sfortiae.

1   Verum ut, his ommissis, ad incoepta revertamur, cum multa et varia in describendis illustrium primordiis ab historicis referri soleant, tum vel maxime in huius vitae exordio plurimorum opinio a nobis imitanda esset, nisi doctiorum auctoritate confirmati, quae minus clara et probata sunt ut inepta sperneremus.

2   Natus est autem Franciscus Sfortia anno Salutis uno et quadringentesimo supra millesimum ex Sfortia, ut praediximus, et

: 3 :

The ignorance of those who have written about him.

It is not without cause that I am moved to wonder at the ignorance (or should I say the impertinence?) of those who have
thought they could record for posterity the outstanding and extraordinary deeds of Francesco Sforza by writing some silly little
verses.[6] These people should know well enough that the work of
mediocre poets carries no authority at all among the learned, and
that it will be rejected and condemned not only, as Horace writes,
before the tribunal of men and gods,[7] but in the judgment of stu-
dents and teachers of rhetoric as well. We on the other hand have
chosen a more sober style of writing. We shall therefore be relating
the deeds of our shining hero in such a way that truth itself will
secure his fame, and brevity will make it lasting.

: 4 :

The birth of Francesco Sforza.

But let us leave such things aside and return now to our subject.   1
Historians are wont to spin many a tall tale when it comes to relating the origins of great men, and I would normally be obliged to
begin this life of Sforza by reviewing a wide range of opinions,
were it not for the fact that — being informed by the best authorities — I am able to pass over legends that have no basis in fact.

Francesco Sforza was born in the year of our Lord 1401. His   2
father, as we said before, was the condottiere Muzio Attendolo
Sforza; his mother was the noblewoman Lucia da Torgiano. The

Lucia de Torsano, illustri muliere, die Saturni decimo Kalendas Augusti in vigilia Divorum Iacobi et Christophori, quorum solemnitas instanti die lunae celebrata fuit, horam paulo ante vigesimam secundam, ascendente primo gradu Capricorni, ut quidam perhibent, ut vero alii contendunt, in occasu solis, in opido Sancti Miniati provinciae Tusciae, quod a Theutonico nomen sumpsit, dum parens eius versus Pisas iter caperet ad Florentinorum civium stipendia ascriptus, qui tum ab Imperatore novo electo, a quo leonis insignia susceperat, abisset; appellatusque est Franciscus a parente suo in fratris Francisci defuncti memoriam, quem unice a Sfortia dilectum fuisse prodidere. Alii addunt Sfortiam paulo ante nativitatem Francisci filii ad stipendia Iohannis Galeaz primi Mediolanensium ducis accessisse, cum urbem Perusiam idem suscepisset, futuraeque felicitatis auspicium ex initio illo portendisse. Natus est igitur anno proximo, quo iubilei solemnitas Romae fuit, Bonifacio nono Ecclesiam regente, biennio post Blanchorum novitatem tota Italia vulgatam. Sed ad instituta redeamus.

: 5 :

De fratribus et sororibus eius et eruditione propria.

1 Fratres habuit Franciscus ex eisdem parentibus Sfortia et Lucia: Leonem, Iohannem et Alexandrum, prae ceteris armis inclitum, paucorum annorum aetate inter se distantes; sororem etiam nomine Lysam, quae Leoneto Sanseverinensi nupta fuit, et eo anno

day of his birth was Saturday, July 23, on the eve of the feast of Saints Jacob and Christopher, whose solemnities were celebrated on the following Monday. The hour of his birth, according to some, was just before six p.m., with Capricorn in the ascendant. Others however contend that his birth occurred at the setting of the sun. The place of his birth was the town of San Miniato, in Tuscany, also known as San Miniato al Tedesco.[8] His father at this time was on his way toward Pisa. He had just assumed command of Florentine forces, having left the service of the newly elected emperor, from whom he had received the coat of arms with the lion.[9] Muzio named his new son Francesco in memory of his own brother Francesco, who had passed away and whom they say he loved most dearly. Other sources add that just before the birth of his son Francesco, Muzio Attendolo had entered the service of Gian Galeazzo Visconti, the first duke of Milan. As this happened just after Gian Galeazzo had seized the city of Perugia, it was seen as a sign of auspicious beginnings.[10] And another thing: Francesco Sforza was born just one year after the Jubilee that was celebrated in Rome under Pope Boniface IX, and two years after the phenomenon of the White Penitents that swept over all of Italy.[11] But let us now return to our story.

: 5 :

His brothers and sisters and his education.

Francesco had the following brothers born of the same parents 1 (Muzio Attendolo and Lucia) as he: Leone, Giovanni, and Alessandro, the latter an outstanding warrior. All three brothers were born over the space of only a few years. Francesco also had a sister named Elisa. She married Leonetto Sanseverino. She was born in

nata est, quo Iohannes Galeaz, de quo supra scripsimus, in Me-
lignano exspiravit, uno scilicet a nativitate Francisci; secundoque
post anno Antoniam, quae Ardizoni Carrariae, viro claro, nupsit;
deinde Bosium alia ex matre; Leonardum quoque alio ex matrimonio genitum; postea Bartholomaeum; novissime Carolum Sfortiam, qui ad Archiepiscopatum Mediolanensem evectus brevi in
dignitate pervixit. Conradum dumtaxat ex eadem Lucia matre genitum fratrem habuit; item sororem Caterinam Bonam nomine ex
eadem matre, quae ex Troilo consorte suo insignes natos peperit.

2   Ipse Ferrariae innutritus apud Marcum Folianum, vitricum
suum, cum undecimum aetatis annum ageret, et cum filiis Nicolai
Estensis tunc urbis principis simul educatus, litterarum rudimenta
facile suscepit. Florentiae quoque, ut fertur, per aliquod tempus
enutritus fuit. Demum a parente suo Perusiam accitus, qua ille in
urbe Ladislai regis stipendia secutus tunc forte morabatur, et patrimonii opida in potestate habebat, ad eum venit.

3   Eodem anno Iohannes Maria, Philippi frater, nonnullorum
civium perfidia interemptus est. Hestor, Bernabovis filius, cum
Iohanne Carolo, nepote eius, Mediolanum occupavit, qui, a Philippo eiectus, infra mensem dominatu cessit. Sed haec alias a nobis
perscripta sunt.

the same year in which Gian Galeazzo Visconti (of whom we wrote above) died in Melegnano, and one year after the birth of Francesco Sforza himself. Two years later came the birth of another sister, Antonia, who married the nobleman Ardizzone da Carrara.[12] Then there was a brother, Bosio, born of another mother, and Leonardo, born from another marriage altogether, and next Bartolomeo, and lastly Carlo, who later became, but only briefly, archbishop of Milan.[13] Francesco also had a brother, Corrado, born of his mother Lucia, as well as a sister named Bona Caterina, also of the same mother.[14] This sister bore her husband Troilo a spate of illustrious offspring.

Francesco spent his childhood years in Ferrara with his step-father Marco da Fogliano. By the time he reached age eleven he had studied together with the sons of Niccolò III d'Este, ruler of the city of Ferrara, and had easily mastered the elements of reading and writing. It is said that he also went to Florence to further his education. His father then summoned him to Perugia. At that time his father happened to be stationed there in the service of King Ladislas and was holding a number of towns of the Patrimony of Saint Peter in his power.[15] So Francesco went to him.

In this same year Giovanni Maria Visconti, Filippo Maria Visconti's brother, was murdered in a conspiracy orchestrated by a number of his subjects. Estorre, the son of Bernabò Visconti, together with Bernabò's grandson Giovanni Carlo, then seized control of Milan. They were however driven out of the city within a month by Filippo Maria. But these are matters we have written about elsewhere.[16]

: 6 :

De prima dignitate comitatus eius.

Non multo post igitur, cognita Francisci virtute atque indole, Tricarici comes a rege Ladislao constitutus est, ac aliorum opidorum, quae rex idem Sfortiae parenti suo dono dederat. Inde Neapolim profectus, et sub Gabrielis Felicis regii camerarii cura delegatus, cum illo permansit; parique modo a Michelino Sfortiae cognato, qui magnam Neapolitani Regni partem sub magistratu continebat, eruditus, praecipua adolescentiae suae incrementa suscepit.

: 7 :

De affinitate parentis eius et coniugio.

Procedente vero tempore, cum rex probitatem, industriam ceterasque virtutes parentis eius admiraretur, et ob id summo in honore a cunctis haberetur, Antoniam de Salimbenis, illustrem mulierem, quae nonnulla opida in Senensi agro possidebat, eidem in uxorem dedit. Qua ex re inductus, Cichus, Antoniae frater, urbem Clusium in dotem illi addidit, veluti filiae suae Arparisae comiti Francisco in uxorem iam promissae pertinentem. Eodem anno Ladislaus idem clarissimus rex Neapoli e vita cessit.

: 6 :

How Francesco Sforza first acquired the title of count.

It was not long afterward that King Ladislas, in recognition of young Francesco's outstanding abilities, made him Count of Tricarico, and of several other towns that he had given as a gift to Muzio Attendolo. Francesco then went to Naples, where he was placed in the care of the royal official Gabriele Felice and remained in that man's service. At the same time he received training from his father's kinsman Micheletto Attendolo, who as an officer of the court held sway over a vast portion of the Kingdom of Naples.[17] Francesco grew and matured under the tutelage of both these men.

: 7 :

The marriage of Francesco's father.

With the passage of time King Ladislas came increasingly to admire the honesty, the energy, and the other qualities displayed by Francesco's father, qualities that earned Muzio Attendolo the highest esteem. So the king arranged for him to marry Antonia de'Salimbeni, a woman of rank whose possessions included a number of towns in Sienese territory. Antonia's brother Cicco felt prompted by this to add Chiusi to her dowry, since that city had been earmarked for his daughter Arparisa, who was already betrothed to Muzio's son Count Francesco. In this same year that most illustrious King Ladislas of Naples passed away.[18]

: 8 :

De honoribus Sfortiae parenti collatis et casibus eius.

Interea Sfortia, defuncto iam rege suo, a Iohanna regina, quae Ladislao fratri ex ordine successerat, Magnus Regni Siciliae Conesta-
bilis creatus est. Itaque immutatis rebus, priore iam defuncta muliere, Caterinam, Pandulfelli cuiusdam non ignobilis sororem, qui
apud reginam plurimum poterat, in uxorem suscipere coactus est.
Nam cum Pandulfelli eiusdem fraude captus a regina teneretur,
nisi affinitate cum eodem inita liberari non potuerat. Eo in loco
cum fortunae propriae maxime diffidens, desperatis rebus, mortem
exoptaret, Francisci filii suavissima oratione ad vitam revocatus
esse dicitur. Cum vero seditionibus in dies emergentibus e Regno
discedere coactus esset, et omnes ex se genitos obsides reginae
tradere, praeterea Michelinum et Marcum cognatos suos derelin-
quere, a rege Iacobo, comite Marciae prius appellato, qui Regnum
eo anno ingressus fuerat, et cui regina ipsa denupserat, in Benevento, urbe Samnii, cum Francisco filio interceptus est, ac per
quatuordecem menses in arce quam Ovi appellant in custodia de-
tentus. In qua demum Margaritae sororis astutia mitiorem in
modum pertractatus est.

: 8 :

Honors conferred upon Muzio and his various fortunes.

With the demise of the king he had served, Muzio Attendolo was made Grand Constable of the Kingdom of Sicily by an act of Queen Giovanna, who had meanwhile succeeded her brother Ladislas. Things changed however and Muzio, whose first wife had died, found himself obliged to marry Caterina, sister of a certain Pandolfello, a man of standing who exercised a huge influence over the queen. For without this close family relationship, Muzio would never have been able to free himself from the captivity he had fallen into through the treachery of the same Pandolfello.[19] It is said that while he was languishing in the queen's prison, losing all hope of his prospects, in complete despair and desiring only death, it was his son Francesco who raised his spirits with stirring words. Once freed, Muzio was forced—events being still very much in flux—to quit the Kingdom of Naples and to consign as hostages to the queen all his children, and to leave behind his kinsmen Micheletto and Marco Attendolo.[20] He was next arrested together with his son Francesco in Benevento, a city in Samnium, and held in detention for fourteen months in the Castel dell'Ovo. The man who had him arrested was King Giacomo, formerly Count of La Marche, who had entered the kingdom in that very year, having married the queen.[21] Muzio's captivity in the Castel dell'Ovo was relatively mild thanks to the clever way his sister Margherita intervened on his behalf.

: 9 :

Exemplum notabile sororis Sfortiae et
eius demum liberatio.

Habitabat tum ea in opido Tricarico et cum Michelino consorte
suo aliisque quibusdam fidissimis arcem tuebatur, cum nunciatum
est Sfortiam fratrem suum a rege captum minus humane detineri.
Itaque cum Neapolitani quidam ex nobilioribus recipiendi opidi
causa ad colloquium cum Michelino et his, quibus arcis cura mandata fuerat, accessissent et, fide praestita, quattuor ex primoribus
ingressi essent, Margarita his detentis neutique fidem ab ullo
praestari posse asseruit se invita, ad quam in primis arcis tutela
pertineret; neque prius egredi passa est, quam fratri nepotique
liberior custodia a rege praeberetur; qui deinde sequenti anno
pariter ex arce liberati sunt. Nam ferunt illustrium quorundam
conspiratione reginam ad convivium invitatam fuisse; quae cum
discedere vellet, clamorem a circumstantibus sublatum contra regem in favorem eius; urbeque tumultu concita, expulsum regem in
arcem se contulisse; nec multo post obsessum a civibus, Sfortiam
vero cum filio liberatum extitisse.

: 9 :

The notable behavior of Muzio's sister and how he was finally freed.

Margherita was living in the town of Tricarico and was in charge — together with her husband Michelino and a few trusted men — of the castle, when it was announced that her brother, the king's prisoner, was being treated inhumanely. So when a number of prominent noblemen from Naples turned up to take over the town, and began to negotiate with Michelino and with the men who held the castle, and four of these envoys of the first rank had been allowed entrance on a pledge, Margherita had them seized, saying that no pledge of safety was valid without her consent because the castle was first and foremost in her charge. Furthermore she would allow no one to leave the castle until she was assured that her brother and her nephew were being properly cared for while held in captivity by the king.[22] In the following year[23] both Muzio Attendolo and his son Francesco were in fact set free. For it is reported that a band of conspirators of rank invited the queen to a meeting, and when she rose to leave, a great cry went up from those present, complaining about King Giacomo and favoring her. The city then rebelled and the king took refuge in the citadel, which not long afterward the Neapolitans besieged. By this time though, Muzio and his son Francesco had been freed.

: 10 :

*De honoribus Sfortiae filio collatis et
Foschini laude.*

1   At vero Sfortia, rege Iacobo e Neapoli primorum vi depulso, denuo a regina ad pristinos honores admissus est donisque maioribus adauctus. Nam urbem Arianum nec non Troiae comitatum assecutus, Franciscum filium, de quo haec scribimus, tum decimum quintum agentem annum, huiusmodi civitatum titulis insignem statuit. Quo quidem tempore Carolus Malatesta, Arimini princeps, a Bracio Montono captus fuerat; ipse vero Bracius Perusiam invaserat.

2   Anno proximo Foschinus, Sfortiae consanguineus, vir praestanti virtute atque fide, cui deinde aetate nostra Mediolanensis arcis a Francisco instauratae cura commissa fuerat, urbem Romam a Sfortia ademptam Bracio Montono, et sub eius custodia ab illo traditam, eiusdem nomine tenebat; eam igitur Sfortiae mandato Iordano, Martini quinti pontificis fratri, reddidit; nam insequenti anno in Constantiensi Synodo pontifex electus ad Urbem accedebat. Eius meriti gratia non multo post Sfortia pontificis opera urbe Manfredonia a regina donatus est, quam Martinus idem post bienium subinde coronari voluit.

: 10 :

Honors bestowed upon Muzio's son, and praise for Foschino Attendolo.

Once King Giacomo had been well and truly driven out of Naples 1
by the armed might of the nobility, Queen Giovanna restored
Muzio Attendolo to his preeminent position in the kingdom and
conferred upon him even greater gifts than before. It was thus that
Muzio, having come into the possession of the city of Ariano and
the county of Troia, decided to make his son Francesco — the subject of our book and still only fifteen years old at the time — the
titled lord of these cities. This happened in the same year in which
Braccio da Montone conquered Perugia, capturing in the process
Carlo Malatesta, the lord of Rimini.[24]

In the following year Foschino — Muzio Attendolo's kinsman, a 2
man of outstanding ability and loyalty to whom in our own day
Francesco Sforza would entrust the custodianship of the newly
rebuilt Castle of Porta Giovia in Milan — was holding Rome in
Muzio's name, for the latter had taken it away from Braccio.[25]
Muzio then ordered Foschino to hand over control of the city to
Giordano Colonna, the brother of Pope Martin V. For in the very
next year the pope (newly elected by the Council of Constance)
set out for Rome.[26] In thanks for such loyal service the pope not
long after prompted Queen Giovanna to reward Muzio by giving
him the city of Manfredonia. And two years later Martin arranged
for Giovanna herself to be crowned queen in a formal ceremony.

: II :

De praesidentia Francisci data a parente eius.

1 Hisdem ferme temporibus Franciscus, Sfortiae filius, in Calabriam a parente missus fuerat, ut comitissam Alti Montis Polyxenam nomine, ducissae Suesanae sororem, connubio sibi adiungeret; quo pariter tempore Sfortia eius parens a regina Iohanna Beneventum suscepit.

2 Cum vero posteriore anno Sfortia ipse a Bracio Montono fortuna quadam bello superatus esset, Franciscus a parente suo ex Calabria Viterbium accitus venerat; quo in loco magna belli clades ab eodem suscepta fuerat, ac protinus eius copiis regendis et exercitui praeficitur; capti siquidem eo proelio fuere plerique spectati milites: Foschinus scilicet, Manibarilis, Georgius Salsavaca, Naymus et Gaspar de Torralto, nec non alii praestantes viri.

3 Erat igitur parenti suo non ignota filii probitas, et quid in posterum acturus esset vir prudens praesagibat animo, ut in illum potissimum mens eius inclinaret, quem fata ad principatum poscerent atque praepararent.

: II :

Muzio places his son Francesco in command of his army.

Around this same time Muzio Attendolo sent his son Francesco to 1
Calabria where he was to be joined in matrimony with the Count-
ess of Montalto, Polissena by name; she was the sister of the
Duchess of Sessa Aurunca.[27] Meanwhile Muzio himself took possession of Benevento at the behest of the queen.

In the following year Muzio through ill luck was defeated in 2
battle by Braccio da Montone; he therefore summoned his son
Francesco from Calabria to join him in Viterbo (which was where
the great military debacle had occurred), and immediately put him
in charge of his own troops and of the entire army. He did this
because among those captured in the battle with Braccio were
some of his very best men: they included Foschino, Manno Barile,
Giorgio Salsavacca, Naimo, Gaspare da Torralto, and many other
outstanding soldiers.[28]

Muzio then was already fully aware of his son's capabilities. A 3
wise man, he knew in his heart what great things Francesco was
going to accomplish in the future. He could foresee that his son
was destined by fate to one day assume power as ruler of his own
state.

: 12 :

Notabile exemplum prudentiae Francisci.

Nam cum antea in Calabriam missus a parente suo, ut praemisimus, contra Raymondum Boilum bellicis artibus instructum armis decertaret, satis conspicua fuerat virtus eius et industria, quod facile hoc exemplo innotuit. Transfugerat ab eo, cum in castris versaretur, militum suorum non contemnenda ad hostes manus, quos cum subinde, novis militibus a parente traditis, proelio adeptus esset, satis conscius quid clementiae suae, quid paternae etiam caritati et oboedientiae tribuendum esset, parenti suo, ut res gesta erat, ex ordine annuntiat, et quid facto opus sit, ab illo exquirit; ac protinus milites omnes non expectato responso liberat. Ex quo secutum est, ut qui paternae clementiae non ignarus fuerat, et oboedientiam erga illum et gloriam sibi ipsi conservaret: nam continuo eos liberandos mandavit pater. Ipse vero milites ultro obsequentes Viterbium adduxit.

: 12 :

A notable example of Francesco's good judgment.

For indeed when Francesco, as we said before, had been sent by his father to Calabria, and was fighting against that most skilled practitioner of the art of war, Ramón de Boïl, he gave tangible proof of his remarkable ingenuity, as the following example will clearly show. A rather large number of his own men had deserted his camp and joined the enemy. Subsequently however, thanks to reinforcements sent by his father, Francesco managed to recapture these same men in the fighting that ensued. Fully aware of the need to show clemency, but also of his duty of obedience to his father's wishes, he reported everything that had happened to his father, and asked him what he should do with the men who had betrayed him: then without waiting for the response he immediately freed them. From this example we see that Francesco — because he knew of his father's penchant for clemency — was able to procure his own glory while maintaining his filial obedience. For as it turned out his father soon responded that the captives should be freed. And Francesco then led these same soldiers — ready ever afterward to follow his orders faithfully — on to Viterbo.[29]

: 13 :

Mors Sfortiae et
Bracii Montoni memoranda.

1 Post haec Sfortia in Regnum profecturus Franciscum filium nec
non Michelinum et Leonetum, comitem Sancti Severini, praeire
iussit, qui illum ad ea opida, quae dictioni suae suberant, expecta-
rent. Anno sequenti Franciscus idem filiam Iacobi Caldorae, viri
inclyti, connubio sibi adiunxit, quam consensu Martini papae deinde ommisit.

2 Eo autem anno, qui vigesimus quartus supra quadringentesimum ac millesimum a Christi Nativitate numeratur, aetatis vero
Francisci vigesimus tercius, Sfortia reginae nomine Neapolim suscepit. Nec longiore intermisso spacio cum exercitum ducturus ad
fauces Piscarae fluminis transitum molitur, in ipso maris aestuan-
tis aditu undis obrutus nusquam inventus est, Romuli imitatus
exitum, qui inter deos relatus iuxta Capream paludem videri desiit.

3 Hic finis Sfortiae tandem fuit, viri armis inclyti, et qui multa in
bello paceque peregisset, exercitus maximos rexisset, urbibus prae-
fuisset plurimis. Nam praeter id, quod dignitatibus multis illustra-
tus fuerat, virtute propria Magnus Regni Siciliae Connestabilis
institutus a regina eius patrimonii totius opida parere sibi compulit; Tricarici comitatum nec non aliorum opidorum filio subesse
voluit; urbium etiam Ariani et Troiae, quarum altera Samnii, altera Apuliae habetur, parem dignitatem illi contulit; Romam praeterea, Bracio ademptam, sub dictione sua tenuit; Manfredoniam,

: 13 :

The memorable deaths of Muzio Attendolo and of Braccio da Montone.

Muzio was now about to set out again for the kingdom of Naples, so he ordered his son Francesco, along with Micheletto Attendolo and Leonetto, the Count of San Severino, to go on ahead and to wait for him in the towns that were already under his control. In the following year Francesco married the daughter of Giacomo Caldora, a man of great fame; but he later had this marriage annulled by Pope Martin.[30] 1

In that same year 1424 since the birth of Christ, Francesco having reached the age of twenty-three, Muzio took control of Naples in the name of Queen Giovanna. Not long afterward, as he was leading his army across the river Pescara at its mouth, he sank beneath the churning waves of the sea, never to be seen again.[31] His death was like that of Romulus, who was borne up into the heavens after vanishing from sight near the swamp of Capra.[32] 2

Such then was the end of Muzio Attendolo, an outstanding man of arms, a man who had accomplished so much in peace and war, who had commanded the greatest armies, who had ruled over so many cities. For alongside the many honors that made him so famous, through his own merits he was named Grand Constable of the Kingdom of Sicily by Queen Giovanna and as such brought the towns that belonged to her by right under his sway; he appointed his son Francesco to rule over the county of Tricarico and other towns; he also made his son the titled lord of the cities of Ariano and Troia, the one located in Samnium, the other in Apulia; he took the city of Rome away from Braccio and ruled it himself; he occupied Manfredonia, Benevento, and other cities; at last 3

Beneventum aliasque civitates adipisci meruit; postremo Neapolim, Regni totius caput, in potestate sua habuit, usque ad ultimum modicis conflictatus proeliis et casibus, dumtaxat invictus semper et felix. Ex quo huiusmodi finem caelitus illi datum confiteri necesse est, ne tot illustribus actis suis fortunae temeritas se immisceret, virtutemque eius fama celebrem calamitate aliqua involveret. Quod annus idem nova clade pariter insignis et Bracii Montoni nece memorandus nos edocuit, qui apud Aquilam bello superatus, amissisque copiis foede trucidatus, Francisci opera et auxilio conficitur. Hinc simultas inter Sfortiae Braciique successores pariter incensa, et ut prius inter duces odium exarserat, sic denuo permansit. Verum nos ad Francisci opera stilum convertemus.

: 14 :

De incrementis virtutis Francisci sub Martino papa.

1 Incrementa igitur laudis eius ac virtutis sub Martino quinto summo pontifice in primis enituere, a quo in Bracium emissus, ut Aquilanos cives ab illo obsessos liberaret, tantam rei militaris peritiam, tantam in bello prudentiam ac fortitudinem ostendit, ut adsistentibus quamquam pontificis et reginae ducibus, adsistente et potentissima Philippi Marie manu, solus tamen victor eo in proelio apparuerit solique gloria et nomen accesserit.

he brought Naples, the capital of the whole kingdom, under his control. He was still engaged in skirmishes and intrigues down to the very end, but always emerged the lucky winner. From this we must conclude that his sudden demise was a gift from heaven, lest bold fortune decide to darken so many bright deeds, casting a pall over his glory with some terrible calamity. For that very same year was equally memorable for the military disaster and violent death that befell Braccio da Montone. Braccio met defeat in battle at Aquila, where he lost his entire army and was foully murdered. The author of his downfall was Francesco Sforza.[33] Thus began the intense rivalry between the successors of Muzio Attendolo and Braccio, a rivalry that continues to this day to be as strong as it ever was between the two historic leaders.[34] But let us now turn to telling of the deeds of Francesco Sforza.

: 14 :

Growth of Francesco's military reputation under Pope Martin.

Francesco's ever-increasing powers and abilities first began to shine forth under the supreme pontiff Martin V. This pope had sent him to fight against Braccio. The mission was to free the citizens of Aquila from the siege Braccio was laying to their city. In carrying out this task Francesco demonstrated such complete mastery of the art of war, such courage and prowess in the heat of battle, that although he had the assistance of the military commanders in the service of Queen Giovanna and the pope, as well as the support of a mighty force sent by Filippo Maria Visconti, he alone emerged as the winner of the battle, and to him alone belonged the glory and credit for having achieved victory.[35]

2   Post haec in Fulginates delegatus, urbi praesidentem ad Ecclesiae obsequium facile pellexit. Ea tempestate Franciscus Carmagnola, vir bello illustris, a Philippo Maria Mediolanensium duce ad
Venetos transivit. Quarto et vigesimo a Christi Nativitate, superi-
oribus additis, elapso anno, Carolus Malatesta, vir fama clarus,
apud opidum Zagonariam bello victus, ad Philippum Mariam
Abbiate deductus est. Franciscus autem Sfortia felici omine insequenti anno ad stipendia eiusdem ducis accessit. Quo Blancha
Maria, ipsius Francisci futura coniunx, ex eodem Philippo et
Agnete Mayna, insigni muliere, quasi quodam divino munere nata
est.

: 15 :

Quae praeclara obvenere insequentibus annis.

1   Eodem anno cum multa praeclara et scitu digna annotata sint,
tum vel maxime miserationem quandam attulisse videtur obitus
Ugonis, illustris adolescentis, qui patrium cubile temerare ausus, a
Nicolao parente suo cum noverca pariter occisus est.

2   Brixia ad Venetos sequenti anno a Philippo defecit, omnis,
quod insequutum est, belli fomes et initium. Nam dum Philippus
urbem ammissam summa vi recuperare nititur, Veneti adeptam
conservare student, Florentinis illis auxilia navantibus, universam
Italiam maximis involvere cladibus, ut latius a nobis in *Philippi Vita*
perscriptum est.

Next he was sent against Foligno, where he easily forced the   2
ruler of that city to submit to the obedience of the Church. At
this same time the famed captain-at-arms Francesco Carmagnola
left the service of the Duke of Milan, Filippo Maria Visconti, and
went over to serve the Venetians. The year of our Lord 1424 also
saw Carlo Malatesta, a man of great fame who had been defeated
in battle near Zagonara, brought before Filippo Maria Visconti at
Abbiategrasso. Francesco Sforza on the other hand was in the following year auspiciously called into the service of the same Filippo
Maria. In that year too, as if the coincidence had been willed by
heaven, Bianca Maria, Francesco's future wife, was born to Filippo
Maria and the noblewoman Agnese del Maino.

: 15 :

Notable things that occurred in the following years.

While many important events worth remembering are recorded as   1
having happened in that same year, the death of the young nobleman Ugo d'Este seems especially to have stirred hearts to the core:
having dared to defile the paternal marriage bed, the young man
was put to death, together with his stepmother, by his own father
Niccolò III d'Este.[36]

In the following year Brescia passed from Filippo Maria Vis-   2
conti into the hands of the Venetians: this event was the origin
and cause of the war that ensued.[37] For with Filippo trying to recover the city he had lost, and the Venetians — aided and abetted
by the Florentines — intent on keeping what they had gained, the
whole of Italy was engulfed in a major conflagration, a situation
about which I have written more extensively in my biography of
Filippo Maria.

3   Praecipue tamen apud Maclodium anno proximo trepidatum est, rebus in ipso ardore belli fluctuantibus, Philippi copiis a Francisco Carmagnola Venetum ductore bello profligatis. Pandulfus Malatesta, vir inter strenuos aetatis suae duces numerandus, Fani Flaminiae defunctus est. Franciscus Sfortia eodem anno ad Castellacium Alexandriae hibernatum concessit. Pax cum Venetis, urbe Bergomo illis tradita, confecta est. Maria, Amadei Sabaudiensis ducis filia, Philippo Marie nupta est.

: 16 :

De conflictu in Genuensi ora et Francisci virtute.

1 Anno deinde proximo novum insecutum est bellum. Quippe Genuenses, pacis et quietis continue immemores, contra Philippum eorum principem insurgere conati sunt variosque in Pulciferae et Bisanis vallibus tumultus concitarunt. Igitur ad eos compescendos Franciscus Sfortia, cum Pulciferam vallem summa audacia magno animo ingressus esset, nonnullorum perfidia ab accolis locorum obsessus est; difficiles enim aditus iter prohibebant, ita ut facile foret, quamquam parva manu, multos destinere accessuque prohibere. Usus igitur ingenio pariter ac vi, militum virtute tandem in tutum relatus est, non sine hostium strage caedeque memoranda, cum ex suis nonnullos praestantes amisisset; cecidit namque eo proelio Gerardus Cutignola affinis eius, vir bello clarus. Ipse in opido, cui Roncho nomen est, ab Iliana Spinula, muliere egregia, e proelio servatus, Mortarium se contulit.

The climax came with the battle fought in the following year at 3
Maclodio: with the outcome of the war hanging in the balance,
Filippo Maria's forces were defeated by the Venetian commander
Francesco Carmagnola.[38] Pandolfo Malatesta, a man to be numbered among the finest generals of his day, died at Fano. That
same year Francesco Sforza retired to winter quarters at Castel-
lazzo, near Alessandria. Peace was made with the Venetians, at the
cost of ceding to them the city of Bergamo. Maria, daughter of
Amedeo, Duke of Savoy, was married to Filippo Maria.[39]

: 16 :

Revolt in Genoese territory and Francesco's skill.

The next year witnessed the beginnings of a new war. For the 1
Genoese, forgetful of the benefits of peace and prosperity, rose up
against their master Filippo Maria Visconti and fomented open
rebellion in the valleys of Polcevera and Bisagno. Francesco Sforza
was sent to quell the revolt. But when he had boldly entered the
Polcevera Valley, he was betrayed and attacked by the local population. The way forward was fraught with difficulty due to its being
relatively easy for a small force to hold back his advance and im-
pede further progress. Using both skill and force Francesco nevertheless managed to spur his men to fight their way to safety, killing
and wounding large numbers of the enemy in the process. He too
lost some of his finest men: his kinsman for example, the illustrious warrior Gerardo da Cotignola was killed in this battle. Francesco himself sought refuge in the town of Ronco, availing himself
of the protection afforded by the noblewoman Eliana Spinola; he
then made his way to Mortara.[40]

2   Quo anno Bononia Martino pontifici quinto rebellavit. Ac Polyxena filia protinus amissa, quam ex Iohanna concubina antea susceperat, aliam eiusdem nominis subinde genuit, quae Sygismundo Pandulfo, Arimini principi, posterius nupta est. Mox elapso anno filium nomine Sfortiam ab eadem procreavit; deinde Tristanum clariore ex femina conceptum Mediolani, quorum alter non perannavit. Tristanus aetate et ingenio praepollens illustris Borsii Mutinensis ducis affinitate conspicuus adhuc viget. Eodem anno Carolus ille senior, Arimini princeps, vir summa sapientia, extinctus est.

: 17 :

De liberatione urbis Lucensium contra Florentinos.

1   Emergentibus deinde in Italia bellis atque discidiis, cum Venetorum ac Florentinorum conatus post bellum cum Philippo gestum non immerito suspicionem afferre viderentur, Florentini praeterea Lucam sibi asciscere tentarent, novo quodam remedio opus erat, ne pars una ita excelleret, ut reliquae opprimerentur. Profectus itaque Franciscus Sfortia a Philippo Maria Mediolanensium duce, cum ab illo discessisset, nec ullo deinceps stipendio aut mercede teneretur, Lucam venit, ut Florentinorum copias duce Nicolao, qui de Stella cognominabatur, urbi imminentes armis ammoveret. Lucam igitur ingressus, Paulum Guinigium illi praesidentem, a quo

In this same year Bologna rebelled against Pope Martin V. And 2
Francesco Sforza, who had suddenly lost Polissena, the daughter
who had been born to his concubine Giovanna, fathered another
daughter to whom he gave the same name. This second Polissena
later married Sigismondo Pandolfo Malatesta, lord of Rimini.[41]
Another year passed and Francesco's concubine Giovanna gave
him a son whom he named Sforza, while with a Milanese noblewoman he fathered Tristano. Son Sforza did not survive, but
Tristano grew in stature and ability: he still lives today, a kinsman
to the illustrious Borso d'Este, Duke of Modena.[42] This same year
also saw the death of Carlo Malatesta, lord of Rimini and a man
of the greatest wisdom.

: 17 :

Francesco frees Lucca from the Florentines.

Discord and war were rife at this time in Italy, caused largely by 1
the justified suspicion that Venice and Florence were attempting to
capitalize on the gains made against Filippo Maria. The Florentines were in fact in the process of trying to conquer Lucca. Some
new remedy needed to be found lest one side gain so much power
that it would be able to crush the others.[43] Francesco Sforza therefore sallied forth. He was no longer in the pay or under any sort of
contract to the Duke of Milan, Filippo Maria, for he had left the
latter's service. He came to Lucca with a purpose: to drive away
the Florentine troops who, under their commander Niccolò Fortebraccio, were threatening to occupy the city by force of arms. He
therefore entered Lucca and, with his usual skill and zeal, set
about protecting the ruler of the city, Paolo Guinigi (on whose

accitus fuerat, singulari virtute summaque constantia ac promptitudine a Florentinorum manibus tutatus est. Sed cum illum beneficii accepti immemorem, clam perfidia crassantem et se Florentinorum consiliis dedentem animadverteret, vim vi repellere coactus, ultro cepit, captumque Mediolanum ad principem Philippum, quo illi gratificaretur, ire iussit; opes omnes, quae ab illo asservabantur, filiis in custodia dimissis, militibus in praedam dedit.

2   Qua in re quid prius laude et commendatione dignum deputem? An qui armis belloque praecellens hostes imminentes vi represserit? An qui intestinum et penitus inhaerentem sibi hostem sua diligentia non evitarit modo, sed oppresserit? Utrumque profecto memoria dignum. Sed ulteriora prosequamur.

: 18 :

De discessu Francisci ex eadem urbe, et quae insecuta sunt.

1   Fuit inter Italos principes Philippus Maria longe praecipuus atque memorandus: plura quippe ingenio quam viribus effecit. Is igitur, Florentinos sibi infensos arbitratus superiore ex bello, Franciscum multis precibus hortatus est, ut illis propicium sese redderet opemque in adipiscenda Luca, quam maxime optabant, polliceretur, liberam suis legibus urbem dimittendo, quo facilior invadendi eam facultas esset. Ea spe allecti, Florentini sequenti anno non mediocrem pecuniae summam Francisco contulere: qua iure suscepta, ut commoditati eorum propria utilitate consuleret, ex Luca

summons he had come), from Florentine aggression.[44] But when he realized that Guinigi, with supreme ingratitude, was plotting behind his back to cut a deal with the Florentines, he was obliged to fight force with force. So he had Guinigi seized and taken captive to Filippo Maria in Milan, knowing the duke would be pleased with such a fine gift. He then turned Guinigi's vast wealth over to his soldiers for plunder, and had the man's sons placed under guard.

Which of these deeds should I single out as the most worthy of 2 praise and commendation? Perhaps I should laud most of all the outstanding condottiere whose forces turned back the advancing enemy? Or should I rather prefer the crafty statesman whose alertness to danger allowed him to expose and spoil the plot of an enemy lurking in his own midst?[45] In truth both of these deeds are eminently worthy of being remembered. But let us now move on.

: 18 :

Francesco leaves Lucca, and what happened next.

Filippo Maria Visconti was by far the greatest and most memora- 1 ble of the Italian princes: more often than not he achieved his ends by using his wits rather than force. He realized from the previous war that the Florentines were hostile to his designs, so he urged Francesco Sforza to become their friend and to pledge to help them acquire Lucca, a thing they most fondly desired. Sforza was to leave Lucca free to live under its own laws, thus making it an easy target for a Florentine invasion. Florentine hopes accordingly soared, and the following year they paid out huge sums of money to Francesco. He rightfully pocketed the cash and left Lucca, having found a way to reconcile his own interests with those of the

cessit. Florentini, novis coactis copiis, Guidonem Montisferetri Urbino praesidentem ad stipendia eorum accivere, simulque in Lucenses movere exercitum, rati facillimum factu fore urbem, defensore vacuam et novis degentem legibus, occupare posse. At vero Philippus alia ex parte Nicolaum Piceninum ad illos misit, quo duce moenia tutarentur cives hostesque depellerent. Ex quo secutum est, ut, profligatis Florentinorum copiis, servatis civibus, Philippus nulla impensa duces suos aleret. Florentini ex pace statum suum augere cupientes, spe simul et pecunia eo anno frustrarentur.

2 Iisdem temporibus Nicolaus marchio Estensis consortem propriam ex Saluciarum nobilissimo genere suscepit, ex qua Herculem Sygismundumque procreavit.

: 19 :

De adoptione Francisci a Philippo Maria ex Blanchae Mariae conubio, et quae ab eodem strenue acta sunt.

1 Eodem anno, qui trigesimus primus post superiores a Christi Nativitate a nobis annotatur, Blancha Maria, Philippi filia, quae nunc cum consorte pariter Mediolanensis populi ducatum possidet, Francisco Sfortiae in uxorem promissa est. Ipse Vicecomitum et soceri sui desumpsit insignia, iam tum quidem Mediolanensium destinatus imperio et in filium accitus a Philippo.

Florentines. They meanwhile mustered new troops and hired Guidantonio da Montefeltro lord of Urbino to be their military chieftain. The invasion of Lucca got underway at once, the Florentines thinking that it would be the easiest of tasks to overcome a city that lacked a defender and was living under new laws. But Filippo Maria had other plans: he sent Niccolò Piccinino to Lucca with orders to organize the defense of the city and repel the invaders. So it happened that the Florentine forces were thoroughly beaten, the city of Lucca was saved, and Filippo Maria managed to maintain both of his condottieri at no expense to himself. Meanwhile the Florentines, who had expected that the Peace of Ferrara would provide them with an opportunity to expand their territory, were that year frustrated in their hopes and despoiled of their money.[46]

At around this same time the Marquis Niccolò d'Este took as   2 his wife a member of that most noble House of Saluzzo. With her he fathered Ercole and Sigismondo.[47]

: 19 :

Francesco is adopted by Filippo Maria through his betrothal to Bianca Maria; his deeds in war.

In that same year, which we number as the year of our Lord 1431,   1 Filippo Maria's daughter Bianca Maria, who today rules over the Duchy of Milan together with her husband, was betrothed to Francesco Sforza. Francesco thus began displaying the Visconti heraldic devices of his father-in-law: clearly he was already at this point destined to rule Milan and had become the adopted son of Filippo Maria.

2   Ea tempestate, cum bellum inter Venetos Philippumque effer-
vescere coepisset, multa et praeclara a Francisco Sfortia facta sunt,
quae longum esset recensere, sive quae Brixiensi in bello, sive aliis
in locis impigre effecit annotare libeat; neque solum terrestri in
proelio, verum etiam navali apud Cremonam, cuius victoriae et par-
ticeps et auctor vel in primis idem fuit. Quae singula cum laude et
commendatione digna videantur, unicum tamen inter cetera insigne facinus ab eodem peractum est. Id autem memoriae com-
mendandum existimavi, quod cum praestantissimo Venetorum
imperatore gestum, fortitudinem eius in re militari prudentiamque
ostendit. Nam cum vir armis inclytus Franciscus Carmagnola, de
quo supra retuli, magna militum manu comitatus—ter mille
nempe ducebat equites—prope Soncinum opidum Sfortiae occur-
risset, qui longe inferiore numero sese obtulerat, proelium subito
inniit, quasi victoria iam parta hostium armis equisque potiturus.
At vero Franciscus, adventu eius nihil territus, pugnam ultro excepit exultantemque solita vincendi fiducia illustrem virum adeo
repressit ac pepulit, ut nullo ex suis fere amisso, multos ex hostibus captivos duceret. Quae res non mediocrem gloriam illi attulit.

3   Eodem anno, ecclipsi solis insigni praecedente, Martinus quintus extinctus est, et Eugenius quartus constitutus pontifex. Venetorum milites Cremonam ingressi sunt, deinde repulsi. Sigismun-
dus Imperator Mediolani coronatus est.

At this time too, with the war between the Venetians and 2
Filippo Maria in full swing again, Francesco Sforza performed
numerous mighty deeds. Relating them all in detail would take us
some time, whether we were to describe what he achieved in the
fighting at Brescia, or on other fronts. Indeed he was active not
only on land, but also in the naval battle near Cremona, where he
was both a participant and the principal architect of victory.[48]
While each and every action of Sforza's would deserve the highest
praise and commendation, there was one deed of his that clearly
stands out above the others. I have therefore decided to single out
for special mention his encounter with the supreme commander
of the Venetian forces, for it illustrates both his courage and his
skill in waging war. It happened that that most outstanding of
generals, Francesco Carmagnola — of whom I spoke earlier — came
up against Sforza near the town of Soncino. Carmagnola was
leading a huge force of three thousand cavalrymen, whereas Sforza
found himself in command of a much smaller number of men.
Carmagnola immediately attacked, certain of victory and expecting to capture the enemy's horses and equipment. But Francesco,
unperturbed, met the challenge head on. And so thoroughly did
he drive back the famous general, who was brimming with confidence that he would win in his usual manner, that he lost hardly a
single man of his own, while he took many prisoners among the
enemy. This victory brought Sforza great glory.[49]

In the same year, following a major eclipse of the sun, Martin V 3
died and Eugenius IV became pope. Venetian forces occupied
Cremona and were then driven out. Emperor Sigismund was
crowned in Milan.[50]

: 20 :

De Piceni adeptione per Franciscum.

1 Franciscus Sfortia anno proximo Iohannem fratrem ad urbium earum regimen ire iussit, quas idem in Neapolitano Regno possidebat. Quo tempore Franciscus Carmagnola in Venetorum civitate, quamquam insons, capite multatus est. Sed haec alias. Verum quo pacto satis memorem virtutem ac praestantiam victoriosissimi ducis nostri in gerendis rebus? Vix credi posset tantum animi ingeniique in illo affuisse, nisi exitus ostenderet. Quippe insequenti anno, qui trigesimus tercius habitus est a superiorum numero, cum a stipendiis Philippi ducis discessisset, aspirantem ceptis suis fortunam aliis in locis experiri cupiens, quo animi sui excellentia aliquo insigni opere elucesceret, quam primum in Picenum iter capere instituit. Nam Eugenius pontifex iampridem ad Synodum a clero evocatus, minus obsequentem se cunctorum votis exhibebat, ut non admonitore solum atque hortatore, ceterum vi et armis opus esset ad Catholicae Fidei statum conservandum.

2 Quam primum igitur eam regionem ingressus est, sic strenuum se ducem praestitit, sic obsequentes habuit milites, sic omnibus in locis nunc legationes, nunc exercitus emittens, partim suasionibus, partim viribus omnes ad se convertit, ut—quod fieri posse vix credendum est—re autem ipsa effectum sit, duorum et viginti dierum spacio Picenum omne, agris, opidis civitatibusque in dictionem redactis, excepto Camerino, ultro sibi asciverit; ut non immerito iisdem verbis gloriari potuerit, quibus Caesarem in

: 20 :

Francesco Sforza seizes the March of Ancona.

In the following year Francesco sent his brother Giovanni to rule 1
over the cities he still possessed in the Kingdom of Naples. At this
same time Francesco Carmagnola was put to death in Venice,
though he was perfectly innocent, but such things need not detain
us. For truly how could I ever devote enough space to praising the
outstanding merits of that most victorious duke of ours in waging
war? It would be hard to believe there was so much courage and
genius in this one man, were it not that his actions offer proof of
the fact. Indeed in the very next year, 1433 by our reckoning, having left the service of Filippo Maria, and wanting to test his rising
fortunes in some new endeavor whereby he might further demonstrate his abilities with some worthy deed, he at once decided to
head for the Marches. Pope Eugenius IV had in fact been summoned by the clergy to appear before the Council of Basel. As he
was increasingly unwilling to submit to the dictates of that assem-
bly, it became apparent that the preservation of the Catholic Faith
would require not just exhortation and admonition, but the force
of arms.[51]

As soon as Sforza entered the Marches he showed himself to 2
be such an energetic leader, to command such loyalty from his
troops, to be capable of sending his emissaries and soldiers to so
many different places at once, that he subdued the entire province,
partly by persuasion and partly by force. It will seem incredible,
but it took him only twenty-two days to conquer the whole of the
Marches: fields, towns, cities—all came under his power, with the
sole exception of Camerino. He might well then have applied to
himself the very same words that Julius Caesar is reported to have

Pharnacis bello usum ferunt: 'Veni, vidi, vici.' Sic enim accessus eius citus, aspectus promptus, victoria facilis illi fuit.

: 21 :

De Piceni marchionatu in Franciscum collato ab Eugenio pontifice.

Annus is profecto magnarum rerum eventu memorandus. Nam Michael ecclesiastici ductor exercitus ad Arzonum opidum, unaque Laurentius, ambo Cutignolae, Leo praeterea, Francisci frater, non longe a Tybure Romano opido insigni proelio cum Nicolao Forte-bracio armis decertarunt. Quo anno Franciscus Sfortia ab Eugenio pontifice Piceni marchio creatus est et Ecclesiae vexillifer, quem confalonerium vocant, institutus. Itaque paulo post urbem Tuder-tum, centum, ut aiunt, opidis insignem, cepit; Interamnem quo-que et Tuscanellam, nec non Flasconi opidum in monte situm de-populatus, quod Nicolai Fortebracii adversae factionis partibus haesisset. Creditumque est a plerisque Nicolaum Piceninum ad balnea finitima accessisse, ut Francisco Sfortiae insidias strueret. Multa enim posterius minus prospere secuta sunt populorum levi-tate; verum ille cum virtute propria, tum Federici, Montis Feretri et Urbini comitis, auxilio confisus, procedente tempore adversa superavit.

used to characterize his campaign against Pharnaces: "I came, I saw, I conquered."[52] So swift indeed was Francesco's entry into the province, so accurate his assessment of the situation, so easy his victory.

: 21 :

Pope Eugenius assigns the marquisate of Ancona to Francesco Sforza.

The year 1433 saw quite a number of memorable events. For Micheletto Attendolo, commander of the papal army, together with Lorenzo, also from Cotignola, and Leone, Francesco Sforza's brother, fought a mighty battle with Niccolò Fortebraccio at the village of Arzono, which is located not far from the Roman town of Tivoli. In that same year Pope Eugenius made Francesco Sforza Marquis of Ancona and Standard-bearer (the official title being *Gonfaloniere*) of the Church.[53] And not long afterward Sforza occupied the city of Todi, said to be the capital of a hundred towns. He also took Terni and Toscanella, as well as laying waste to the hilltop town of Montefiascone, for this latter place had chosen to side with his opponent Niccolò Fortebraccio. Many believe that Niccolò Piccinino had meanwhile gone to the nearby baths in order to spring a surprise attack on Francesco Sforza.[54] A number of less fortunate events later ensued on account of the fickleness of peoples. But in the course of time Sforza prevailed over adversity, his success being due to his own skill as well as to the aid he received from Federico da Montefeltro, Count of Urbino.[55]

: 22 :

De favoribus collatis Ecclesiae Romanae a Francisco.

Neque tamen minus clara aut conspicua habentur, quae sequuntur. Populus nempe Romanus, nulla lege ad arma concitatus, Eugenium quartum summum pontificem, virum singulari virtute et religione, per vim detinere meditatus, universam urbem seditionibus turbisque replevit. Multae igitur contentiones atque pugnae memoratu dignae per Franciscum Sfortiam tentatae in Ecclesiae favorem; multae secus a Nicolao Picenino excitatae non longe ab urbe Roma, in quibus Francisco inferior Nicolaus semper fuit; resque Italae in discrimen maximum adductae sunt amborum dissensionibus, nisi Philippi Mariae prudentia continuo obstitisset. Is nempe inter utrosque pacem meditatus, seu potius odii et simultatis missionem, litem avertit. Sic ducibus inter se divisis quies insecuta est. Sed haec a nobis liberius in historiis perscripta sunt. Sequenti anno Ludovicus tercius rex in Consentia Calabriae extinctus est.

: 23 :

Memorabile de Philippi Mariae clementia et liberalitate,
quam Franciscus imitatus est.

1 Trigesimus quintus annus a superiorum ordine reliquos excellere visus est, memoria captivitatis Alfonsi regis, cunctorum praestantissimi, qui a Genuensibus navali bello superatus, Mediolanum ad Philippum Mariam, Genuensium principem, adductus est:

: 22 :

Francesco Sforza serves the cause of the Church.

The events that followed were no less illustrious or deserving of mention. The Roman populace staged an armed revolt aimed at capturing Pope Eugenius IV, a man of singular virtue and holiness. The entire city of Rome was filled with turbulence and bloodshed. Francesco Sforza fought long and hard on the side of the Church, while Niccolò Piccinino stirred up trouble on the outskirts of Rome. But in these contests Niccolò was always inferior in skill to Francesco.[56] The battles between these two men might well have brought Italian affairs to a pretty pass, had it not been for the prudent arbitration exercised by Filippo Maria Visconti. In order to establish peace between the warring parties, or at least achieve a cessation of hostilities, Filippo brought their quarreling to an end. With the leaders thus pacified, a period of calm ensued. But these are things we have described more extensively in our Histories.[57] The next year King Louis III of Naples died at Cosenza, in Calabria.

: 23 :

The noteworthy clemency and generosity of Filippo Maria Visconti is imitated by Francesco Sforza.

The year 1435 stands out from the others because it witnessed the   1
capture of Alfonso of Aragon, that most worthy king among all kings. Defeated by the Genoese fleet at sea, he was brought a prisoner to Milan to face Filippo Maria, ruler of Genoa. Here truly

unicum profecto spectaculum memoratu dignum, regem ipsum cum fratribus duobus, quorum alter rex fuit, intueri; tot vero praestantes principes atque duces una captos, ut nusquam relatum aut scriptum audiverimus patrum nostrorum memoria tam insignem illustrium procerum catervam uno in proelio conspirasse, simulque adversae fortunae impetu oppressam extitisse; nullam etiam maiore laude et commendatione liberalitatem visam aut auditam, quam quae a Philippo Maria duce clementissimo erga illos impensa est, cum omnes liberasset.

2   Quam Franciscus Sfortia in ingressu civitatis nostrae non minore gloria imitatus est, cum omnes cives tam adversos suis partibus, quam faventes, pari modo salvos esse voluit, ut a nobis inferius annotatum est.

3   Eodem anno Iohana secunda Neapoli defuncta est, cum Regno praesideret. Sed nos ad Franciscum ipsum revertemur.

: 24 :

De recuperatione urbis Bononiae
Ecclesiae Romanae per Franciscum.

1 Is nempe superiore anno Venetorum Florentinorumque exercitibus stipatus, pontificis Eugenii nomine, sub cuius imperio, pace inter utrumque facta, militabat, Bononiam obsedit eamque, licet populo pecuniisque florentem, et Ecclesiae iugum ferre recusantem, sua industria ad parendum compulit. Ex quo indulctum

was a remarkable spectacle to recall: to see the king himself with his two brothers, one of whom was a king in his own right; to see in addition so many outstanding princes and generals all taken prisoner together! Never before had we ever heard tell or write about such a worthy band of illustrious leaders, all participants in a single battle, all being suddenly overwhelmed by adverse fortune. Nor had anyone ever heard of or seen such liberality as that which the most clement Duke Filippo Maria showed to these captives by granting them all their freedom, an act worthy of the highest praise and commendation.[58]

Francesco Sforza earned himself no less glory by imitating this 2 act when he entered our city of Milan, for he wanted all of our citizens, those who had opposed him as well as those who had favored him, to enjoy the same guarantees of safety, as we shall relate later in our story.[59]

In that same year Giovanna II died in Naples, while ruling over 3 the kingdom. But we return now to telling of Francesco Sforza himself.[60]

: 24 :

Francesco recovers the city of Bologna for the Church.

In the year noted above Francesco Sforza, supported by the armies 1 of Venice and Florence, laid siege to Bologna in the name of Pope Eugenius, in whose service he had been fighting ever since peace had been made between the two of them. Although Bologna was a large and wealthy city, and resolutely opposed to being ruled by the Church, Sforza worked hard and eventually forced it into submission.[61] As a reward the pope gave him permission to occupy

illi a pontifice, ut Barbianum sibi acquireret, ad quod opidum veluti Ecclesiae vexillifer profectus est. Eo anno filium suscepit nomine Sfortiam ad Criptas ortum Picenias, secundum ab illo qui
prius interierat.

2   Eodem fere tempore Isabella, Renati regis uxor, Gaietam urbem
cum filio ingressa est, nec multo post Philippi Mariae opera reiecta
et exclusa.

: 25 :

*De rebus strenue gestis contra conspirantes in eum a Francisco
et defensione urbis Pisarum.*

1   Nihil tamen intermissum est laboris aut industriae a Francisco
Sfortia priore ex bello. Nam cum Bononiae finitimus apud Po-
ledranum pontem sequenti anno conspirationem in se factam
cognovisset a plerisque praeclaris ducibus — erant enim eius conscii
Petrus Iampaulus, Petrus de le Testis, Rodulfus Perusinus ac Petrus Navarinus, Baldesaris Ufidae opera — exercitum in eos statim
movit; quos impigre aggressus, sic profligavit ac fudit, ut nullus ex
tot ducibus tantisque copiis superesset aut resisteret arrepta fuga,
maiorque pars eorum interciperetur.

2   Quo quidem anno Florentinorum opes sua industria pariter
tutatus est, addita celeritate summa in gerendis rebus. Nicolaus
quidem Piceninus Philippi mandato Pisas versus iter ceperat, ut
urbem, milite et defensore vacuam, per proditionem caperet; quam
profecto invasisset, ni Franciscus, re praecognita, trium dierum

Barbiano, to which town he now repaired as Standard-bearer of the Church. That year too a son was born to him at Grottamare in the Marches and was named Sforza Secondo after the son who had earlier died.[62]

At this time too Isabella, wife of King René of Anjou, entered 2
the city of Gaeta with her son. But not long afterward she was forced to leave the city and prevented from ever returning by Filippo Maria Visconti.[63]

: 25 :

Francesco Sforza reacts vigorously to suppress a conspiracy,
and his defense of Pisa.

Francesco had no time to rest from his labors after the taking of 1
Bologna. For in the following year, at the bridge of Poledrano quite near the city, he learned that several of his key generals were plotting against him. The conspirators included Pietro Giampaolo Orsini, Pietro della Testa, Rodolfo da Perugia, and Pietro di Navarrino. Their ringleader was Baldassarre da Offida. As soon as Sforza discovered the plot he ordered his army to attack. His action was so sudden that he totally dispersed and destroyed the plotters. Not a single one of them was able to rally his men to resist. They fled in all directions and most of them were captured.[64]

That same year also saw Sforza exert himself to protect the 2
might of Florence, providing yet another example of swift and decisive action. Niccolò Piccinino, on orders from Filippo Maria Visconti, was on his way to Pisa. His mission was to occupy that undefended city, with help from supporters among the Pisans. He certainly would have succeeded had not Francesco Sforza, learning

itineratione ex Flaminia Pisas usque appulisset. Quo facto debili-
tatis conspiratorum animis, urbs ipsa a periculo servata est.

3   Eodem anno Genuensium civitas Philippo rebellavit foedusque
cum Venetis Florentinisque coniunxit.

4   Sequenti vero nata est Francisco filia Drusiana nomine, dum e
Luca sublatis copiis Regium Lepidum versus tenderet, ex Iohanna,
de qua supra retuli, quae comiti Iacobo Picenino nupta apud parentem asservatur.

: 26 :

De liberatione urbis Veronensium per Franciscum.

1   Verum longe maiora atque illustriora fuere quae sequuntur. Crevit
enim cum aetate virtus eius atque industria, de quibus deinceps
scribere ordiemur.

2   Veneti Florentinique magnis proeliis a Philippo Maria exagitati,
duce Nicolao Picenino, cum imperatorem illi parem aut certe su-
periorem habere cuperent, Franciscum Sfortiam in quinquenium,
ingenti comparato exercitu, denuo ad stipendia sua conduxerant.
Nam Brixiam summa vi magnis copiis undique obsessam, fame
propterea et peste laborantem, sine huius auxilio servari posse dif-
fidebant. Ille igitur cum primum ad Venetos accessit, qui iam Li-
niaco opido amisso, transmisso Athesi ab hostibus copiis, nihil
tuti in continenti retinebant, non solum trepidationem ex eorum
mentibus exemit, verum sic libera omnia et secura reddidit quae in

of the plan, rushed down from Romagna, reaching Pisa in just three days. Sforza's sudden arrival broke the spirit of the Pisan conspirators and the city was thus saved.[65]

That same year the Genoese rebelled against Filippo Maria and 3 joined an alliance with Florence and Venice.[66]

And the year after that Francesco Sforza's daughter Drusiana 4 was born, while he was moving his troops from Lucca to Reggio Emilia. Drusiana, whose mother was the same Giovanna that I mentioned before, was betrothed to wed Count Giacomo Piccinino and is currently in the keeping of her father.[67]

: 26 :

Francesco frees the city of Verona.

But still greater and more stunning deeds were to come, for Fran- 1 cesco's skills were increasing with each passing year, as we shall now attempt to demonstrate.

The Venetians and the Florentines had made no real progress 2 in their ongoing battles with Filippo Maria Visconti, whose general in the field was Niccolò Piccinino. Since they wished to have a supreme commander who would be equal or even superior to Piccinino, they again signed Francesco Sforza up to a five-year contract and placed him in charge of a mighty army.[68] They were in fact convinced that without Sforza's help they would be unable to hold on to Brescia, which was besieged on all sides by a huge hostile force and was in addition laboring under the double distress caused by famine and plague. When Francesco arrived on the scene the Venetians had already lost the town of Legnago and the enemy had crossed the Adige: Venice's entire mainland empire appeared to be under threat. Francesco not only strengthened

dictione eorum fuerant, ut, brevi immutata belli fortuna, Philippus ipse vix intra Mediolanensium urbis moenia se tutum arbitra-
retur esse.

3   Decem enim milia equitum, peditum sex milia in armis deduce-
bat, quae ipso praeside non Italae solum nationes, sed barbarae
trans maria horrescerent. Itaque cum Nicolaus non Philippi dumtaxat copiis innixus, verum etiam Iohannis Francisci, qui Mantuae
praeerat, militibus stipatus, Veronam noctis tempore per insidias
cepisset, nemo erat, qui Venetos universa quae in continenti habe-
rent ammissuros eo anno non existimaret, nisi Franciscus per
montium invia incredibili celeritate, extremam rerum omnium
passus inopiam, ad eorum opem accurrisset. Tenem enim tunc
obsidebat opidum in asperrimis locis situm, cum adventu eius
fama solum et opinione debellati, hostes Veronam reliquere, quamquam praesidiis suffultam maximis. Sic effectum est, ut quo die
Philippus victoriae solennia laetus celebrabat, eadem ad Venetos
descivisse urbem maestus intelligeret, et quantum Franciscus Nicolaum anteiret, subinde agnosceret.

Venetian resolve, he also recovered and secured all of the city's territory on the mainland. His success was such that the fortunes of war were reversed and Filippo Maria Visconti himself no longer felt safe within the walls of Milan.

Sforza was in fact leading an army composed of ten thousand cavalrymen and six thousand foot soldiers. Such a force, especially with him as leader, was bound to strike fear into the hearts not only of the Italians, but even of those barbarous nations across the seas. Thus when Niccolò Piccinino, with the support not only of Filippo Maria's troops but those of Gianfrancesco Gonzaga, lord of Mantua, as well, had occupied Verona in a night raid, and everyone thought that Venice was again about to lose its grip on its mainland possessions, Sforza came rushing to the scene with incredible speed, forging a path over impassable mountains and enduring extreme privation in order to rescue the city. He had been besieging the town of Tenno at the time, located as it was in quite rugged terrain, and with his arrival the enemy, demoralized and defeated simply on account of his reputation, abandoned Verona, despite the city's being eminently capable of mounting a defense. And so it happened that on the very day that Filippo Maria Visconti was joyfully celebrating a major victory, his joy turned to sorrow in learning that Verona had slipped back into the hands of the Venetians.[69] On that day too he suddenly came to realize how far superior Francesco Sforza was to Niccolò Piccinino.

: 27 :

De victoria Francisci contra Philippi exercitus.

Nam infeliciora his secuta sunt, Philippo acceptam belli cladem novo quodam labore sarcire cupiente; iusserat enim Nicolaum Piceninum, derelictis Ligurum partibus, in Etruriam transire, ut Florentiam inopino bello opprimeret, ratus Florentinos Franciscum Sfortiam ab incepto avocaturos, omnemque belli cladem in eos decisuram. Nec vane movebatur: Florentini quippe tam repentino casu territi, vix rebus suis consilium afferre poterant, omni milite et tutore destituti. Iam quidem universa colonorum manus cum armentis filiisque ac mulieribus in urbem confluebat; trepidabant cives, nec qua se verterent aut se ipsos tutarentur satis norant. Eugenius praeterea pontifex Florentiam delatus, cum omni comitatu suo veluti carceribus inclusus, formidabat; actumque erat de civium salute ac libertate, factiosis omnibus ad arma consurgentibus, nisi Franciscus Sfortia tam ingentis discriminis fortunam meditatus, cum ab excellenti viro Cosmo Medico cive Florentino adhortaretur, cuius salubre consilium in plurimis et arduis rebus expertus fuerat, ne de universae Italiae imperio aut servitute pariter certamen sperneret, hostiles Philippi copias apud opidum Soncinum castra metantes propria virtute aggressus oppressisset. Quibus actis Nicolaus Piceninus, ut Philippi afflictis rebus subito assisteret, copias suas Anglarium versus deducere coactus est; quo in loco conspirantibus in unum Florentinis et Ecclesie militibus,

: 27 :

Francesco is victorious over the armies of Filippo Maria.

Much worse things were in store for Filippo Maria, who was eager
to wipe away the stains of defeat with some bold new enterprise.
He had ordered Niccolò Piccinino to leave Lombardy and to move
into Tuscany. His plan was to spring a surprise attack on Florence
in the belief that the Florentines would call Francesco Sforza to
come to their aid, thus bringing the war into their own backyard.
The plan worked: the Florentines, panic-stricken at this sudden
turn of events, were in no position to defend themselves, being
entirely leaderless and without protection. Soon the city was over-
flowing with the steady arrival of peasants, accompanied by their
livestock, children and womenfolk. The city dwellers too were in
complete disarray, not knowing where to turn for protection, and
being as they were quite incapable of defending themselves.[70] Pope
Eugenius had taken up residence in the city at this time as well.
Fearing for his life, he shut himself up behind prison-like walls,
together with his entire retinue. It might well have been the end of
Florentine prosperity and freedom (for the specter of armed fac-
tionalism had reared up again), had not Francesco Sforza taken
the measure of this critical moment. Following the advice of that
most judicious man, Cosimo de'Medici, a citizen of Florence upon
whose wisdom he had so often relied in difficult times past, Francesco realized he had to act, for the fate of all Italy was hanging in
the balance. He therefore engaged Filippo Maria's army near the
town of Soncino and skillfully defeated it.[71] This forced Niccolò
Piccinino to retreat from Florence and move his army toward Anghiari, from where he would be able to bring aid to Filippo Maria.
But at Anghiari Piccinino found himself facing the combined
might of the Florentine and papal forces and was thoroughly

ingenti certamine prostratus corruit. Sic Francisci fortitudine et prudentia in Liguria pariter et Etruria Philippi exercitus victi concidere; Veneti vero ac Florentini ingenti periculo servati sunt, demumque victores simul evaserunt. Hoc tam illustre proelium anno aetatis eius nono et trigesimo confectum est, quod magnam illi gloriam et laudem peperit, solumque militaris rei principem in Italia esse docuit.

: 28 :

De oppugnatione Martinengi et pace praebita a Philippo.

1 Sequenti anno adhuc magis Francisci Sfortiae virtus enituisse visa est eventu rei, actumque esset de belli summa, nisi Philippi Mariae auctoritas et in magnis casibus probata virtus sua prudentia intercessisset, qui iam utriusque ducis vires et peritiam expertus, felicitatem praeterea animo concipiens, pace potius periculo occurrendum esse censuit, quam ulterius probanda arma.

2 Nicolaus quidem post cladem apud Anglarium acceptam Mediolanum venerat, ut quoquo modo statum heri sui dubio inhaerentem gradu tueretur. Quamobrem pecunia suffultus, secundam belli aleam subire cogebatur, ut vel minus prospere acta corrigeret, aut certe quae supererant in deterius omnino labi prohiberet. Recuperata igitur Adduae Glarea — sic enim ea regio Mediolano finitima appellatur —, apud Martinengum castra habebat. Franciscus

beaten in a great battle.[72] So Francesco Sforza's courage and skill resulted in Filippo Maria's armies being destroyed in both Lombardy and Tuscany. Venice and Florence were not only saved from disaster but emerged victorious. The famous battle of Anghiari took place in Francesco Sforza's thirty-ninth year and brought him immense glory and fame. He had now claimed for himself sole ownership of military supremacy in Italy.

: 28 :

The siege of Martinengo and the offer of peace from Filippo Maria Visconti.

Francesco's skills were even more in evidence in the following year, as events were to prove. In fact the war would soon have reached its climax had not Filippo Maria brought his authority to bear on the situation, for trying circumstances had always revealed him to be a capable decision maker. He had now had occasion to test the strength and prowess of the two leading generals of his time. Desirous in his heart of enjoying some respite, he decided it was better to risk the hazards of peace, rather than to pursue any further the dangers of war.

After his defeat at Anghiari Niccolò Piccinino had returned to Milan, hoping to offer protection to his lord and master Filippo Maria, whose power over his dominions was beginning to wane. He therefore set out on a new campaign, his coffers bursting with money. His aim was to try to recover his lost prestige, but also and more importantly to prevent any further dismemberment of the Visconti state. He began by reconquering the Ghiaradadda, which is the name of a region situated very near to Milan itself. He then set up his camp at Martinengo. Francesco Sforza was besieging

alia ex parte opidum, quamquam defensore validum, enixius op-
pugnabat. Erat quippe in eo Iacobus Gayvanus ad tutanda moenia
longe peritissimus, cum pax subito a Philippo oblata est, quae litem abstulit concordiamque firmavit.

3   Quo eventu satis patuit, neque minus ex his quae secuta sunt,
quanti faceret Philippus princeps Franciscum ducem et quantum
Nicolao illum anteponeret.

: 29 :

De Blancha Maria a Philippo tradita Francisco,
et eiusdem varietate fortunae.

1   Nempe qui eodem anno, repudiatis ceterorum fortunis et obse-
quiis, novo foedere Franciscum placare studuit, cum Blancham
Mariam unicam filiam suam, quam illi iampridem matrimonio
desponderat, multis etiam precibus a se petitam longa spe distule-
rat, non solum restituerit, verum Cremonam dotis nomine ultro
addiderit. Et ex eo tempore Franciscus se vexilliferum Romanae
Ecclesiae semper appellavit, quamquam ligae esset universae.

2   Sic perfecta pace, affinitate coniuncta in Padi ripa, in templo
Divi Sigismundi, Franchino Castellioneo Philippi consiliario commissa peragente, iam tandem omnibus clare innotuit Philippum
Mariam post multa proelia resque praeclarissime gestas Francisci
felicitati virtutique cessisse, solumque ex cunctis eligisse cui summam status sui imponeret successoremque pararet.

Martinengo at that time at the head of an enemy force, though the town was being valiantly defended. Giacomo Gaivano was in charge of the defense and was showing great skill, when suddenly Filippo Maria offered peace terms that removed the source of contention and established a basis for lasting harmony.[73]

It is clear from this turn of events, as well as from what followed, how highly Filippo Maria regarded Francesco Sforza and the extent to which he valued him above Niccolò Piccinino. 3

: 29 :

Filippo Maria gives Bianca Maria to Francesco Sforza in marriage; Francesco's mixed fortunes.

Indeed in that same year Filippo Maria spurned the offers and 1 blandishments of others and sought instead to forge a new agreement with Francesco Sforza. For he now took his only daughter Bianca Maria (long promised in marriage to Sforza but withheld from him despite frequent petitioning) and delivered her up to him, adding Cremona as her dowry.[74] From that time forward Sforza continued to style himself the Standard-bearer of the Church of Rome, even though he was now actually the Standard-bearer of a vast alliance.

And so with peace proclaimed, and the marriage vows ex- 2 changed in the Church of San Sigismondo on the banks of the River Po in the presence of Filippo Maria's agent, Franchino Castiglioni, it finally became clear to all that Filippo Maria, having witnessed so many battles and great deeds of valor, had at last acknowledged Sforza's superior abilities and had selected him above all others to assume full control of the duchy and to rule as his successor.

3   Eodem anno illustris Nicolaus marchio Estensis, de quo supra
retuli, Mediolani defunctus est, cui Leonellus successit filius. Proximo deinde anno Alfonsus rex, per aquaeductum praemissis militibus suis, Renato rege vi depulso, Neapolim intercepit. Iohannes
autem Francisci frater, quem in Regno missum prius scripseramus,
minus prospere cedente proelio, a gubernatione urbium fratris sui
confestim excidit.

4   Anno praeterea quadragesimo tercio plurima a Francisco per-
acta sunt, saeviente fortuna. Nam modo rege Alfonso sua sponte
in illum depugnante, modo suadente Philippo socero suo, tot
proeliis oppressus est, tot periculis agitatus, instante Nicolao Picenino, ut non ab exteris solum, sed a militibus suis destitueretur.
Quae omnia magno animo, summo ingenio virtuteque superavit.

5   Anno deinde quadragesimo quarto natus est Francisco filius nomine Galeaz ex Blancha Maria Firmi, Piceni urbe, quo tempore
Beatus Bernardinus Ordinis Minorum in Aquilana civitate ad su-
peros migravit. Is igitur comitatu insignis, affinitate etiam Lodo-
vici Gonzagae Mantuani principis illustrior effectus veluti parentis
avique successor, amborum meritis et honore decoratur.

6   Per idem tempus Nicolaus Piceninus non longe a Mediolano,
quasi novo principi loco cederet, e vita sublatus est. Insequenti
anno Asculani cives, novo tumultu exciti, Francisco rebellarunt. Et
eodem anno filia illi ex eadem Blancha nata est nomine Hippolita,
singulari pietate et forma praedita; quae Neapolitani regis filio in
matrimonium promissa apud parentes asservatur. Sic Francisco
pariter adversa felicibus veluti fato quodam permista contigere.

That same year the illustrious Marquis Niccolò d'Este, whom 3
we mentioned earlier, died in Milan. His son Leonello succeeded
him. Then in the following year King Alfonso conquered Naples
by sending his troops into the city via an aqueduct and driving
King René out by force of arms. Sforza's brother Giovanni, whom
we noted earlier had been sent to the kingdom, was less fortunate
in battle and was consequently obliged to give up governing the
cities his brother had entrusted to him.[75]

In the year 1443 Sforza himself campaigned in adverse circum- 4
stances. For at times King Alfonso made war against him on his
own initiative, while at other times he did so at the instigation of
Sforza's father-in-law Filippo Maria. Sforza was as a consequence
beset by warring parties on so many sides, and faced so many dangers, with Niccolò Piccinino always at his heels, that he found
himself abandoned not only by his allies but even by his own soldiers. And yet he overcame all adversity thanks to his courage, his
skill, and his military genius.[76]

In the year 1444 Bianca Maria bore Sforza a son named Ga- 5
leazzo. He was born at Fermo, in the March of Ancona. At
around the same time the Franciscan friar San Bernardino departed this life in the city of Aquila. Galeazzo, graced with the title of count and pledged to wed a daughter of the lord of Mantua,
Ludovico Gonzaga, has become a worthy successor to both his
father and his grandfather. He combines the merits and distinction of both lines of his descent.[77]

In this same year Niccolò Piccinino died near Milan, as if yield- 6
ing his place to the man destined to be the new ruler. The next
year the citizens of Ascoli rose up once again and rebelled against
Francesco Sforza. And that same year Bianca Maria gave birth to
Ippolita, a daughter endowed with singular beauty and gentleness.
Betrothed to the son of the king of Naples, she is meanwhile in
the keeping of her parents.[78] And so fate dealt Francesco Sforza a
mixed bag of welcome and unwelcome developments.

: 30 :

De bello Philippi contra
Franciscum apud Cremonam.

1 Quod insequentium eventu etiam magis comprobatum est, ut qui ad felicitatis et honoris culmen esset ascensurus, tardiusculis rerum incrementis non sine iugi labore ad summa perveniret. Sic enim fortunae diuturnitatem spondere nobis possumus, cum laetis tristia, sollicitis grata miscentur. Qui autem ad felicitatem rapidis feruntur gressibus, nec ulla doloris interposita affliguntur nota, praecocem quendam nec longe progressurum significare creduntur instabilitatis casum.

2 Quamobrem novo labore opus erat, ut Francisci fortuna in maius elucesceret. Suspicionibus itaque plurimis exagitatus Philippus, nec iam sibi ipsi satis fidens, etiam ad Franciscum convertit odium. Missus est igitur mandato eius exercitus haud contemnendus contra Cremonam, quam pridem illi in dotem destinaverat. Ceterum Venetis opem afferentibus, quibus Francisci salus tutelae eorum coniuncta videbatur, Philippi exercitus non longe a Casali opido, quod Maius appellatur, Michaele Cutignola duce assistente, insigni proelio dissipatus est, cum Franciscus, victoriae perceptae nescius, apud Gradarium castra haberet, quinto et quadragesimo aetatis suae anno. Quo quidem nuncio, cum maxime exultaret, continuo Firmum a se descivisse allatum est, Alexandrumque fratrem cum parente sua inde abscessisse intelligit.

: 30 :

Filippo Maria unleashes war on
Francesco Sforza in Cremona.

Subsequent events showed even more clearly that the man des-   1
tined to ascend to the towering heights of fame and glory reached
the pinnacle only little by little and after years of struggle. Thus
truly are we able to promise ourselves ever-changing fortunes,
where good and bad, the happy and the unhappy, are all mixed
together. But those who rise to the top with rapid steps, and never
feel an ounce of pain or adversity, are believed to be earmarked for
an early fall from grace, which will not be long in coming.

And so there was still more work to do before Francesco's for-   2
tunes reached their peak. Filippo Maria was a man so tormented
by suspicion that he hardly trusted even himself. He thus turned
his fury on Francesco Sforza. He ordered a powerful army to attack Cremona, the very city he had previously assigned to Sforza
as part of the marriage agreement. But the Venetians came to
Sforza's aid, since they saw him as the guarantor of their own
safety. Filippo's army was thus defeated in a major battle near the
town of Casalmaggiore, under the generalship of Micheletto Attendolo.[79] Francesco Sforza meanwhile, unaware of the victory
won, was encamped at Gradara, in his forty-fifth year. As he was
celebrating after hearing the news, he was suddenly informed that
the town of Fermo had revolted.[80] He then learned that his
brother Alessandro had escaped from there with his mother.

: 31 :

De novis foederibus Philippi cum Francisco
et eius Philippi obitu.

1 Philippus igitur undique diffisus animo, cum nullam aliam afflictis casibus fortunam sperare posset, Franciscum denuo conciliare et novo foedere amiciciam cum eo firmare instituit. Iacta sunt igitur inter eos fundamenta pacis, nec non novi stipendii condictiones acceptae ab utroque anno Salutis septimo et quadragesimo supra millesimum et quadringentesimum, Petri Pusterlae opera, viri clarissimi et utrique fidissimi. Quo quidem anno Eugenius quartus Romanorum pontifex vita migravit; Nicolaus autem quintus institutus est.

2 Cum igitur ad Philippum tamquam ad parentem supplex filius accessum parat, omnia voluntati suae concessurus et a Pisauro in Liguriam venturus esset, apud opidum Catholicam metatus est; nec multo post Bononiam se transtulit, qua in urbe certior effectus est Philippum Mariam vita decessisse.

3 Animo igitur dubius, nec quid ageret tanta in re satis gnarus, Parmam primum, deinde Cremonam petere decrevit. Ad quam delatus Mediolanenses libertatem cepisse intelligit, ordinemque rei publicae suae posuisse; se autem non ingratum illis adventare, Venetis eorum urbes foede invadentibus; iam enim Placentiam Laudamque interceperant. Ob id ea quae a Mediolanensibus ultro offerebantur laetus admittens, eorum tutelam suscipere meditatus est, ne civitas clarissima a Venetis oppressa universam Italiam servitute et clade involveret, ipseque et successione sibi debita et dig-

: 31 :

Filippo Maria Signs a new agreement with Francesco Sforza;
the death of Filippo Maria.

Filippo Maria Visconti was now thoroughly discouraged. As he   1
had no other option in these dire straits, he turned once again to
Francesco Sforza and decided to strike a new deal with him.
Through the agency of the most illustrious Pietro Pusterla, a man
who enjoyed the confidence of both camps, the foundations of
peace between the two were laid, along with a new contract signed
by both sides.[81] The year was 1447. That year too the Roman pontiff Eugenius IV died. Nicholas V became the new pope.[82]

Sforza meanwhile was on his way to Filippo Maria, every bit   2
the humble son seeking out his father and ready to obey his every
wish. While on his way from Pesaro to Lombardy Sforza camped
at the town of Cattolica. Not long afterward, when he had reached
Bologna, he received news that Filippo Maria had died.[83]

Sforza was uncertain as to what his next move should be at this   3
critical juncture. He decided to head for Parma first, and then
Cremona. When he had reached the latter place he discovered that
the Milanese had recovered their freedom and set up a republican
form of government.[84] News of this event did not displease him,
for the Venetians had already invaded the duchy and had occupied
Piacenza and Lodi.[85] In view of these circumstances Sforza was
quite happy to accept the conditions offered him by the Milanese:
he was ready and willing to act as their protector in order to prevent the Venetians from occupying that most glorious city of Milan, an act which would enslave and eventually spell disaster for
the whole of Italy while also depriving Sforza of his rightful inher-

nitate privaretur. Instituerat nempe Philippus ipse Blancham Mariam, filiam suam, legitimam heredem dominatus sui.

4   Sicque eorum imperator in bello eligitur.

: 32 :

De adeptione urbium Papiae et Placentiae per Franciscum.

1   Composito cum Mediolanensibus foedere, ut exercitus sui dux contra Venetos bellum gereret, Sanctum Columbanum, quod illi interceperant, iter dirigit; quo opido potitus, dum illic moram agit, oratores Papiensium ad se venisse urbemque dictioni eius obtulisse intelligit; nam a Gallis Venetisque magnis pollicitacionibus sollicitabantur. Quamobrem arce suscepta opera Bolognini fidissimi custodis, comitem Rubertum Sanseverinensem, qui urbem obtineret, emisit. Eoque modo Franciscus urbis Papiensium, cunctarum Liguriae pulcherrimae atque ornatissimae, et ad magnas res agendas opportunissimae, dominus effectus est. Sic sensim ad maiora susceptis viribus, auctoritate firmata, non timeri solum, sed amari et in honore esse cepit.

2   Veneti quoque maioribus se copiis tutari satagebant ac primum Placentiam, paulo ante interceptam Mediolanensibus, equestribus pedestribusque militibus firmare accelerant. Franciscus, quo maior belli moles imminebat, eo velocius discrimini occurrendum arbitratus, exercitum omnem Placentiam obsidere iubet. Quae eo difficilius obsidebatur, quo maioribus fulta praesidiis, hostiles impetus longe repellebat. Tandem magno ducis robore, militum

itance. For had not Filippo Maria himself made his daughter Bianca Maria the legitimate heir to the duchy?[86]

And so it transpired that Francesco Sforza became the supreme   4 commander in charge of the Milanese forces.

: 32 :

Francesco Sforza occupies Pavia and Piacenza.

Having negotiated a contract with the Milanese whereby he was to   1 lead their army into war against the Venetians, Sforza set out for San Colombano, a place the Venetians had seized. Sforza took it back, and while he was still there he learned that a delegation of citizens from Pavia had come to offer him the lordship of their city, for both the French and the Venetians were making overtures to them. Sforza first assured himself of possession of the citadel, which he obtained thanks to the cooperation of its reliable custodian Bolognino. He then sent Roberto Sanseverino to occupy the city itself.[87] In this manner Sforza became the ruler of Pavia, the most beautiful and graceful of all the cities of Lombardy, as well as being a place of immense strategic importance. Sforza's power was thereby considerably enhanced, and his authority increased. He now began to be not only feared, but loved and honored.

The Venetians called up reinforcements: they hastened in the   2 first place to shore up the defense of Piacenza—a city they had only recently taken from the Milanese—with an injection of fresh troops. Sforza, believing it best to act swiftly at the decisive moment in order to bring things to their crisis, ordered his entire army to focus on the siege of Piacenza. The siege was the more arduous in that the massive force that had been mustered to defend the city managed for a long time to repel the invaders. But in the end the city fell, thanks to the iron will of the commander and

tolerantia et fortitudine expugnata capitur. Tadeus marchio, Venetorum in bello ductor, cum omnibus suis ad Franciscum perducitur. Urbs praedae exposita exercitum per multos menses ita aluit, ut stipendio non egeret, nempe cum praede precium, captivis manubiis armisque militum simul pensitatis, quingentorum milium aureorum summam facile excesserit.

3   Haec victoria tantam Francisco invidiam attulit, ut non Veneti modo, sed ipsi Mediolanenses falsis rumoribus agitati contremiscerent; tractatumque est inter utrosque de concordia paceque ineunda, quamquam iniquissimis condictionibus, ut Veneti scilicet parva quaedam opida, quae in transitu Adduae sita erant, restituerent sublata priori bello; Mediolanenses vero urbem Laudam illis traderent. Verum haec consilio prudentum, populi tumultu excito, repudiata maiorem Francisco gratiam et laudem attulerunt.

∶ 33 ∶

De vexillis Francisco concessis per Mediolanenses
et bello navali apud Cremonam.

1   Iam igitur Francisco felicitatis suae thronum fortuna praeparabat, et vexillis Mediolanensium ad eum allatis, anno aetatis suae quadragesimo septimo, omnibus certum erat non exercitus dumtaxat imperium, sed civitatis principatum ad eum ferri, maioraque in dies portendi, ne Philippi sedes vero successore et duce fraudaretur.

the endurance and courage of his men. The Venetian forces, led by Marquis Taddeo d'Este, were delivered over to Sforza. The city was then put to the sack.[88] It provided so much plunder for Sforza's army that there was no need to pay the men for many months, for the value of the weapons and other enemy booty seized easily totaled in excess of five hundred thousand gold ducats.

This victory earned Sforza so much ill will that not only the 3 Venetians but even the Milanese themselves, who were becoming prey to false rumors, began to tremble with fear. So Milan and Venice turned to negotiating a peace deal, though the conditions being discussed were iniquitous, for the Venetians were conceding only a few small towns on the Adda river crossings, towns they had seized in the previous war and were now returning, while the Milanese on the other hand were supposed to hand over the city of Lodi to Venetian control. The Milanese government, however, made the wise decision to reject these terms after an uprising of the people, all of which increased the standing and prestige of Francesco Sforza in the city.[89]

: 33 :

The Milanese bestow their standards on Francesco Sforza;
the naval battle near Cremona.

The fates then were already paving the way toward Francesco's ul- 1 timate triumph: with the forty-seven-year-old Sforza now in possession of the standards of the Milanese people, everyone was certain that he had received not only the supreme command of the army, but lordship over the city itself, and that still greater deeds would follow, lest Milan, the capital of Filippo Maria's duchy, be shorn of its rightful lord and heir.

2 Transmissis igitur felici omine a Cremona in Adduae Glaream militibus suis, quo hostilibus copiis propior assistens bellum caperet, cuncta trepidacione pavoreque repleverat. Quibus ex causis commoti Veneti, ingentem classem magno apparatu Cremonam versus statim adduxere, ut ponte interciso, qui Pado imminebat, commeatu simul et praesidiis urbem spoliarent. Eo loci magna vi ab utraque parte certatum est, plurimique ex Venetis vulneribus affecti in pugna cecidere. Nec longe repulsa classis denuo Cremonam versus rediit. Franciscus obviam ad Casale Maius progressus Castelletum cepit praedeque exposuit. Verum, instante classe, visum est ipsi non ulterius differre proelium, verum fortunam sese offerentem ultro arripere, instructaque ex adverso classe sua, quam Papiae paratam iampridem continebat, bellum cepit.

3 Longum esset enarrare qua animi magnitudine, qua alacritate militum, quo robore navium, quanto labore id proelium a Francisco ceptum, perfectum profligatumque sit. Veneti omni ex parte superati in fugam vertuntur. Naves hostiles captae et incensae sunt. Urbibus et oppidis Pado imminentibus pax et securitas brevi parta a Francisco. Id bellum perdifficile visum est, cum, Andrea Quirini Venetum classem in primis deducente, victoria omnino desperari videretur prudentia ducis, nec minus propugnatorum multitudine et robore.

Sforza next moved his troops from Cremona into the Ghiara-   2
dadda region in order to bring the war to the enemy. This happy
move sowed fear and trepidation throughout the whole area.
Wherefore the Venetians were prompted to order a huge and well-
armed fleet to head immediately toward Cremona. The Venetian
plan was to destroy the bridge on the river Po and to deprive the
city thereby of its lines of supply and defense. A great battle ensued in that place, with both sides fully engaged. A goodly number
of the Venetians were badly wounded and killed in action. But it
was not long before their forces regrouped and returned once again
to attack Cremona. Francesco Sforza meanwhile had reached
Casalmaggiore. He occupied Castelponzone and put it to the sack.
However, seeing the Venetian fleet still in action at Cremona, he
decided it would be imprudent to delay the decisive encounter any
further; better to seize the favorable moment and test his chances.
So he deployed his fleet in battle formation—having kept it in
reserve at Pavia all this time—and attacked the Venetians.

It would be a long business to tell in detail with what fighting   3
zeal, with what disciplined soldiers, with what powerful ships and
hard work Sforza undertook, prosecuted, and won that battle.[90]
The Venetians were overcome on all sides and the battle turned
into a rout. The Venetian ships were captured and burned. Within
a very short time Francesco Sforza had restored peace and security
to the towns and cities located along the Po. It should be stressed
that this battle had initially appeared impossible to win, for with
Andrea Querini in charge of the Venetian fleet there seemed to be
no hope of victory on account of this commander's great skill and
the mighty fighting force that was at his disposal.

: 34 :

De victoria Francisci contra Venetos apud Caravagium.

1   Laeto victoriae auspicio inde digressus, Franciscus Caravagium pervenit, quod opidum a Venetis summa vi continebatur. Nam eo loci terrestres eorum copiae maiore adhuc apparatu suffultae venerant totiusque belli molem subiturae videbantur. Ludovicus Mantuae princeps vires suas eorum copiis adiunxerat. Michael, Francisci affinis, vir illustris et bellicis artibus expertissimus, exercitum ducebat. Nihil deerat ad consumandam Francisci gloriam, nisi ut palam omnibus fieret Venetos non propria auctoritate aut opum vi, sed illius virtute et prudentia Philippum superasse, postquam et ipsi denuo ab eodem devicti sunt.

2   Affuere eo in bello ab utraque parte insignes copiae: Venetorum equitum ac peditum quindecim milia, Francisci autem exercitus inferiore militum numero continebatur. Cum iam inter se opido appropinquassent, alteraque ex parte Venetorum copiae, altera Mediolanensium Francisco duce castra metarentur. Hostes, rati Francisci exercitum inopine aggredi incautumque opprimere posse, continuo immeditatos invadunt. Erat enim solenni die, hora non expectata, absentibus hinc inde plurimis, quos armis exutos subito aggressi inscios offendunt. Conseritur primum inter occurrentes pugna. Iacobus Piceninus primo impetu saucius acie excessit. Alexander, Francisci frater, vir armis inclytus, periculo accepto, pontem, qui castris intercesserat, Coclitis exemplum imitatus, celeri custodia occupat, ac dum ceteri arma capiunt, transitum tuetur. Accedunt subinde ex intervallo subsidia, et atrox pugna fieri coepta est. Franciscus ad omnia praesens, nunc movendo, nunc

: 34 :

Francesco defeats the Venetians at Caravaggio.

Riding the wave of victory Francesco decamped and came to Cara-   1
vaggio, a fortified town that the Venetians were holding with a
large force. The Venetian ground troops had been moved into
place here, and were now well-armed and ready to bear the brunt
of a major battle. Ludovico Gonzaga, the lord of Mantua, had
joined his forces to those of the Venetians. The famous and highly
skilled condottiere Micheletto Attendolo, a close relative of Sforza's, was in charge of Venetian operations. The scene was set for
the consecration of Francesco's glory, for it was about to become
clear to all that the Venetians had formerly defeated Filippo Maria,
not by their own merits or resourcefulness, but solely on account
of Sforza's skill and courage; now indeed it was the Venetians' turn
to taste defeat at the hands of their former commander.

Both sides had engaged their best troops: the Venetian cavalry   2
and infantry numbered fifteen thousand men; Sforza's army was
somewhat smaller in number. When both armies had approached
the town, they made camp on opposite sides, with Caravaggio between them. The enemy, believing it could catch Sforza's army
unawares and destroy it, mounted a sudden surprise attack. It was
a Sunday, at a time of rest and repose. Sforza's men were scattered
here and there, unsuspecting and unarmed, when suddenly the
enemy swooped down upon them. The fighting began on the run.
Giacomo Piccinino was wounded in the first exchanges and had to
leave the battlefield. Francesco Sforza's brother, Alessandro, an
outstanding soldier, quickly and boldly seized the bridge that sepa-
rated the two camps, holding the enemy at bay like a new Cocles[91]
while the men leaped to their arms. Meanwhile reinforcements
arrived and the real battle got underway. Francesco was everywhere

hortando, plerumque subsidia hinc inde emittendo, proelium sustinet; postremo solita virtute et felicitate usus, hostes invadit. Funduntur continuo adversae acies: duces Veneti ab impetu repulsi cedunt, milites, undique arrepta fuga, terga vertunt. Sic quisque praestantior in bello capitur: Gentilis, Guido Rangonus, Rubertus Montis Arboti ad Franciscum deducuntur.

3   Bernardinus Titignanus Urbetensis balistariorum ductor, ex Francisci exercitu, dum acriter pugnat, sagitta saucius confestim periit. Postremo, dissipatis Venetorum gentibus, victoria a Francisco parta est: qua nulla illustrior usquam aut clarior aetate nostra habita fuisset, nisi spes ambiguas et incertas tutiora consilia reliquissent; nam Italiae perpetuam pacem ipsi Francisco imperium longe amplius cum laude et gloria fortasse peperisset. Verum ita Deo placuisse visum, a quo feliciora securioraque ad tempus praeparantur.

: 35 :

De dissensione populi Mediolanensis et
pace Francisci cum Venetis.

1 Profligatis Venetorum copiis illustri pugna, Franciscus, ut maiora moliretur, Brixiam versus exercitum progredi et urbem obsidere imperat. Nam Franciscus Piceninus cum parte copiarum, Lauda

at once, always on the move, keeping the men's morale high, sending in fresh troops wherever they were needed, and generally holding the line. When he saw the time was ripe he summoned up his usual courage and turned the attack on the enemy. All of sudden the Venetian front line caved in. Overwhelmed by this sudden reversal, the Venetian general staff retreated. This was the signal for their soldiers to turn tail and run in all directions. Several of the leading figures were captured and hauled up before Francesco Sforza: their number included Gentile da Leonessa, Guido Rangoni, and Roberto da Montalboddo.

Bernardino Titignano da Orvieto, commander of the Sforza 3 artillery, was hit by an arrow in the thick of the action and died of his wounds. But in the end, with the Venetian army annihilated, victory belonged to Sforza.[92] And it might well have been the sweetest and most famous victory of our age had not the safer policy option prevailed over vague and uncertain hopes. For the victory at Caravaggio might well have given rise to perpetual peace in Italy, while also delivering to Sforza a much higher command, along with praise and glory. But it seems God had dictated otherwise: happier and more secure times would have to wait for their appointed moment.

: 35 :

Milan plunges into civil turmoil and
Francesco Sforza makes peace with Venice.

Having defeated the Venetian army in this famous battle, Fran- 1 cesco sought to capitalize on his gains: he ordered his forces to head for Brescia and to place that city under siege. Meanwhile Francesco Piccinino was besieging Lodi with another band of

obsessa, cives ad deditionem incitabat, quam deinde Laudenses
ultro obtulere.

2   Interea Mediolanenses varie inter se fluctuabant: quidam victoria elati Franciscum ad astra praecipuis laudibus ferebant; alii
verbis dumtaxat libertatem praedicabant, verum impense onus
curamque detractabant; erant, quibus servitus libertate potior videretur esse, et hi dominum in primis afectabant. Ceterum non
eadem nitebantur via: nam alii Venetos, alii Franciscum ipsum
exoptabant; quibus autem vivendi cum principe consuetudo inerat,
quo in numero vir insignis Petrus Pusterla et alii fuere, Franciscum veluti Philippi filium et afflictis rebus succurrere potentem
magnopere laudabant; e contra, quibus mercatorum familiaritas et
usus aderat, quorum minima pars fuit, Venetos ut divinos quosdam homines praeponendos dictitabant. Nihil in medium con-
sulebatur, sed, ut vulgo mos est, studia in contraria incerti scinde-
bantur. Sic confusis civium voluntatibus, plebs omnium ignara
libertatis, dumtaxat nomen sibi asciverat, et nullo salubri consilio
perducta in optimum quemque, simplici confisa dominatu cras-
sabatur.

3   Itaque maior pars ad Franciscum oculos flectere et ab illo in
tanto rerum discrimine salutem deposcere et precari videbatur. Eas
ob causas permotus, Franciscus, ne civitas, deteriori consilio se-
ducta, in peius laberetur, sibique et ceteris bonis perniciem afferret, cum Venetis foedus inire statuit, veritus ne illi, diversa via

troops and negotiating for that town's surrender. The citizens of
Lodi eventually agreed to terms and handed over their city.

All the while the political climate in Milan itself was becoming   2
increasingly unstable. There were those who, elated by the victory
at Caravaggio, went about praising Francesco Sforza to the skies;
others preached the virtues of liberty with fine words, but then
steadfastly refused to assume the duties and responsibilities that
liberty entails. Some preferred servitude to freedom, and these
people longed above all for a strong ruler. But there was no agreement as who should assume command. Some favored the Venetians, while others leaned toward Francesco Sforza. Those men
who had been accustomed to live under a prince, and their number included Pietro Pusterla and other noblemen, were wont to
praise Francesco Sforza as the adopted son of Filippo Maria Visconti and as a man capable of rescuing Milan from the dire straits
in which it presently found itself. On the opposite side stood those
who gravitated around the merchants, a smaller group. These men
supported the Venetians, seeing them as possessing almost divine
qualities. There was no room for compromise: rather, as often
happens, the lukewarm too were now splitting up along mutually
opposed party lines. And with the citizenry thus divided, the plebeian masses, entirely ignorant of the true meaning of the word
liberty, but adopting it as their slogan, launched an unprincipled
hate campaign against the city's nobility, confident of total mastery.[93]

Most people thus began to look to look to Francesco Sforza as   3
their savior, and to call for him to put an end to the crisis. Moved
by such pleas, Francesco decided to seek a separate peace with
Venice. His aim in doing so was to prevent the situation in Milan
from getting any worse. He reasoned that if things continued to
deteriorate it would spell disaster for him and for other good men.
He feared that the Venetians would look to their own interests

necessitati suae consulentes, universa in utilitatem suam commutarent, maxime cum iam Mediolanenses, se inscio et excluso, pacem cum Venetis quaerere et meditari cognovisset. Colloquio igitur cum illis habito, et pacis conditionibus ultro oblatis, si in adipiscenda dignitate sua vires impartirent favoresque praestarent, foedus firmavit; quod ab illis cupidissime susceptum est. Nam longa belli impensa permoti, nec minus fortunae clade fatigati, omnia bello potiora fore existimabant.

4   Eoque modo Veneto proelio finis tandem a Francisco datus est.

: 36 :

De bello Francisci contra Mediolanenses.

1   Foedere cum Venetis inito, confestim Franciscus Placentiam versus castra movit, quam urbem, anno superiore a Venetis ademptam, Mediolanensibus belli iure restituerat. Placentini, adventu Francisci cognito, portas statim illi reserant laetisque ominibus sublatum in dominum assumunt. Ipse, praemissis signis, nulla interposita mora, Binascum versus agmen movet, quod opidum per decem milia passuum a Mediolano situm distat. Nec multum commoratus, intercepto opido, ut omnes aditus civitatis intercluderet, Abbiate pervenit. Id opidum situ peramoenum et Philippi Mariae iampridem iocunda mansio, etiam Blanchae, filiae suae, ab

and find a way to turn everything to their advantage. Indeed he had just learned that the Milanese authorities were already negotiating behind his back for their own separate peace with Venice. So Francesco entered into talks with the Venetians and an agreement was finally reached whereby the Venetians, as one of the conditions, were obliged to help Sforza obtain Milan, the prize that was his by right.[94] The Venetians accepted this condition most willingly. Their treasury was now exhausted by protracted war, and they were tired of suffering abrupt turns of fortune. In short they had reached the point where they thought anything preferable to more war.

It was in this manner that Francesco Sforza at last brought the conflict with Venice to an end.   4

: 36 :

Francesco Sforza prosecutes war against Milan.

Having forged an alliance with Venice, Francesco immediately set out with his army for Piacenza. That city had fallen to the Venetians in the previous year, but Francesco had then reclaimed it for Milan as a prize of war. When the people of Piacenza heard that Francesco was back they at once opened the gates of their city and joyously accepted him as their lord and ruler.[95] Francesco did not stop here, however. Sending ahead his standards he moved his forces on toward Binasco, a fortified town located some ten miles from Milan. He did not tarry there for long either. Having taken control of the place he marched on to Abbiategrasso, hoping to shut down all the access points to the city of Milan.[96] Now Abbiategrasso is a lovely town and was once a residence much favored by Filippo Maria Visconti. It was also the place where Bianca Maria,

incunabilis domus fuerat; ob id illud ab omni machinarum iniuria
tutum servare studuit.

2   Quo pariter potitus parvo temporis spacio, faventibus populis,
Novariam, Parmam, Dertonam, Alexandriam aliasque urbes dictioni suae subdidit. Ceterum in Novariae adeptione plurimum
laudis et commendationis meruisse visa est Ruberti Sanseverinen-
sis viri illustris in agendo diligentia, qui comitibus Urso et Dulci
sotiatus, Campanellam, non instrenuum virum, Mediolanensium
ductorem, cum ducentis equitibus Novariam tendentem, in ipso
itinere delevit vicitque. Quae res obtinendae urbis occasionem
praebuit.

: 37 :

*De variis contentionibus Mediolanensium et
pace eorum cum Venetis.*

1   Auspicio tanti principatus assistentibus fere cunctis, Mediolanensium res in deterius labi coepere. Nam duce destituti, dissiden-
tibus inter se civibus, deteriora prioribus in dies pullulabant. Non
publica munera a populo rite gubernari, non divites onera con-
ferre, non iussa quisquam exequi poterat, sed veluti tempestate
disiecta classis, inundante pelago, hinc inde ferebatur. Si qua in
residuis militibus spes affulxerat, Caroli Gonzagae ambitione tur-
babatur, qui ad populi dominatum improbe aspirans, longa suspicione cuncta destinebat. Qua ex causa desperatione et pavore
squalebant omnia. Coniurationes ad haec a quibusdam perpetratae

Filippo's daughter, had been raised from infancy. For these reasons Sforza ordered that the town be spared from bombardment by his artillery.

Once Abbiategrasso had been taken it was not long before 2 other cities, their populations clamoring for change, also submitted to Sforza's rule. The list included Novara, Parma, Tortona, Alessandria, and others still.[97] It should be noted that in the taking of Novara Roberto Sanseverino's decisive action was deserving of the highest praise and commendation. This great man, acting together with Counts Orso Orsini and Dolce dell'Anguillara, managed to intercept and destroy a Milanese force of two hundred horsemen headed for Novara under the command of a quite capable commander by the name of Campanella.[98] It was Sanseverino's defeat of this force that delivered Novara to Francesco Sforza.

: 37 :

Civil conflict intensifies in Milan and
the city makes peace with Venice.

With practically everything that was happening calling for strong 1 leadership, events in Milan began to go from bad to worse. Without a leader the citizens could reach no agreement on policy. Each day brought with it a further deterioration. The people were incapable of following proper rules of governance. The wealthy citizens were excluded from holding office. No one was able to follow orders. The situation was like that of a fleet of ships buffeted by a storm: the waves flood the ships and the fleet is tossed about in all directions. Any faint glimmer of hope in a military solution was negated by the ambitions of Carlo Gonzaga. This man was secretly plotting to overthrow the government: his designs cast a

maiorem adhuc sollicitudinem singulis iniecerant, capti siquidem plerique nobilissimi cives et supplicio affecti sunt. Sed nec ullorum caede mali atrocitas leniri poterat, cum extrema paterentur, Carolo potissimum urbem Laudam Francisco concedente.

2   Qua amissa, et Piceleonis opidum, quod Adduam fluvium ponte intersecat, illi traditum. Sic diuturnitate belli afflictis civibus, quod per bienium fere exactum fuerat, populus fame laborare coeperat. Boni praeterea, officiis exuti, nec sibi aut aliis prodesse utiles, silentio languebant; plebs vero inter spem metumque coniecta onus tolerabat, dominatus dumtaxat nomine exultans, et plurimorum seductionibus frustra inhians; multa enim a Ludovico duce Sabaudiae, multa vicissim a Carolo Aurelianensi in dies polliceri, plura a Gallis, quamquam vana et inepta, ut civitatem calamitatibus affectam tentarent, potius subigere optantes, quam subsidia ulla aut opem ferrent. Quod documentum ceteris praestare potuit, quantum alienigenis et praesertim Gallis fidei speique ad magna opera adhibendum sit, maxime cum celeritate opus esse videamus.

3   Versae sunt demum et ad Federicum Imperatorem spes inanes, Enea oratore aures civium dulci et ornata allocutione demulcente, qui nunc, ad pontificatum maximum elatus, Pii secundi nomen habere meruit. Mihi quoque ea provincia a populo collata est, ut Federico civitatem traderem, quam ultro renui. Turpe quidem

long shadow of suspicion over the entire scene. Thus everything in the city was tainted with the stench of fear and despair. Sporadic conspiracies heightened the general feeling of insecurity. A number of the most prominent citizens were arrested and put to death. But killing them brought no end to the suffering.[99]

The military situation worsened when Carlo Gonzaga surren- 2 dered Lodi to Francesco Sforza.[100] The loss of Lodi brought the downfall of the fortress of Pizzighettone, with its bridge over the river Adda. The very length of the war was taking its toll on the Milanese: hostilities had been dragging on now for almost two years; the populace was beginning to feel the pangs of hunger.[101] Meanwhile the best men in the city, excluded as they were from office and thus unable to help either themselves or others, lan-guished in silence. The plebian masses on the other hand, torn between hope and fear, bore the full burden of government. Thrilled by the illusion of power, they gaped in vain at the seduc-tive offers of help that came pouring in from various quarters. Many promises came tumbling forth from the lips of Ludovico, Duke of Savoy,[102] as well as from those of Charles d'Orléans. The French promised more, but their promises were empty and coun-terproductive. It was all too clear that their plan was to take ad-vantage of the city's desperate plight in order to subjugate it, rather than to come to its rescue with aid and reinforcements. Here we have tangible proof of how little faith and trust can be placed in foreign and especially French help when it is most required: such help is particularly useless in an emergency.[103]

Vain hopes were also being entertained at this time regarding 3 the emperor Frederick III, for his ambassador Enea Silvio Piccolo-mini swayed public opinion in his master's favor with a slick and seductive speech.[104] Enea by the way has since been deservedly el-evated to the high office of pope as Pius II. I myself was duly ap-pointed by the Milanese government to negotiate the devolution of our city to Emperor Frederick, but I refused, for it seemed to

mihi videbatur, si ducalem dignitatem, quam parens olim meus
cum Petro de Candia, Novariensi episcopo, qui postea Alexander
quintus fuit, pro Iohanne Galeaz duce primo a Venceslao Imperatore olim impetrasset, ipse et genitura et baptismate utrique ob-
noxius, auctor restituendi fierem.

4   Ceterum universa in cassum nitebantur, urgente fame, civibus
plurima expertis in extremis casibus, quos nec Caroli Gonzagi
victoria ad opidum Modiciam, nec reditus Francisci Picenini in
urbem a tantis malis liberare potuisset. Nam Viglevanum, muni-
tissimum opidum, prisco foedere Mediolanensibus adiunctum, Piceninus sub tutela sua receperat; et cum bellum sustinere putare-
tur, a Sfortia expugnatum, cladem omnem ad urbem deferebat.
Quae cum Venetis innotescere coepissent, libido solita eos invasit
non civitatis modo, sed Liguriae universae confestim occupandae.
Missis itaque clanculum legatis suis, qui civium mentes blanda
oratione perverterent, pacem polliceri coepere, porro auxilia adversus Franciscum, ut libertatem tuerentur hostemque depellerent,
non quod pacem multi facerent, sed ut inani spe allectos homines
et pecuniis exutos, simulque Franciscum bello fatigatum, sollerti
consilio opprimerent.

5   Eoque modo pax inter utrosque, Francisco inscio, firmata est.

me dishonorable to become the instrument whereby the ducal title would be returned to the empire. To comply would have been to betray both my birthright and my baptism. Indeed it was my father—together with the bishop of Novara, Pietro di Candia, later elected pope as Alexander V—who had initially obtained from the emperor Wenceslas the imperial investiture for the first duke of Milan, Gian Galeazzo Visconti.[105]

In Milan then, confusion reigned supreme, the famine grew worse, and the citizens—having already been through so much—reached their breaking point, so that neither Carlo Gonzaga's victory at Monza, or the return of Francesco Piccinino to the city, could provide release from all these troubles.[106] Piccinino had undertaken to protect the heavily fortified town of Vigevano, which was closely bound to Milan by ancient ties of loyalty. And although it was believed that the place could withstand a siege, Sforza nevertheless took it by force. The fall of Vigevano brought the wrath of war to Milan's doorstep. When the Venetians saw how things were going, their long-standing ambitions were rekindled: here was their chance to seize not just Milan alone, but the whole of Lombardy. So they secretly sent their envoys to the city with instructions to speak in such a way as to convince the citizenry that Venice wanted only peace, that she would lend help against Francesco Sforza, that she would defend liberty and repel the invader. But the real intention behind these overtures was not to establish peace, but simply to lead the cash-strapped populace astray by spreading false hopes. The Venetians were banking too that Francesco Sforza was tired of war, leaving them free to crush both him and the Milanese by their trickery.

This is how Milan and Venice reached a peace agreement between themselves, without Sforza's knowledge.[107]

4

5

: 38 :

De victoriis Francisci et adeptione civitatis Mediolanensium.

1 Exhilarari primo aspectu visa civitas et aliquantum a cladibus perpessis respirare, cum omnia in contrariam partem conversa sunt. Spes quoque vanae in dies elucescere, fame ingruente, coeperunt. Unicum igitur supererat remedium aspectus Leonardi Venerii oratoris Veneti, qui timore dumtaxat et spe urbem impleverat, et ut plebem ad se alliceret, confictis litteris rumores componebat. Desperationi igitur et inediae non deerat locus: nam Francisci mentem cives intuentes adversitatibus nullis fatigatam, indesinenti subsidio nitentem mirabantur, quippe qui Venetorum intellecta pace, dissimulato periculo, spem pacis dederat. Deinde hortantibus plurimis et illustribus viris, inter quos et Franciscus Vicecomes fuit, multisque precibus illum circumstantibus, et ne nobiles urbe eiectos deserere vellet, impensius orantibus, solito acrior ad arma consurrexerat, obsessisque itineribus ad urbem confluentibus famem geminabat.

2 Magna in Sygismundo Pandulfo spes illis fuerat, sed hunc quoque contra Franciscum insurgere conantem, cum ad Brippii opidum castra metaretur, victum intellexerant; Cotroni marchionem praeterea novis foederibus diu sollicitatum apud Canturium a Francisco praeventum et captum extitisse; Iacobum etiam Piceninum, unicum periclitanti patriae subsidium, repulsum vicissim a Francisco in Briantina ora et auxilii spe exutum. Quid amplius

: 38 :

Francesco Sforza is victorious and obtains Milan.

The city had hardly begun to exult and to find some modicum of   1
relief from its sufferings when everything it had planned fell to
pieces. Vain hopes were dashed as hunger continued to take its
toll. The one remedy left to the citizens was the Venetian emissary
Leonardo Venier, a man who had filled them in turn with hope
and fear and who now — to keep the multitude on his side — was
reduced to circulating rumors with false news bulletins. Starvation
and despair were everywhere, as people realized that Francesco
Sforza was undeterred by adversity. They were filled with wonder
too at his ability to carry on the fight with seemingly endless resources. Sforza on the other hand, having learned of the city's
making peace with Venice, ignored the danger and renewed his
own offer of peace to the Milanese. Then, at the urging of several
prominent citizens of Milan, whose number included Francesco
Visconti,[108] and whose voices were seconded by still others, all eagerly exhorting him not to abandon the cause of the noblemen
who had been ejected from the city, he resumed the fight with
more determination than ever before, and redoubled the grip of
hunger on the city by shutting down the last access roads leading
into it.

The Milanese had placed high hopes in Sigismondo Pandolfo   2
Malatesta,[109] but they soon learned that he too had met defeat
against Francesco Sforza while encamped at the fortified town of
Brivio. They then got wind of events at Cantù, where Sforza had
hemmed in and captured the Marquis of Cotrone, whose forces
had only recently been engaged to intervene in the struggle. On
top of this came news that Sforza had checked the advance of
Giacomo Piccinino in Brianza.[110] Piccinino had represented a last

sperare poterant aut conari destituti cives, nisi incumbenti fortunae cedere et Franciscum pacem affectantem, pacem afferentem
in dominum assumere? Perstabat tamen nonnullorum sive constantia, sive credulitas, ut quaecumque servitute potiora ducerent,
cum Deus miserandis civibus tandem opem afferre statuit.

3   Quarto igitur Kalendas Martii divino instinctu optimorum civium in unum concita non mediocris pars, Gaspare Vicomercato
viro magnanimo in primis duce, adversus renitentes arma sumpsit,
expugnataque ducali curia, residuum civilis status, Leonardum
etiam Venerium, oratorem Venetum, consilio assistentem et inter
trepidantes sese occulentem, subito rumore aggressa per tumultum
interemit. Reliqui factionis comites ex fuga elapsi in diversa abiere;
Francisco Sfortiae Mediolanensium civitas consono cunctorum
clamore patefacta est, cum ipse Vicomercati castra haberet: anno
Salutis quinquagesimo supra quadringentesimum atque millesimum, qui Francisco ipsi alterius nativitatis principium videtur attulisse, ut qui iubileum insequente anno, Bonifacio nono regente
Ecclesiam, in lucem editus primum fuerat, insequenti iubileo sub
Nicolao quinto altiorem lucem gloriamque penetraret.

desperate attempt to save the fatherland: the Milanese were now shorn of all hope. They were left destitute, with no other option but to yield to the course of events and to accept Francesco Sforza — the bringer and bearer of peace — as their lord and master. And yet there were still those diehards (were they showing courage, or just being foolish?) who continued to regard any solution preferable to servitude under a new prince. It was at this point that God finally decided to put an end to so much misery.

So on February 26 a large number of the leading men of the   3
city, moved by divine inspiration, came together under the valiant leadership of Gaspare Vimercate and took up arms against the last adherents of the dying republic.[111] Storming the offices of the government, they put an end to what was left of the civil authority. They found the Venetian commissar Leonardo Venier in a meeting. He tried to hide himself among the cowering officials, but he was seized in the tumult and killed. The rest of the rump government fled the scene and disappeared; with a single voice the entire city of Milan now proclaimed itself ready to welcome Francesco Sforza, who was at that time encamped at Vimercate. The year of our Salvation 1450 thus seemed to offer Francesco Sforza the promise of a rebirth: just as his actual birth had occurred in the year following the Jubilee proclaimed by Pope Boniface IX, so now his entry into the full light of glory was occurring in the subsequent Jubilee year proclaimed by Pope Nicholas V.

∶ 39 ∶

De clementia et facilitate Francisci in ingressu civitatis
Mediolanensium erga omnes.

1   Quid nunc clementiam eius ac facilitatem in conservandis ab omni
iniuria civibus, amplexandis, colligendis praedicem? Quis diei illius laeticiam abunde referre queat? Quis gratulationem nobilium?
Quis hilaritatem totius populi? Quis intuentium securitatem?
Longum esset enarrare. Hostis enim loco principem, salvatorem,
protectorem advenisse mirabantur: nam populum fame enectum,
praemissis undequaque ad vitam necessariis, summa opulentia
ditavit et in pristinum gradum abundantiamque restituit.

2   Quid deinde plausum accurrentis turbae, cum paulo post Blancha Maria consorte sua comitatus Mediolanum ingressus est?
Accelerabant universi, angiportus populo affluente replebantur,
unusquisque assistere, gratulari, manu significare cupiebat. 'Vides
Franciscum?' 'Blancham vides?' 'Quam concorditer incedunt, quam
iocunde colloquuntur!' Nemo prae studio visum satiare poterat,
dum alternos summa cupiditate intuerentur.

3   Quod deinde spectaculum illud fuit, cum in templo maximo
totius civitatis, assistente inter ceteros Angelo Aciarolo, illustri
equite, Florentinorum oratore, universo iubilante populo, ducalis
dignitatis sumpsit insignia! Stupebant intuentes ac se ipsos tardi-
tatemque et suspicionem accusabant quod principem suum,

238

: 39 :

*Francesco Sforza shows clemency and kindness toward
all on his entry into Milan.*

What now shall I say about Sforza's clemency and kindness in   1
keeping our citizens free from harm, in caring for their immediate
needs, in reconciling them to one another? Who could sufficiently
describe the joy the city experienced on the day of his entry, the
acclamation shown by the nobility, the euphoria of the populace,
the feeling of safety and security that descended on the crowds?
Such scenes would take forever to relate. Everyone was amazed
that the man who had been their enemy was now entering the city
as their savior, their protector, their prince. For Sforza's men
showered the starving population with an abundance of every kind
of foodstuff, thereby returning Milan to the times of plenty.

What then too of the shouts of jubilation that rose up from the   2
seething crowds as Sforza himself, shortly thereafter, made his
entry into the city in the company of his wife Bianca Maria? The
crowds surged forward, and every alleyway was filled to over-
flowing; everyone wanted to witness the event, to salute the new
ruler by waving their hands. "Did you see Francesco?" "Did you
see Bianca?" "How nicely they advanced together in perfect uni-
son!" "How happily they spoke to one another!" No one could get
enough of seeing the couple, as eager eyes roved from one to the
other.

Then what a spectacle in the Duomo! Here, in the presence of   3
(among others) the famed knight and Florentine ambassador Angelo Acciaiuoli, Francesco Sforza took up the trappings of the ducal office as the crowd roared its approval.[112] Those looking on
wondered at their own stupidity: why had they not realized sooner
that Sforza was their true prince, that he was offering them peace,

pacem, copias et securitatem afferentem non celerius cognovissent, non humanius suscepissent, et calamitatum suarum causam sibi ipsis ascribebant. Sed haec minima, cum clementiam erga infimos quosque, etiam partibus suis adversos, contemplarentur, cum benignitatem in audiendo, facilitatem in iudicando, mansuetudinem in parcendo pensitarent, cum mutationem denique animorum erga illum quem, cum hostem omnibus advenisse crederent, non principem modo aut ducem, sed patrem patriae adesse cernerent.

: 40 :

De bello et victoria Francisci contra Venetos
et pace Italiae.

1 At Veneti novo Francisci dominatu animo perculsi, cum illum ambitione et gloria aestuantem universa, Mediolano adepto, sibi subicere velle existimarent, alias denuo copias, aliud bellum ordiri efflagitabant.

2 Franciscus e contra, qui pacem Italiae dumtaxat, Mediolanensibus quietem securitatemque quaesiverat, pacem illis offerre, pacem summopere per oratores poscere et precari non cessabat. Verum frustra tentabatur, spe iampridem inhaerente animo, quam effectu comprobarant, nihil aliud quaerentes quam ut, exhaustis Mediolanensium facultatibus, Francisco pecunia attrito, ipsi Mediolanum sibi ascisserent. Perstabat enim ambitiosissimae

prosperity, and protection? Why had they not welcomed him sooner with open arms? They alone were to blame for the calamities that had befallen their city. But it was no matter now, as they contemplated their new ruler's clemency toward even the most humble, toward even those who had opposed him; or when they considered the way he listened to everyone, his leniency in passing judgment, the ease with which he pardoned those who had offended him; or when they saw the way everyone changed their minds about the man they had thought was coming to town as their enemy and who now showed himself to be, not only their prince and ruler, but the father of their country.[113]

: 40 :

*Francesco is victorious in war against Venice;
peace comes to Italy.*

The Venetians meanwhile were upset at Francesco's installment as   1
Duke of Milan, for they saw him as a man burning with ambition and lusting for power. Surely, they thought, with Milan in his grasp, he would now try to extend his conquests as far as was possible. The only proper response for Venice was to raise a new army and to make preparations for war.

Francesco on the other hand sought only peace, an Italian peace   2
that would guarantee security and tranquility for Milan. So he made repeated offers of peace to the Venetians, sending his emissaries to them with ardent pleas.[114] But all his efforts fell on deaf ears. The Venetians clearly had never abandoned their original plan: their one desire now as before was to occupy Milan themselves once that city's resources were exhausted and Sforza's war chest emptied. They were in fact still obsessed, as even the greatest

cupiditatis pertinax libido, quae maximis ingeniis ut plurimum inesse solet, nec mentes fiducia sublatas quiescere sinebat. Franciscus, eorum voluntate perspecta, cum nullam paci viam adesse cerneret, bellum et ipse agere instituit. Foedere igitur cum Florentinis icto, Gallorum regem in amiciciam pariter accire studuit, ut, eius auxilio si opus esset, statum suum populosque tueretur; et opportuno aspirante tempore, non expectato hostium insultu, donec ipsi in Mediolanensi agro castra ponerent, Brixienses invadere statuit.

3   Per id tempus Federicus tercius Romanorum Imperator, de quo supra verba fecimus, cum uxore, Portugaliae regis filia, Romam venerat, et repudiato Mediolanensi diademate, ut Venetis faveret, a Nicolao quinto summo pontifice coronatus fuerat.

4   Veneti igitur comparato ingenti exercitu, etiam pontem Adduae fluvio magna impensa machinarumque apparatu maximo imposuere, per quem non Laudam modo ac finitimas partes, verum etiam Mediolani oram excursionibus praedaque popularentur. Sic incensis animis utraque ex parte bellum acriter fieri coeptum. Ceterum admirari licuit in tanto rerum turbine tantisque undique imminentibus periculis, quam eximia fuerit Francisci prudentia, magnanimitas, tolerantia. Quippe cum omni ex parte bella streperent, hinc finitimi Veneti instarent, illinc Guillielmi Montisferrati, viri illustris, copiae urgerent et trans Padum turbarent omnia, in Parmensi agro Corrigienses viribus animisque pollentes moverent arma, Franciscus omnibus in locis praesidia mittebat, ubique aderat, instabat, hortabatur; nec solum se suosque tuebatur a tam numeroso hostium exercitu, verum eos ubique repellebat,

minds will often be, with an irresistible craving to realize their grandiose scheme, even though their intelligence told them it was now too late. Francesco saw where they were heading: since there was no way to convince them to accept peace, he decided to opt for war. Having first negotiated an alliance with Florence, he then sought to obtain an agreement with the king of France whereby the latter would come to his aid to protect his territory and his peoples, should the need arise.[115] Finally, he determined that at the appropriate moment he would take the initiative and attack Brescia rather than wait for the enemy to move its troops onto Milanese soil.

At this same time the emperor Frederick III, whom we mentioned earlier, had come to Rome with his wife, the daughter of the king of Portugal. Spurning the Milanese coronation in order to please the Venetians, he had himself crowned by Pope Nicholas V.[116]

Next the Venetians, having fielded a huge army, built a bridge over the river Adda at great effort and expense; by using it they were able to stage attacks not only on Lodi and its surrounds, but even on the outlying districts of Milan itself. Both sides were now fully engaged in an increasingly brutal war. Here we can pause to admire how — in the midst of so much turmoil and hemmed in on all sides by impending danger — Francesco Sforza retained his composure, his skill, and his energy. For with war raging on all fronts at once — with the Venetians marching ever closer to Milan, with troops under the command of the famed Guglielmo di Monferrato pressing forward and creating havoc beyond the river Po, and with the powerful Correggiani up in arms in the Parma region — Francesco continued to send help wherever it was most urgently required.[117] He himself was present everywhere, bolstering morale and encouraging his men to continue the fight. And not only did he manage to protect himself and his men from such a massive enemy offensive, he even succeeded in repelling the

reiectisque assiduis oppugnationibus, opida eorum expugnabat. Postremo militum robore et constantia fretus in extremis casibus, hiemis etiam tempore ab inimicorum offensione nequaquam destitit, quo ad Brixiensium opida omnia in dictionem suam redegit; ponte denique intercepto, quem tanta impensa, tot machinis munierant, omnes eorum conatus avertit.

5   Ex quo postremo effectum est, ut qui pacem prius recusaverant, primi pacis munus implorarent, quaererent, precarentur. Nam iisdem temporibus Constantinopolis a rege Asiae, quem Turcum vocant, per vim capta et praedae tradita, Iohanne Imperatore foede interempto, nonnihil pavoris Venetis iniecerat. Sic magna Francisci gloria bis victis Venetorum copiis, ceterarum potentissimis, pax ab illis quaesita et concessa est, quamquam praecipuis ducibus in re militari et militum multitudine abundarent et tot praesidiis fulti victoriam adipisci crederent. Opida omnia, quae Adduae fluvio imminebant et in Mediolanensem agrum iter dederant, ab illis Francisco concessa sunt, ut tuta pace quietaque frueretur.

6   Ipse Mediolanum victor reversus est, ac veluti ex Italis triumphum referens, ingenti civium gratulatione et laeticia susceptus, cum omnes illum beatum dignumque maiore imperio et laude praedicarent. Nempe virtutem eius admirantes, magnanimitatem, clementiam et in primis felicitatem, haud satis eum pro meritis extollere posse fatebantur, tam eximia consorte praeditum, tam illustribus filiis, Galeaz videlicet primogenito eius, et Hippolita, praestantissima ornatissimaque virgine, nec non iuniore Sfortia,

Venetian advances, thwarting their attack, and turning the tide of battle against their own strongholds. Relying then on the strength of his men and their steadfastness in adversity, he maintained his offensive right through the winter months, until he had taken each and every fortified town in the Brescia region. By next destroying the bridge on the Adda—the one the Venetians had built at huge expense and surrounded with elaborate fortifications—he blocked any further move on their part to invade Milanese territory.

The result in the end was that the very same men who had   5
earlier refused to discuss peace now became the first to see its merits, and to seek, nay even to beg for peace.[118] For at this same time an Asian king, known as the Turk, stormed and sacked Constantinople, murdered the emperor John, and struck fear into the hearts of the Venetians. And so it was that the Venetians, most powerful of the powerful, yet twice defeated by the glorious Francesco Sforza, sought and obtained peace, even though—with their military strength intact, their leadership undiminished, and so many resources at their disposal—they still believed victory was theirs for the taking. By the terms of the peace they conceded to Sforza all the fortified towns along the river Adda, towns that had previously offered them such easy access into Milanese territory. This concession was meant to guarantee Sforza's security on his eastern front.

Sforza himself returned to Milan victorious and was given a   6
hero's welcome, as if he were the conqueror of Italy. Everyone cheered and congratulated him, praising him as being wholly worthy of holding the highest authority in the city, for they admired his courage, his generosity, his clemency, and most of all his success. Indeed they could hardly praise him enough for all his merits. There he was, flanked by such an excellent wife and surrounded by such outstanding children! Among these latter were his firstborn son Galeazzo, the lovely and highly cultivated maiden Ippolita, as well as the second-born son, Sforza Maria. Each of

quos ille affinitatibus principum regumque coniunxit. Reliquos vero filios suos, insignes adoloscentes, ex Blancha Maria consorte sua vicissim procreatos, Philippum scilicet Mariam, avito nomine illustrem, Ludovicum et Ascanium, nec non Octavium et eorum sororem Elisabeth, connubiis maximis et clarissimis optatos, virtutibus in primis illustrare studuit.

7 Conversus deinde ad excolendam urbem, vicis harena latereque constratis, arcem Portae Iovis populi tumultu antea disiectam e fundamentis erigi magnificentissime curavit. Curiam etiam priscorum ducum vetustate fatiscentem non solum restituit, sed ampliavit ornavitque. Aquaeductum quoque ex Addua, defosso solo, per viginti miliaria deduci iussit, quo agri finitimi irrigarentur populoque necessariae copiae suppeterent. Mediolanenses cives ab inordinariis tributis immunes praestitit. Nec propterea quiete propria contentus, Ecclesiam Romanam sub Nicolao, Calisto Pioque pontificibus ab omni iniuria illaesam praestitit.

8 Sic Deo praeside felicissima prole auctus et ad summum principatum pariter evectus, Mediolanensium civitate vicissim illustrata, ab exterorum populorum incursibus et periculis in pace constitutam defendit Italiam.

these three he joined by marriage ties to other royal and princely houses.[119] As for the fine younger children he fathered with his wife Bianca Maria, namely Filippo Maria (whose name recalled the boy's illustrious grandfather), Ludovico and Ascanio, as well as Ottavio and their sister Elisabetta—all of whom were much sought after as marriage partners by the best houses—he made sure they were brought up to embody the finest accomplishments.[120]

Turning next to the embellishment of the city, he had the streets of Milan paved with brick and sand. He then rebuilt with the utmost magnificence the Castle of Porta Giovia, which had previously been destroyed in a popular uprising.[121] He also restored, extended and improved the Corte dell'Arengo, the former seat of the Visconti that had since fallen into ruin and decay.[122] In addition he ordered that a canal twenty miles long be dug from the river Adda, its purpose being to irrigate the fields nearby and to supply the needs of the people.[123] He exempted the citizens of Milan from all extraordinary taxes. Not content with having thus assured the tranquility of his own state, he made sure that the Roman Church under Popes Nicholas, Calixtus, and Pius remained free from all harm.

And so with God as his protector, waxing in his numerous progeny, standing at the very pinnacle of power, and with the city of Milan basking in all its renewed glory, Francesco Sforza set about defending a now peaceful Italy from the dangers of invasion by foreign peoples.

7

8

APPENDIX

This Appendix consists of three letters concerning the composition and publication of Decembrio's biography of Filippo Maria Visconti. All three letters as reproduced here are contained in Genoa, Biblioteca Universitaria, MS C.VII.46.[1] It should be noted that while the first two letters are not dated as to year, the missing information is easily supplied by the date of the third letter, which clearly alludes to the earlier correspondence. Since Filippo Maria Visconti died on August 13, 1447, and his death is described in Decembrio's biography, the first two letters were written in 1447.[2]

Letter of Leonello d'Este
to Pier Candido Decembrio
[October 22, 1447]

Leonellus Marchio Estensis P. Candido salutem.

Vitam Philippi Mariae a te editam legi, et iterum legi, quae mirum in modum mihi placuit, adeo graphice et adeo historice rem ipsam mira quadam brevitate complexus es. Itaque ago tibi gratias quod libellum mihi legendum iudicandumque reliquisti. Eum igitur ad te remitto, sicuti eram tibi pollicitus. Ceterum cum omnia mihi placeant quae in eo scripta sunt, tecum libere et ingenue loquar, te oratum esse velim, ut partem illam quae de secreto et nunquam referendo vitio loquitur, aut penitus deleas, aut punctim, et ut aiunt per transenam[1] de ea verba facias, ita ut quamquam breviter loquaris, brevior et obscurior adhuc fias. Quod si ea omnia cunctis mortalibus esse nota dixeris, tamen per huiusmodi scripta tua, quae immortalia erunt, posteris patefacienda non sunt. Vale, et ne nimiam hac in re esse censueris meam arrogantiam apud te, qui in huiusmodi scribendi genere et aliis probe calles.

Ex Porto XXII Octubris.

Letter of Leonello d'Este
to Pier Candido Decembrio
[October 22, 1447][3]

Marquis Leonello d'Este to Pier Candido, greetings.

I have read and reread your biography of Filippo Maria. The work pleased me immensely, so vividly and accurately have you managed to capture the subject, and in so remarkably few words. So I thank you for allowing me to read the book and to express my opinion, and I accordingly return it to you just as I promised you I would. But while it is true that everything written therein pleases me, I will speak with you quite freely and frankly with regard to the chapter that talks about a secret and never to be mentioned vice: I really would urge you to delete this passage completely, or else to make your language here more subtle and allusive, for even though your present treatment of the matter is brief, I would like you to be briefer still, even to the point of obscurity. Because while you may say that the whole business is common knowledge among those of us living today, there is still no reason to pass such information on to posterity through these literary works of yours, which are destined to become immortal. Farewell and please do not think that my comments reflect a feeling of superiority toward you, for in biography as well as in the other genres of writing you are rightly to be regarded as a master practitioner.

Porto,[4] *October 22.*

: II :

Letter of Pier Candido Decembrio
to Leonello d'Este
[*October 31, 1447*]

P. Candidus Leonello Marchioni Estensi salutem.

Delectatus sum admodum epistola tua, princeps illustrissime, et quod scripta mea tibi non ingrata fuerint, nec eorum iudicium proferre recusaveris. Amavi principem illum, qui me a pueritia aluit, qui studiorum quietem et modum mihi adhibuit; nam illius facultatibus adiutus facile adiscendi tempus inter curas adeptus sum. Nulla mihi peregrinatio nisi iocunda et utilis eo auctore ascripta est; licuit inter montes, campos, mariaque peragranti non solum regiones noscere earumque aspectu delectari, sed etiam inter itinera libris studiisque vacare. Ingratus mihi videbar admodum, ni ex lucro partem facerem auctori bonarum mercium; ob id vitam eius scribere institui absolvique, ut vides. Nundum tamen edidi in publicum, nec edam iudicio tuo admonitus quousque satisfactum erit voluntati tuae. Non enim ita edideram ut infamiam pareret principi meo, sed laudem potius et gloriam. Quod si errare tibi visus sum, id egi solum ne errarem. Nihil in historico mendacio est turpius. Timui igitur ne, si quae notiora fuerant omitterem, minus fidei promererer in his quae laudem et commendationem

: II :

Letter of Pier Candido Decembrio
to Leonello d'Este
[October 31, 1447][5]

Pier Candido to Marquis Leonello d'Este, greetings.

I was quite delighted with your letter, most illustrious prince, both because my writings found favor with you, and because you did not hesitate to pass judgment on them. I loved that prince of mine: he took me under his wing from my earliest childhood; he provided me with the leisure and means to pursue my studies, for thanks to his support I managed rather easily to find the time, in the midst of my administrative duties, to devote to learning. None of the diplomatic missions I undertook on his behalf were ever boring or without some profitable outcome. Whether I happened to be traveling through mountains or crossing fields or seas, I not only came to know and take pleasure in visiting foreign lands, but I even found time for my books and studies during such journeys. It seemed to me that I would be most ungrateful if I failed to repay some part of the debt I owed to the author of so much good fortune. This is why I decided to write his biography. And as you see, I have completed it, but I have not yet published it, nor will I do so, given the reservations you have expressed, until I have satisfied your demands. After all, I have not composed this book to cover my prince with opprobrium, but to spread his fame and glory. But if I seem to you to have erred, I did so only so that I might not err. Nothing is more reprehensible in a historian than lying. My fear therefore was that if I failed to mention these notorious things you refer to, my account would lack credibility when it came to treat the areas where my prince was deserving of praise

merebantur. Sed postquam honestius tibi apparet posteritati de-
servire, id agam, sed adeo moderate et concinne, ut intelligi potius
voluerim quam audiri.

Vale. Ex Mediolano ultimo Octubris.

: III :

Letter of Leonello d'Este
to Pier Candido Decembrio
[August 19, 1448]

Leonellus Marchio Estensis P. Candido salutem.

Tandem evellimus a manibus Pisani pictoris numisma vultus tui,
et illud his annexum ad te mittimus, retento exemplari ab eo, ut
intelligas quanti te tuaque faciamus. Emendationem autem per te
adhibitam in Philippi ducis vita plurimum commendamus, nam
quamquam honesta illa essent in historico, haec tamen ut hones-
tiora reputamus.

Vale Ferrariae XVIIII Augusti 1448.

and commendation. But since it seems to you more important to keep posterity in mind, I shall carry out the revisions, executing the task so subtly and concisely that my meaning will be intelligible without being explicit.

Milan, October 31.

: III :

Letter of Leonello d'Este
to Pier Candido Decembrio
[August 19, 1448][6]

Marquis Leonello d'Este to Pier Candido, greetings.

I have finally managed to pry from the hands of the painter Pisanello the medal containing your portrait.[7] I am sending it along with this letter, and keeping a duplicate for myself, so that you will see how much I value you and all that pertains to you. I am also exceedingly pleased with the correction you have made to your biography of Duke Filippo. For although what you wrote before was worthy of the historian in you, I consider this new version to be worthier still.

Ferrara, August 19, 1448.

Note on the Texts and Translations

❧❦❧

The present edition of Decembrio's two most important biographies is the first to be published since the standard edition began to appear almost one hundred years ago. That edition, with texts established by Giuseppe Petraglione and notes by Attilio Butti and Felice Fossati, took over half a century to produce and ran to 989 large folio pages covered from top to bottom in minute print. Of the three editors, only Fossati lived to see the final pages make their long-awaited appearance in 1958.[1]

The reason the standard edition took so long to produce, and filled nearly a thousand folio sheets, lay in the copious notes that accompanied the texts. Fossati in particular took a dim view of Decembrio's reliability as a historian and therefore felt it to be incumbent upon himself as editor to (1) demonstrate the inadequacies of Decembrio's *Lives* from a strictly historical point of view, and (2) rewrite from scratch the history of the entire period.[2] This immense task required space, and the notes accordingly grew in proportion, eventually threatening to crowd Decembrio's text right off the page. The result is that while the standard edition contains an incredibly rich store of documentation, and indeed remains a definitive scholarly landmark in its own right, it also has the unfortunate consequence of rendering Decembrio's text itself virtually unreadable. With regard to the *Life of Filippo Maria Visconti*, the latter defect was remedied to some extent by the publication in 1983 of an Italian translation. It is this edition that is most often cited today, even though it does not always accurately reflect the original. In addition to this considerable drawback, the Italian translation does not reproduce Decembrio's Latin text, nor does it contain the companion biography of Francesco Sforza.[3]

If the present edition has one overriding purpose it is to bring Decembrio's texts themselves back from the wilderness to which the standard edition consigned them last century. To this end, Massimo Zaggia has carefully reviewed the manuscript tradition and restored the Latin original, correcting earlier readings wherever they were defective. The notes, by Gary Ianziti, have been kept to an absolute minimum, in order to let the texts breathe. To the extent possible, we have tried to allow Decembrio at last to speak for himself, in his own words. If this sometimes challenges the modern reader, then so be it. We strongly believe that works like Decembrio's *Lives* should not be allowed to become mere pretexts for the display of modern erudition. The primary function of the philological and historical disciplines is to render the author's meaning accessible across the abysses of time, place, and language. If the relatively sparse notes serve this humble purpose, they will more than have done their job.

The same philosophy applies when it comes to the accompanying translation, the first ever into English. Decembrio's Latin is not easy, and it would be unreasonable to expect even the few well-equipped modern readers of that language to find themselves in a position to cope with it. The phraseology often verges on the obscure: it is full of ablative absolutes, long-winded subordinate clauses, and recondite vocabulary. Such linguistic features make the text especially difficult to translate into contemporary English. A particular problem has been the episodic quality of the style, for example, the occasional terseness (*brevitas*) of the original, which is impossible to imitate in English, as to do so would drain the translation of its color. As a consequence, I have frequently been obliged to expand and expatiate where Decembrio contracts, my purpose being to make his meaning—or what I take to be his meaning—clear to the reader. This represents a betrayal (*traduttore, traditore*, as the Italians say), albeit a necessary one if the text is to continue to exist as a living entity in our own time. Specialists may well quibble with some of my choices, but I have decided to remain faithful to the spirit, if not always to the exact letter of the texts. My main question in translating has been: what would this sound like if Decembrio had written it in our language? And in the end I have been most comforted by the fact that the Latin text will always be there on the facing page as a guide to any future reader capable of working through its intricacies.

Gary Ianziti

VITA PHILIPPI MARIAE TERTII LIGURUM DUCIS

Among the manuscripts that preserve the *Vita Philippi Mariae*, three witnesses stand out, all of which are recognized as having been vetted and approved by the author:[4]

A   Milan, Biblioteca Ambrosiana, MS Trotti 418, a codex of
       Milanese appearance, undated but produced around the
       middle of the fifteenth century, originally held by the
       Milanese monastery of Sant'Ambrogio.

H   Cambridge, MA, Harvard University, Houghton Library, MS
       Richardson 23, containing the collected *Opuscula historica* of
       Pier Candido as organized by the author; on fols. 22v–55r
       the *Vita* is placed after the *De laudibus urbis Mediolanensis*,
       fols. 4r–22v, and before the *Panegyricus de laudibus Nicolai
       Picenini* and the *Breve epitoma Romanae historiae*, fols. 55r–83r,
       83r–97v; the codex is elegantly decorated and has a
       dedication to Borso d'Este, lord of Ferrara and Modena,
       datable to 1460–1465.

P   Paris, Bibliothèque Nationale de France, MS N.A.L. 846, a
       codex of Milanese appearance, undated but produced
       around the middle of the fifteenth century, with notes
       indicating provenance from late fifteenth-century Urbino.

Besides these author-approved witnesses, there are four more manuscripts dating from the second half of the fifteenth century:[5]

Florence, Biblioteca Medicea Laurenziana, MS Ashburnham 1659, dated
    1476, with a note indicating that it was in the possession of Fabrizio
    Marliani of Milan, bishop of Piacenza.
Madrid, Biblioteca de la Universidad Complutense, Archivo Histórico
    Universitario, MS 129, fols. 121r–54v, part of a miscellany of various
    humanistic materials, with marginal notes in the hand of Angelo
    Decembrio.
Perugia, Biblioteca Comunale Augusta, MS F. 71 (formerly 397),
    fols. 189r–233r (following the *Historia Mediolanensis* of Andrea Biglia,
    fols. 1r–185v).

Rome, Biblioteca Nazionale Centrale, MS Sessoriano 413, fols. 1r–22v, the opening work in a massive (comprising 496 folios) miscellaneous collection of Latin and vernacular prose and verse circulating in Milan toward the end of the fifteenth century.

Three further manuscripts document the fortunes of the text within collections of various Milanese historical materials, from the sixteenth to the seventeenth century:

Milan, Biblioteca Ambrosiana, MS B 173 Sussidio, seventeenth century, fols. 1r–68v.
Milan, Archivio Storico Civico e Biblioteca Trivulziana, MS 104, sixteenth century, fols. 1r–31r.
Milan, Archivio Storico Civico e Biblioteca Trivulziana, MS 1273, seventeenth century, lost.

The first printed edition of the text appeared, without the editors' names, in 1630, as part of an illustrious collection of Milanese historiography (including works by Tristano Calco, Giorgio Merula, and Paolo Giovio) promoted by the council of the sixty *Decurioni* of the City of Milan. The second edition, edited by Ludovico Antonio Muratori, with the assistance of Filippo Argelati, was published in volume 20 of the *Rerum Italicarum Scriptores*. The third and most recent edition appeared in five fascicles published between 1925 and 1935 in the new edition of the *Rerum Italicarum Scriptores*, edited by Giuseppe Petraglione (Latin text), Attilio Butti (notes and historical commentary, chaps. 1–29), and Felice Fossati (notes and historical commentary, chaps. 29–71). All three of the existing editions were based on an incomplete knowledge of the manuscript tradition: until quite recently scholarship was unaware of the author's presence in A and P, while H remained entirely unknown.

The present edition is the first to be founded on a thorough investigation of all of the surviving witnesses. The codices not reviewed by the author have proved to be irrelevant for the purposes of constructing a critical edition of the text, though they are of interest from another point of view, insofar as they can serve to document the various fortunes of the work, including the critical reactions it gave rise to. Particularly interesting in this regard is the Complutense codex (MS 129), with marginal comments by Angelo Decembrio.[6]

The present edition has been conducted chiefly on the basis of the author-approved codices, all three of which offer a guarantee of authorial oversight: A has 279 marginal notes in the hand of Pier Candido, plus a further 66 corrections to the text that have definitely been made in his hand (along with 8 corrections in another, unidentified hand, and 26 deletions); H has 4 marginal notes and 60 corrections to the text in the author's hand (along with 14 more corrections most likely made by the author, and 12 deletions); P has two marginal notes and 17 corrections made in Pier Candido's hand (plus 6 more in another hand and 10 deletions; 14 further corrections can be safely attributed to other copyists), and it has two long passages (chaps. 45 and 53–57) that have been personally transcribed by the author. However, nearly all of Pier Candido's direct interventions on the text have as their goal the correction of the many small errors introduced by the copyists in transcribing the original.

It was nevertheless necessary to check to see whether Pier Candido's interventions contain significant authorial variants, and whether they might possibly represent two or even three different stages in the author's elaboration of the work.

The answer is substantially negative: there are no important variants in terms of the work's basic ideology, in particular in chapters 46 (the most controversial, with its homosexual overtones) and 71 (with its problematic concluding reference to the nascent Ambrosian Republic).[7] The only important variant is the absence of chapter 44 in P, this chapter being regularly present in both A and H. It should be added that the same P presents chapter 45 as a marginal addition in Pier Candido's own hand, at fol. 25v.

The three manuscripts do nevertheless exhibit a series of small variants that can be grouped into three different categories: variants in spelling and phonetics (243: starting with the first chapter, *auctor/autor, sita/syta*; plus another 68 variants that concern proper names, for example *Oppizo/Opizo, Vercellas/Vercelas*, also in the opening chapter); small variants of a lexical and syntactical nature (66: for example *Papiam urbem/Papie urbem* at the beginning of the third chapter, or *fecit/effecit* in chapter

45); and small but substantive variants (24 in all, but occurring in the second half of the text, starting with chapter 29 where, in place of the reading *novissime abscessisset* given in A and H, MS P has *turpissime aufugisset*).

In the present edition we shall signal (in the notes) only the principal variants that relate to content. These concern the addition or modification of several proper names: see the notes to chapters 29, 46, 63, 64.

The comparison of the variants allows us to establish the chronological order in which the three author-approved codices were produced. The variant in chapter 63 is revealing in this regard: the text of P names (with overtones of contempt) *Antonius Panormita poeta Siculus*; A contains an obvious erasure, over which one finds the correction, made in the hand of Pier Candido, of *Antonius Panormita poeta Siculus* to read *Franciscus Barbula poeta Greculus* (= Francesco Filelfo); the third codex reads, in the hand of the copyist and without erasure, *Franciscus Barbula poeta Greculus*. Similarly, in chapter 39, P has the reading *eam recusaret*; A still has *eam recusaret*, but with an ink slash over *eam* that indicates deletion; H has only *recusaret*. It thus becomes quite clear — through the study of these and other variants — that the chronological order is the following: P represents the first phase, A the second, and H the third and final phase. It is nevertheless necessary to repeat that in general the textual differences concern only minor details (chiefly the addition or substitution of a few names), so that one cannot really speak of three different redactions of the work.

As a consequence, the text printed in this edition is essentially the latest one in point of time, that of H. I have intervened only to eliminate the errors that went unnoticed in the author's own revision (twenty-four in all). And I have accepted a correction made in all three previous printed editions concerning a reading that is obviously erroneous, even though it is present in all three of the author-approved manuscripts (P, A, H): *nec* for *ne* at the end of chapter 28. This has all the appearances of being an "authorial error," which was already present in Decembrio's (lost) autograph copy and which from there was passed on in the first instance to all three author-approved copies. It is in fact well known that small but insidious "authorial errors" are present in many autograph manuscripts, given that such errors are capable of evading even the most attentive scrutiny by the author himself.

I have in addition given preference to the reading in H in cases where there are differences in spelling, phonetics, syntax (that is, word order), or vocabulary between the three author-approved codices. I have made an exception only in relation to chapters 45 and 53–57, where I have followed the reading given in P, which in these passages (fols. 25v, 31v–34v) represents a transcription in the author's own hand, and thus provides further insights into the *usus scribendi* of Pier Candido. In general, however, I have followed H, even reproducing its morphological oscillations, for example, *biennium/bienium, commoditas/comoditas, vendicare/vindicare*, as these were evidently tolerated by the author. Even so, in chapter 51 I have corrected the form *vita*, given in all three author-approved manuscripts, to read *vitta*, because the meaning requires that we understand "fillet" here rather than "life" (quite possibly this should be classified as yet another "authorial error"). Among the three author-approved copies, H is also the only one to adopt the use of diphthongs in the manner of the revived classical Latin of mature humanism: this edition therefore normalizes the use of diphthongs throughout, which also makes for easier reading.

Finally, one of the three author-approved copies, A, contains a large number (279) of marginal notes in the hand of Pier Candido: on examination, however, these prove to be mere *notabilia* emphasizing the proper names of persons and places mentioned in the text. I have therefore decided not to reproduce these in the present edition. There are only two marginal notes by Pier Candido in P, while there are four in H: these too are of little relevance for the purposes of interpreting the text. I have nevertheless included a few useful indications from these authorial remarks in the notes to chapters 19, 46, and 62.

ANNOTATIO RERUM GESTARUM IN VITA ILLUSTRISSIMI FRANCISCI SFORTIAE

The *Annotatio in vita Francisci Sfortiae* is preserved in three fifteenth-century manuscripts:[8]

S   Paris, Bibliothèque Nationale de France, MS Lat. 5890, dated
1462, a copy prepared for Francesco Sforza (with a large
capital F on the original binding) and formerly housed in
the library of the dukes of Milan.

M   Madrid, Biblioteca Nacional, MS 18657/30, a codex without
indication as to its provenance, but seemingly copied in
Northern Italy in the third quarter of the fifteenth century.

U   Città del Vaticano (Vatican City), Biblioteca Apostolica
Vaticana, MS Urb. lat. 227, fols. 179v–205v (within a
miscellaneous collection of various humanist writings), a
codex signed by the celebrated copyist Federicus Veteranus
and produced for Duke Federico da Montefeltro, therefore
dateable prior to 1482.

The most important codex is clearly S, since it was the official copy prepared for Francesco Sforza. In fact, this codex exhibits a remarkable formal elegance, even if it is not richly decorated. The two previously
printed editions of the text — that of Ludovico Antonio Muratori (with
the assistance of Domenico Vandelli, 1731) and that of Petraglione-Butti-
Fossati (1935–1958) — were based solely on S. Both editions however are
characterized by a number of mistakes in transcription, as well as by decisions about punctuation and syntax that are not always convincing.

Manuscript S, with its elegant, rounded *littera antiqua*, is the work of a
professional copyist, but it also contains numerous interventions in the
hand of Pier Candido Decembrio: these include several brief additions in
the margins or between the lines (six in all, at fols. 7r, 9v, 10r, 11v, 15r, 19r;
plus thirteen further corrections or deletions, probably by Pier Candido
as well, at fols. 4v, 11r, 14r, 16r–v, 21v, 23r–v, 26r, 28r, 30r–v) and also a
certain number of marginal notes (twenty-one, at fols. 8r, 15r, 17r, 18v, 19r,
20r, 28r, 30r). For this reason, S deserves to be considered, if not a
proper autograph copy, at least one that has benefited from the direct
surveillance of the author. Previous editors were unaware of the author-
approved character of S.

The present edition too is obviously based chiefly on S. However,
even when dealing with an author-approved manuscript, it is an editor's

duty to be on the lookout for eventual "authorial errors," that is for the presence of mistakes that have managed to elude even authorial vigilance. For this type of work, the comparison of S with the other two witnesses, M and U, is most instructive. It is true that neither M or U can boast authorial approval, but an examination of the text shows that the two manuscripts do not derive from S, but that each one descends independently from Decembrio's autograph copy. In fact, M contains a certain number of erroneous readings (36), and U contains even more of these (136), yet none of the errors are shared in common between the two manuscripts. We can therefore construct a genealogical tree of the manuscript tradition, placing the (lost) autograph copy at the top, and the three witnesses descending from it, each one independent of the others: S (author-approved), M, and U.

In cases where there are divergences in the readings given by the three witnesses, the alliance of two witnesses against one certifies the authenticity of the majority reading, and allows us to isolate the *lectiones singulares* of the lone witness.

The most instructive case comes at the end of chapter 37, where S reads *invadendae*. On the surface this would seem to be a perfectly acceptable reading (*libido Liguriae invadendae*), and it is taken as such in the Petraglione-Butti-Fossati edition (whereas the Muratori edition erroneously reads *invadere*). But on closer inspection, we note that the main verb is *invasit*, and it seems highly unlikely that a writer of Decembrio's caliber would tolerate such a jarring repetition (*invasit libido Liguriae invadendae*). In fact, M and U both read here *occupandae* (*invasit libido Liguriae occupandae*), which is surely a much better reading. It is to be remembered that M and U never ever contain, in any portion of the text, errors or innovations that they share in common. Therefore *occupandae* cannot be descended from a common ancestor, but must necessarily come from the autograph copy itself.

A similar case occurs halfway through chapter 34, where S reads *proelio* (*proelio accepto*), but M and U have a much better reading, one that also perfectly suits the context: *periculo* (*periculo accepto*). And yet another noteworthy case comes halfway through chapter 16, where S gives the name *Niana Spinula* (accepted in both the Muratori and in the Petraglione-

Butti-Fossati editions), while M and U read *Iliana Spinula*. In point of fact, in all of the historical sources, as well as in her autograph letters, this woman's name is consistently given as *Eliana Spinola* (see Fossati's note, p. 585), and therefore there can be no doubt that the authentic reading is that of M and U, and not that of S.

This being said, the cases where an alliance of M and U forces us to correct the reading of author-approved S are few in number (eleven in all), and they are all, with the exception of the three indicated above, of minor importance, being almost solely matters of formal variation.

There is only a single case, at the beginning of chapter 29, in which all three witnesses contain what appears to be an erroneous reading: in the text, the subjunctive verbs *restituerit* and *addiderit* require the conjunction *cum*, which is missing in the three manuscripts but was reintegrated in the previous editions of Muratori and Petraglione-Butti-Fossati. It has seemed only right and proper to integrate *cum* into the present edition as well: the omission of *cum* in all three witnesses suggests this must be an "authorial error," which in all probability was already present in Decembrio's autograph copy.

With the exception of these particular cases, the present edition faithfully reproduces the quite correct author-approved S. Given this manuscript's status as a text reviewed by the author, I have also respected its irregularities in spelling and phonetics, as well as its few morphological oscillations (thus, *biennium/bienium*, *Connestabilis/Conestabilis*, *oppidum/opidum*, the latter frequent). On the other hand, it should be noted that S does not use diphthongs: I have nevertheless decided to introduce these into the present edition, in order to achieve uniformity with the text of the *Vita Philippi Mariae*, which has here been published according to the usage adopted in H.

In addition, S contains numerous marginal notes (255, of which 21 are in the hand of Pier Candido). But on examination, these turn out to be mere *notabilia*, whose limited function is to underscore dates and the names of persons and places mentioned in the text. The marginal notes have therefore been left out of the present edition.

A final philological issue concerns the preliminary chapter contained at the beginning of M and U under the title (possibly applicable to the entire *Annotatio*): *Actorum militarium victoriosissimi principis Francisci Sfortiae epitoma foeliciter incipit*. This chapter is absent in S, but it should be noted that S as preserved today is shorn of its first folio, meaning that the chapter's absence there is due to purely material circumstances. In the present edition, therefore, I have reintegrated the chapter as transcribed in M and U, even though it is missing in S.

Massimo Zaggia

NOTES

1. For details of publication, see the Bibliography under *Life of Filippo Maria Visconti* and *Deeds of Francesco Sforza*.

2. See in particular Fossati's negative evaluation of Decembrio *qua* historian, *Vita Philippi Mariae*, 333–46.

3. The *Vita di Filippo Maria Visconti* is a serviceable, but far from flawless translation. The interested reader can compare its version of chapter 41 (pp. 82–84) and/or chapter 57 (pp. 107–108) with the Latin, to see what I mean. The German translation too (*Leben des Filippo Maria Visconti und Taten des Francesco Sforza*) has its shortcomings, as pointed out by Fossati in his notes to *Vita Philippi Mariae*, pp. 263, 408, 424, 428, 430. This being said, no translation will ever be perfect, and no translation (including my own) can ever substitute for the original. Which is why, in contrast to previous translations, the present one appears together with Decembrio's Latin texts.

4. The identification of Pier Candido's hand in A is by Mirella Ferrari, "La biblioteca del monastero di S. Ambrogio: Episodi per una storia," in *Il monastero di S. Ambrogio nel Medioevo: Convegno di studi nel XII centenario, 5–6 novembre 1984* (Milan, 1988), 82–164, at 147; in H it is by James Hankins, *Italian Humanists in Ten Manuscripts from the Houghton Library: An Exhibition on the Occasion of the Annual National Meeting of the Renaissance Society of America* (Cambridge, MA, 1988), 4–5, and then by Pyle, "Harvard Ms Richardson 23," 196; in P it is by Zaggia, "La traduzione latina da Appiano," 237.

5. Kristeller, "Pier Candido Decembrio," 562–63, gives the most complete listing. The Perugia codex was added by Zaggia in Massimo Zaggia, Pier

Luigi Mulas, Matteo Ceriana, *Giovanni Maria Bottigella cortigiano, uomo di lettere e committente d'arte: Un percorso nella cultura lombarda di metà Quattrocento* (Florence, 1997), 209. The manuscript that once belonged to the Maggi family's private collection is presently either lost or missing: it was in any case a codex transcribed sometime between 1483 and 1489 (see Fossati's preface to *Vita Philippi Mariae*, iv–v) and could therefore not have contained any further corrections by Pier Candido, who died in 1477.

6. Vincenzo Fera, "Filologia in casa Decembrio," in *I Decembrio*, 155–59.

7. A noteworthy addition contained only in P concerns the final sentence, where it is said that, at the death of Filippo Maria, the Milanese *felici omine libertatem assumpserunt*: in P, at fol. 43r, the addition of *haud* between the lines, just before *felici*, changes the original political meaning of the sentence to its opposite. However, the hand in which the word *haud* is written is not that of Pier Candido, but that of one of the three or four other hands that are recognizable as having subsequently tampered with the codex.

8. A listing of the manuscripts can be found in Zaccaria, "Sulle opere," 38–40, and in Kristeller, "Pier Candido Decembrio," 563.

Notes to the Texts

☜§?☞

1. *Marginal gloss in Decembrio's hand in H:* Allobroges Sabaudienses sunt, ut Cesar scribit.

2. *This name is absent in A and P but is added in H.*

3. Captus est . . . custodiae iniicitur] *This sentence is cancelled by Decembrio's brother Angelo in MS Complutense 129, fol. 136r.*

4. *Decembrio's brother Angelo expresses his moral disapproval of this chapter in a marginal note to MS Complutense 129, fol. 140v:* Capitulum turpitudinis et infamie.

5. thoro] *This word was left out by the copyist of H but reintegrated in the margin by Decembrio. In the place of* thoro, *P and A both read* cubiculo.

6. pedotrivi] *Marginal gloss in Decembrio's hand in H:* Pedotrivus est puerorum exercitator.

7. Hoc solum proprium . . .] *A marginal note in Decembrio's hand calls attention to this passage in P: it reads* Attende (*that is, "Take notice"*).

8. Franciscus Barbula poeta Greculus] *This is the reading of H, but P, chronologically the first of the three MSS approved by the author, had* Antonius Panormita poeta Siculus, *a reference to the poet Antonio Beccadelli, called Panormita. The change is visible in A, where the original reading* Antonius Panormita poeta Siculus *is corrected to read* Franciscus Barbula poeta Greculus (*Decembrio's nickname for his rival Francesco Filelfo*).

9. Thomam Ferentinum] *In P the name is* Thomam Reatinum; *in A it is* Thomam Ferentinum, *written over an erasure; in H it is once again* Thomam Ferentinum, *but a marginal gloss in Decembrio's hand signals* Reatinum. *In any case, the person being referred to is Tommaso Morroni da Rieti.*

10. Iohannis Balbi et Iohannis Mathei nec non Thomae Bononiensis opera] *All three names are listed in H (Giovanni Balbi, Giovanni Matteo Bottigella, and Tommaso Tebaldi), but P, chronologically the first of the three MSS ap-*

proved by the author, mentions only Iohannis Balbi, *while A, second in point of time of the three approved MSS, lists* Iohannis Balbi et Iohannis Mathei.

VITA FRANCISCI SFORTIAE

1. *An anonymous marginal gloss in MS M indicates that the polemical target in this chapter is the* Sphortias *of Francesco Filelfo:* Nota, Philelphe.

APPENDIX

1. sc. transennam

Notes to the Translations

స్⁀స

ABBREVIATIONS

Biglia   Andrea Biglia, *Rerum mediolanensium historia*, in *RIS* 19 (Milan 1731), cols. 9–158

Cognasso   Francesco Cognasso, "Il ducato visconteo da Gian Galeazzo a Filippo Maria," in *Storia di Milano* (Milan 1955), 6:3–383

DBI   *Dizionario biografico degli italiani* (Rome, 1960–), online at www.treccani.it/biografico/

Il ducato   *Il ducato di Filippo Maria Visconti, 1412–1447*, ed. Federica Cengarle and Maria Nadia Covini (Florence, 2015)

RIS   *Rerum italicarum scriptores* (Milan, 1723–51); 2nd ser. (Città di Castello and Bologna, 1900–1975)

Simonetta   Giovanni Simonetta, *Rerum gestarum Francisci Sfortiae Mediolanensium Ducis commentarii*, ed. Giovanni Soranzo, in *RIS*, 2nd ser., vol. 21.2 (Bologna, 1932–59)

LIFE OF FILIPPO MARIA VISCONTI

1. In the original Latin, Decembrio accords Filippo Maria the title of *Ligurum Dux*. Literally translated this would yield "Duke of the Ligurians." Such usage, however, reflects the tendency among Visconti humanists to designate Lombardy as *Liguria* and its inhabitants as *Ligures*, or Ligurians. Thus Petrarch, *Seniles* 3.1.25, calls the city of Milan itself *Ligurum caput*, by which he means "the capital of Lombardy." In his numerous letters on the issue of nomenclature, Decembrio makes it clear that his choice of the title *Ligurum Dux* is deliberate and is intended to stress that the Visconti (and later Sforza) dukes exercised authority not just over Milan and its district but also over a much wider territory, one more or less identifiable with the Lombard plain and its adjacent territories: see, for example, Genoa, Biblioteca Universitaria, MS C.VII.46, fols. 45v–47v; 48v–49v. In the text that follows, Decembrio consistently uses the

term *Liguria* when he means to refer to Lombardy in this broad sense: see below, chapters 14, 23, 25, 69.

2. This first chapter is closely modeled on Suetonius, *Augustus* 1. Decembrio cautiously connects the Visconti to the counts of Angera but does not trot out the fabulous genealogy that traced the family's origins through those mythical figures all the way back to the Trojans. For an example of this latter type, see the fantastic genealogy compiled by Pietro da Castelletto in 1402 as part of his funeral oration for Gian Galeazzo Visconti: *RIS* 16 (Milan, 1730), cols. 1046–48. On such genealogies in general and the Visconti case in particular, see Roberto Bizzocchi, *Genealogie incredibili* (Bologna, 1995).

3. The reference here is to the famous Visconti heraldic device showing a giant snake swallowing a child, or perhaps a Saracen: see Dante, *Purgatory* 8.80. The actual origins of the device are unknown. Decembrio's hesitations reflect the confusion inherent in the tradition: see Bonvesin de la Riva, *Le meraviglie di Milano*, ed. Paolo Chiesa (Milan, 2009), 126–29, 237–38.

4. Ottone Visconti (1207–95) was appointed archbishop in 1262 by Pope Urban IV. His victory over the rival Della Torre family in 1277 is commonly seen as the beginning of Visconti lordship over Milan, initiating a dynasty that would rule almost continuously until 1447. For details see Francesco Cognasso, *I Visconti* (Milan, 1966), 47–80.

5. Matteo Visconti (1250–1322) was appointed imperial vicar by Adolf of Nassau in 1294. He abdicated in favor of his son Galeazzo Visconti in 1322. For the references to Vercelli and Novara, see Pliny the Elder, *Natural History* III, 124. Larius is the ancient Latin name for Lake Como, while the city of Como itself was commonly designated as Novum Comum after Julius Caesar had it moved from its original hilltop location to the lakeside position it enjoys today.

6. On Azzone Visconti (1302–39), as well as on the other early Visconti rulers mentioned here and in the previous chapter, Decembrio's main source was the prolific fourteenth-century Dominican chronicler Galvano Fiamma (1283–1344). See, for example, Fiamma's *Manipulus florum*, in *RIS*

11 (Milan, 1727), cols. 537–740; his *Opusculum de rebus gestis ab Azone, Luchino, et Johanne Vicecomitibus*, ed. Carlo Castiglioni, in *RIS*, 2nd ser., vol. 12.4 (Bologna, 1938); and the *Annales Mediolanenses*, in *RIS* 16 (Milan, 1730), cols. 641–714. For a convenient summary of Fiamma's life and works, see *DBI* 47:331–38. Modern research substantially confirms Decembrio's picture of Azzone: see Patrick Boucheron, *Le pouvoir de bâtir: Urbanisme et politique édilitaire à Milan* (Rome, 1998), 108–26; Jane Black, *Absolutism in Renaissance Milan: Plenitude of Power under the Visconti and the Sforza* (Oxford, 2009), 38–48; Federica Cengarle, "La signoria di Azzone Visconti," in *Tecniche di potere nel tardo medioevo*, ed. Massimo Vallerani (Rome, 2010), 89–116.

7. The French king ransomed by Galeazzo II (1320–78) was John the Good (1319–64), captured by the English at the battle of Poitiers in 1356.

8. The reference here is to Petrarch, *Seniles* 5.1.9, where Galeazzo II is described as "a man superior to others in many things, but surpassing even himself in the magnificence of his building" (vir in multis alios, in aedificandi magnificentia sese vincens).

9. Galeazzo II erected the Castle of Porta Giovia in the 1360s as the principal defensive fortification guarding the city of Milan. Under Filippo Maria the castle was to become the ducal residence and seat of the Visconti court. The castle was dismantled by order of the Milanese authorities after the demise of Visconti rule in 1447.

10. Gian Galeazzo Visconti (1351–1402) was married to Isabelle (1348–72), daughter of the French king John the Good, in 1360. The couple's only surviving offspring was their daughter Valentina Visconti (1371–1408), who eventually married into the French royal family and became the Duchess of Orleans.

11. Gian Galeazzo was invested with the title of Duke of Milan in 1395 after protracted negotiations with the imperial authorities. On the significance of this title for the Visconti, the best source is now Jane Black, "Giangaleazzo Visconti and the Ducal Title," in *Communes and Despots in Medieval and Renaissance Italy*, ed. John E. Law and Bernadette Paton (Farnham, UK, 2010), 119–30.

12. A passage inscribed on Gian Galeazzo's funeral monument in the Certosa di Pavia reads ". . . Hierosolymis sacellum et aras erexit . . .": see Otto Aicher, *Theatrum funebre* (Salzburg, 1673), 189.

13. One hundred and twenty-five years are reckoned from the establishment of Visconti rule in Milan in 1277 to the death of Gian Galeazzo in 1402, a period of almost unbroken territorial conquest and expansionism. This was followed by the dismemberment of the duchy under the nominal rule of Gian Galeazzo's elder son, Giovanni Maria (1388–1412).

14. Decembrio records the date, time, and place of Filippo Maria Visconti's birth with the exactitude required by Suetonian biography: cf. Suetonius, *Augustus* 5. Such information was also important in determining the astrological calculations referred to in the next chapter.

15. On the special position enjoyed by Giovanni Antonio Rambaldi at the court of Filippo Maria Visconti, see Decembrio's remarks in chapters 46 and 47 below. More information on Rambaldi's career can be found in Maria Francesca Baroni, "I cancellieri di Giovanni Maria e di Filippo Maria Visconti," *Nuova rivista storica* 50 (1966): 367–428, at 412–13.

16. Facino Cane (1360–1412), formerly a condottiere in the service of Gian Galeazzo Visconti, used his private army to build a power base after the latter's death in 1402. Taking full advantage of the collapse of the Visconti system, Cane gradually occupied large portions of the duchy, eventually becoming its effective coruler along with the young duke Giovanni Maria. He took control of Pavia in 1410. See *DBI* 17:791–801, and below, chapters 38 and 40.

17. Giovanni Maria was assassinated on May 16, 1412, in a conspiracy orchestrated by the heirs of Bernabò Visconti. Facino Cane died of natural causes a few hours later on the same day.

18. The date of birth of Beatrice Cane (d. 1418) is uncertain, but she was probably born circa 1372. The chronicler Andrea Biglia (1395–1435) writes that in 1412 she was old enough to be young Filippo Maria's mother: see Biglia, col. 38. For her ultimate fate, see chapter 39 below.

19. The date May 16, 1412, here must necessarily be wrong: see note 17 above. Perhaps Decembrio meant to write *Iulias* rather than *Iunias*. In this case the actual date would be June 15. On that day in fact, almost one

month after the events of May 16, Filippo Maria appeared with his troops before the walls of Milan and began military operations against his enemies: see Cognasso, 156.

20. A major programmatic statement that reflects Decembrio's intention to follow Suetonian organizational principles in presenting his material: cf. Suetonius, *Augustus* 9.1.

21. See chapter 19 below.

22. Decembrio's sentence reworks the opening words of Suetonius, *Augustus* 10. The following chapters (12–26), corresponding to *Augustus* 10–20, rapidly review the various wars conducted by Filippo Maria throughout his career.

23. Decembrio summarizes here events described in much greater detail in Biglia, cols. 39–40.

24. The two men were captured in August 1416 and perished soon thereafter: cf. Biglia, cols. 43–44.

25. Decembrio is very rapidly describing Filippo Maria's reconquest of the territories formerly ruled by his father. Many of these (including Lodi, Como, and Piacenza) had been occupied after 1402 by local strongmen, such as those mentioned in this chapter. For a recent account of Filippo Maria's gradual restoration of Visconti rule throughout the duchy, see Federica Cengarle, *Immagine di potere e prassi di governo* (Rome, 2006): the study details on pages 19, 23, and 140 how Filippo Maria dealt with Loterio Rusca.

26. On Filippo Arcelli and his brother Bartolomeo, see *DBI* 3:751–52; Cengarle, *Immagine di potere*, 19–21, 136.

27. Fondulo (1370–1425) was a mercenary soldier who had seized control of Cremona and made himself its ruler by force of arms in 1406: see *DBI* 48:586–89; for his ultimate fate, see below, chapter 40.

28. Cremona fell to Filippo Maria in 1420; Bergamo and Brescia also came under Visconti rule in a series of closely related maneuvers that unfolded from 1419 to 1421.

29. A reference to the battle of Montichiari, October 8, 1420: see below, note 62.

30. According to Biglia, col. 49, Parma willingly returned to Visconti rule after a brief period (1409–20) under Niccolò d'Este. Reggio remained under Este control, thanks largely to Venetian mediation, as a fief held from Filippo Maria Visconti: see Cognasso, 188–89; Cengarle, *Immagine di potere*, 48, 95–96, and 141.

31. The reference is to an earlier, unsuccessful attempt (1418) by Filippo Maria's forces to cower Genoa into submission: see Cognasso, 184–86.

32. Genoa came under Visconti rule in 1421; Decembrio's account of these events closely follows, but considerably condenses, the narrative to be found in Biglia, cols. 57–60. On Tommaso Fregoso and his brother Battista, see *DBI* 50:387–88, 448–51.

33. Significantly, this is the first mention of Carmagnola's role in the almost unbroken string of military victories that characterized Filippo Maria's early years in power. In fact, Carmagnola's brilliant generalship was instrumental in assuring Visconti success in most of the instances related so far: see *DBI* 15:582–87.

34. Carmagnola's forces defeated the invaders at Arbedo on June 30, 1422: see the detailed account of the battle given by Biglia, cols. 55–57. The Suetonian passage Decembrio refers to can be found in *Augustus* 95.

35. The battle took place on July 28, 1424. As we will learn later (chap. 31), Carlo Malatesta was captured and taken prisoner. For a detailed description of the battle and its aftermath, see Biglia, cols. 66–69.

36. In keeping with the principle of *brevitas* typical of Suetonian biography (see above, chap. 10), Decembrio's coverage of these events is extremely compressed. The discussions leading to the Florentine-Venetian military alliance date from the second half of 1424; the defection of Carmagnola to Venice occurred in early 1425; there followed the fall of Brescia to the Venetians in 1426, with Filippo Maria subsequently forced to ratify the Treaty of Venice; his failure to respect the terms of this treaty brought on the decisive battle at Maclodio, October 12, 1427; Piccinino saved Lucca by defeating the Florentines on December 2, 1430. Thus in the space of a few lines Decembrio dispatches more than six years of complex diplomatic, military, and political history, on which see Cognasso, 213–65.

37. The pact between the Houses of Savoy and Visconti was signed on December 2, 1427. The move was a desperate attempt on the part of Filippo Maria to shore up his position after the defeat at Maclodio. For his relations with his second wife, Maria of Savoy (1411–69), see below, chapter 39.

38. The reference is to the Treaty of Ferrara (April 19, 1428), by the terms of which Filippo Maria was forced to accept the loss of Brescia and Bergamo to Venice.

39. Decembrio described this battle (June 21–22, 1431) in detail in the concluding pages of his *Panegyric in Praise of Milan*, written in 1435: see Petraglione, "Il *De laudibus* ."

40. Carmagnola's arrest, trial, and execution took place between March and May 1432. On Carmagnola, a controversial figure, see further chapters 27 and 29, and Battistella, "Una lettera inedita."

41. Piccinino defeated and captured Corner at Delebio in November 1432. For the prisoner's fate see chapter 42 below.

42. The peace terms are those proclaimed at Ferrara, April 1433; Piccinino's victory at Imola occurred on August 28, 1434.

43. Genoa had been under Visconti rule since 1421: see chapter 15 above. The Genoese fleet defeated the naval forces of King Alfonso of Aragon off the island of Ponza on August 5, 1435. Alfonso and his entourage were taken prisoner and conveyed to Milan. The revolt of Genoa was caused less by Genoese hubris than by popular indignation at Filippo Maria Visconti's generous treatment of Alfonso and his release of the king in October 1435, on which see chapter 31 below. Cf. the version of these events provided by Leonardo Bruni in his *Memoirs*: Leonardo Bruni, *History of the Florentine People*, ed. and trans. James Hankins and D. J. W. Bradley (Cambridge, MA, 2001–7), 3:380.

44. Decembrio had already produced a detailed account of the career in arms of Niccolò Piccinino (1386–1444), Filippo Maria Visconti's preferred military commander: see his *Panegyricus in funere illustris Nicolai Picenini ad cives Mediolanenses*, ed. Felice Fossati, in *RIS*, 2nd ser., vol. 20.1 (Bologna, 1958), 991–1009. For a parallel account of Piccinino's 1436 expedition to Genoa, see page 999 of this funeral oration, written in 1444.

Therein Decembrio had already criticized the Visconti officials in similar language for surrendering the citadel early in 1436, before Piccinino's arrival: Genoa, he wrote, was Piccinino's for the taking ". . . si arcem urbis osservantibus tanta in sustinendo praesidio spes fuisset, quanta illi in mittendo celeritas affuit."

45. On the humanist and statesman Francesco Barbaro (1390–1454), see *DBI* 6:101–3. His heroic defense of Brescia in 1439 is related in detail by Biondo Flavio, *Historiarum ab inclinatione romani imperii decades* (Basel, 1531), 534–40, 547–48.

46. Once again, Decembrio has compressed five years of complex Italian history, 1437–41, into a short paragraph. The main events referred to here include (1) Piccinino's siege of Brescia and the valiant defense of that city organized by the Venetians under Francesco Barbaro, June 1438 to April 1439; (2) Piccinino's successful sweep through Venetian territory, culminating with his occupation of Verona, November 17, 1439; (3) Francesco Sforza's immediate retaking of Verona for Venice, November 20, 1439; (4) Piccinino's Tuscan expedition, ending with his decisive defeat at Anghiari, June 29, 1440; (5) Sforza's marriage to Bianca Maria Visconti, October 1441; (6) the peace of Cavriana, November 20, 1441, which ended Filippo Maria Visconti's fourth Venetian war by reestablishing the *status quo ante* in Lombardy (except for the cession of Cremona to his now son-in-law Francesco Sforza). Decembrio provides a more detailed account of the events of 1438 to 1440 in his *Panegyricus in funere illustris Nicolai Picenini*, in *RIS*, 2nd ser., vol. 20.1, 1001–8.

47. Decembrio's war-driven narrative jumps ahead here to 1446, the year in which Filippo Maria unleashed his last campaign against Venice. The initial objective was Cremona, but on September 28 the Visconti forces were defeated in a major battle at Casalmaggiore. This military disaster left Filippo Maria at the mercy of his enemies: he died in Milan on August 13, 1447. On these events and those mentioned in the previous chapter, see Cognasso, 319–83.

48. On which see chapters 15 and 18 above.

49. This statement has affinities with Suetonius (cf. *Aug.* 20: "Externa bella duo omnino per se gessit. . . . Reliqua per legatos administra-

vit . . ."), but it is also grounded in the concrete practices of surveillance
and control described below in chapter 28. See in particular Maria Nadia
Covini, "Per la storia delle milizie viscontee: I famigliari armigeri di
Filippo Maria Visconti," in L'età dei Visconti, ed. Luisa Chiappa Mauri,
Laura De Angelis Cappabianca, Patrizia Mainoni (Milan, 1993), 35–63, at
56–62. As Covini points out, these practices are independently confirmed
in the surviving documentation, e.g., Stilus cancellariae: Formulario visconteo-
sforzesco, ed. Alfio Rosario Natale (Milan, 1979), 41–42. For further docu-
mentary confirmation, see Cengarle, Immagine di potere, 115.

50. On Trotti see Covini, "Per la storia delle milizie viscontee," 55.

51. Arasmino Trivulzio (1384–1459) was indeed one of Filippo Maria
Visconti's most trusted military captains and advisors: see Covini, "Per la
storia delle milizie viscontee," 38, 48, 49, 54–55, 58–62. Appointed governor of Genoa in 1435, he was among the Visconti officials who took refuge in the citadel when the city broke into open rebellion on December
27: see chapter 22 above, where Decembrio—without mentioning Trivulzio by name—contrasts the Visconti officials' lack of courage with the
heroism of Niccolò Piccinino.

52. Giorgio Annoni's career as an agent of ducal policy is detailed in the
relevant entry of the DBI 3:358–59. Documents dating from 1442 onward
show Annoni reporting to Filippo Maria Visconti on the activities of the
Visconti armies in the field: see, for example, Documenti diplomatici tratti
dagli archivi milanesi, ed. Luigi Osio (Milan, 1864–72), 3.2:280, 281, 294,
444. See too the general profile in Franca Leverotti, Diplomazia e governo
dello stato (Pisa, 1992), 114–16.

53. Originally from Parma, Antonello Arcimboldi (1398–1439) moved to
Milan with his family in 1420 after Parma (as described by Decembrio in
chapter 14 above) came under Visconti rule. In Milan he served as a condottiere under Filippo Maria Visconti and later rose to become one of
the duke's closest associates: see Covini, "Per la storia delle milizie viscontee," 56–61. He was the brother of the high-profile jurist Nicolò Arcimboldi, mentioned below in chapter 34.

54. On Angelo della Pergola (d. 1428), see DBI 37:135–40; Luigi dal
Verme (d. 1449) entered the service of Filippo Maria Visconti in 1436.

He was the son of the more famous Iacopo dal Verme (d. 1409): for father and son see *DBI* 32:262–67, 273–77.

55. That is, in the *Panegyricus in funere illustris Nicolai Picenini*, on which see notes 44 and 46 above. Piccinino was the leading representative of the military tradition stemming from Braccio da Montone (1368–1424) and as such Francesco Sforza's main rival at the Visconti court: see *DBI* 83:175–77.

56. Bernardino Ubaldini della Carda (d. 1437) entered the Visconti service in 1431 and figured prominently in the 1432 Battle of San Romano, later immortalized in the famous series of paintings by Paolo Uccello.

57. At the time of his death (1428), the condottiere Sicco da Montagnana held the exalted title of *marescallus exercitus*: see Covini, "Per la storia delle milizie viscontee," 37, 49, 51, 54. "The one more useful for his counsel" is presumably Guido Torelli, on whom see below, chapter 64.

58. Not to be confused with the famed condottiere of the same name (*DBI* 1:639–42) who died in 1409. On Alberico da Barbiano junior (d. 1433), see *DBI* 6:196–98: captured by the Milanese at Zagonara (chap. 17 above), he was subsequently set free and became a loyal servant of the Visconti cause.

59. Niccolò Mauruzzi da Tolentino (d. 1435) is best known as the Florentine commander whose equestrian portrait by Andrea del Castagno graces the wall of Santa Maria del Fiore in Florence. He did however serve under Filippo Maria Visconti for a brief period (1429–31) before returning to lead the Florentine forces to defeat in his final battle.

60. A selective cavalcade of names, some obscure, some famous: Luigi da Sanseverino (d. 1447) entered Filippo Maria's service in 1438, late in his career; the future Marquis of Monferrato Guglielmo Paleologo VIII (1420–84) was signed on in 1445, according to the entry in *DBI* 60:769–73; Carlo Gonzaga (1413/23–56), the second son of the Marquis of Mantova Gianfrancesco Gonzaga (chap. 23 above), served under his father, who joined the Visconti in 1438 (*DBI* 57:693–96); Ladislao (sometimes Venceslao) Guinigi da Lucca (b. 1404) was the son of Paolo Guinigi, the man who ruled Lucca from 1400 to 1430; Pietro Giampaolo Orsini (d. 1443) served the Visconti from 1435; Ludovico Colonna (d. 1436) served

from 1428 (*DBI* 27:361–65); Italiano Armuzzi, also called Taliano Furlano, (d.1446) joined the Visconti service in 1438.

61. Filippo Maria Visconti nourished a deep and abiding interest in emblematics. The evidence shows that he frequently sought the advice of his humanists on heraldry and its uses. On at least one occasion, circa 1430–31, he asked Decembrio to design a new device, and Decembrio obliged, proposing a palm branch flanked on either side by a lioness: for details, see Petrucci, *Petri Candidi Decembrii Epistolarum iuvenilium libri octo*, 373–92. Among the devices Decembrio mentions in this chapter, two are well-known: the Visconti serpent (n. 3 above), and the solar motif once ascribed to Petrarch but now thought to be of French derivation through Gian Galeazzo Visconti's marriage to Isabelle of Valois (n. 10 above); see Federica Cengarle, "Il sole ducale (1430): A proposito di una divisa viscontea," in *Il ducato*, 230–46.

62. Lodovico Migliorati (d.1428), an ally of the Malatesta, was taken prisoner after his defeat at Montichiari, October 8, 1420: see above, chapter 13. He was released from captivity in March 1421.

63. On Filippo Maria's tender feelings for his former tutor and protector Carlo Malatesta (1368–1429), see Biglia, col. 69. For the aging condottiere's defeat at Zagonara, see above, chapter 17 and note 35.

64. See chapter 21 above. Filippo Maria's surprise release of his prisoners in October 1435 signified a complete reorientation of his political alliances. At first hostile to Alfonso of Aragon's designs on the Kingdom of Naples, he now struck a deal whereby he offered his support to the Aragonese cause: see Francesco Somaini, "Filippo Maria e la svolta del 1435," in *Il ducato*, 107–66. The most immediate result of this policy shift was the revolt of Genoa.

65. Decembrio alludes here to the battle of Varna, November 10, 1444.

66. John VIII Paleologus visited Milan in 1424: see Giorgio Giulini, *Memorie spettanti alla storia . . . di Milano* (Milan, 1854–57), 6:267.

67. Sigismund came to Milan in 1431 at Filippo Maria's invitation. He was crowned in the Church of Sant'Ambrogio by the archbishop of Milan, Bartolomeo Capra, on November 25 of that year. Filippo Maria did not attend the ceremony and famously avoided meeting his illustrious

guest; see *Der Briefwechsel des Enea Silvio Piccolomini*, II Abteilung, ed. Rudolf Wolkan, Vienna, 1912 (= *Fontes rerum Austriacarum, Diplomataria et acta*, 67), 171: ". . . superbus tamen Sigismundo Filippus fuit, qui nec alloqui suum dominum nec dextram porrigere dignatus est."

68. Stefano de'Federici (d. 1440), long-standing ducal chamberlain (*ducalis camerarius*), also known as "Todeschino," was an influential figure. His role as a corrupt official in charge of the distribution of ecclesiastical benefices is confirmed by Enea Silvio Piccolomini: see *Der Briefwechsel des Enea Silvio Piccolomini*, I Abteilung, ed. Rudolf Wolkan, Vienna, 1909 (= *Fontes rerum Austriacarum, Diplomataria et acta*, 61), 118.

69. Oldrado Lampugnani (1380–1460) was another powerful player in the intrigues surrounding the Duke of Milan; see Biglia, col. 72: "Multo vero civitati nostrae id salubrius, eiusmodi homines nunquam natos esse . . . per quos nihil ad Ducem referri posset, quam quod placere arbitrarentur" (It would have been far better for our city if such men had never been born . . . for on account of them nothing could be communicated to the duke except what they deemed appropriate for his ears). See also the entry in *DBI* 63:280–83, as well as Maria Nadia Covini, "Le difficoltà politiche e finanziarie degli ultimi anni del dominio," in *Il ducato*, 71–105: at page 93 Covini notes Lampugnani's removal from power after 1437.

70. Decembrio's father was Uberto Decembrio (d. 1427), the well-known humanist and translator — with the aid of Manuel Chrysoloras — of Plato's *Republic*. Uberto also served as secretary to Giovanni Maria Visconti: see Baroni, "I cancellieri," 389–90. Under Filippo Maria, he was appointed *podestà* of Treviglio in 1422, and his appointment was later reconfirmed, possibly thanks to his son. See also below, chapter 40.

71. The decree was issued in 1432: see Covini, "Per la storia delle milizie viscontee," 44–45.

72. The careers of Giovanni Francesco Gallina (1370–1442) and Franchino Castiglioni (d. 1462) are detailed in Baroni, "I cancellieri," 398–400, 402–3, as well as in the entries in *DBI* 51:672–74 and *DBI* 22:148–52. Both men were members of Filippo Maria's *Consiglio segreto*, or Privy Council, on which see Francesco Cognasso, "Istituzioni comunali e

signorili di Milano sotto i Visconti," in *Storia di Milano* (Milan, 1955), 6:489–92, and Franca Leverotti, "La cancelleria dei Visconti et degli Sforza signori di Milano," in *Chancelleries et chanceliers des princes à la fin du Moyen Âge*, ed. Guido Castelnuovo and Olivier Mattéoni (Chambéry, 2011), 39–52.

73. The jurists Nicolò Arcimboldi (1404–59) and Giovanni Feruffini were members of Filippo Maria's *Consiglio di giustizia*, which had jurisdiction over civil cases: see Leverotti, "La cancelleria," 51. Arcimboldi is by far the better known of the two: for details see his entry in *DBI* 3:779–81. Arcimboldi was a personal friend of Decembrio's and the dedicatee of the latter's *Historia peregrina*, on which see Zaccaria, "Sulle opere," 18–20.

74. Recent research substantially confirms Decembrio's picture: see Stefania Buganza, "Note su Filippo Maria Visconti committente d'arte," in *Il ducato*, 247–84, at 249–53 (Castle of Porta Giovia), 253 (Cusago), 253 (Vigevano), 255 (Pizzighettone). Buganza suggests that Decembrio's description of the fortress of Pizzighettone cannot be documented, but independent confirmation comes from the Sforza secretary and historian Giovanni Simonetta; see Simonetta, 303: "est enim id oppidum in Cremonensium finibus ad Adduae ripam positum ingenti murorum et altitudine et latitudine a Philippo duce conditum" (that fortified town is located on the banks of the river Adda, just inside Cremonese territory; it is characterized by the towering and massively thick defensive walls erected by Filippo Maria Visconti).

75. Buganza, "Note," 256–70. confirms most of the details contained in this chapter: see in particular 265–67 (on the Duomo of Milan), and 268 (on the recycled columns used in the construction of the *chiostro grande*, or *chiostro dei morti*, located in the Dominican monastery at Sant' Eustorgio).

76. Decembrio here opens an entirely new subject area, signaling the change in words that deliberately echo Suetonius, *Augustus* 61.1.

77. See above, chapter 8 and notes 17 and 18. For political expediency, the marriage was hastily contracted in the second half of May 1412, while the actual ceremony took place two months later, on July 24: see Cognasso, 155.

78. See above, chapter 19 and note 37.

79. A serious mistake: the newborn child (and future Duke of Milan, 1466–76) was named Galeazzo Maria, as decided by his grandfather Filippo Maria Visconti; on the strategic implications of the name choice, see Simonetta, 139.

80. Biglia, cols. 50–52, relates the tale in a manner that is highly sympathetic to Beatrice, stressing her innocence: at col. 51 he describes her as "Foemina quidem, si vitae ac morum ratio spectetur, nullo coniugio indigna" (A woman who, if we consider her high moral principles and exemplary life, was eminently worthy of any husband). See *DBI* 7:343–47.

81. For Filippo Maria's mother, Caterina Visconti (1368–1404), see above, chapter 4. Her death in mysterious circumstances gave rise to rumors she had been murdered. Cabrino Fondulo's surrender of Cremona in 1420 is covered above, in chapter 13. As for Sperone da Pietrasanta, he served as a highly placed official in the Visconti administration before being abruptly dismissed in 1431. According to Felice Fossati (in Decembrio, *Vita Philippi Mariae*, 244–47), Decembrio is our sole source for the story of Sperone's execution.

82. Uberto Decembrio was arrested and jailed sometime toward the end of the year 1410. He remained incarcerated until the death of Facino Cane in May 1412: see Baroni, "I cancellieri," 389–90.

83. Gabriele (1385–1408) was the illegitimate son of Gian Galeazzo Visconti and his lover Agnese Mantegazza. Antonio too (b. 1402) was an illegimate son of Gian Galeazzo, but born of a different, possibly peasant mother. The date of his death is unknown. See also chapter 71 below.

84. Giacomo, born circa 1405, died sometime after 1451. In 1429 he was legitimized by Filippo Maria Visconti and made his heir, but with certain restrictions, including the precedence in the line of succession to be accorded to Filippo Maria's own children, should any be born from his recent marriage with Maria of Savoy. For further details, see Fossati, in Decembrio, *Vita Philippi Mariae*, 252–57. See also chapter 71 below.

85. On the ominous significance of silence as the exclusive prerogative of the prince, see Elias Canetti, *Crowds and Power*, trans. Carol Stewart (New York, 1973), 333.

86. See above, chapter 20. Corner (1374–1439) remained a prisoner for seven years and left behind an account of the appalling treatment that was meted out to him during his captivity: see *DBI* 29:210–12. According to Biondo Flavio, *Historiarum ab inclinatione Romani imperii decades*, 472, Filippo Maria announced Corner's death in 1433 in order to circumvent the terms of the recently concluded peace treaty with Venice (n. 42, above), one of the conditions of which was that both sides immediately proceed to release all prisoners captured during the war.

87. On Giovanni Carlo Visconti, see chapters 8 and 11 above. Giovanni Carlo had two sons; it is not known to which of them Decembrio is referring.

88. On Cabrino Fondulo, see chapters 13 and 40 above. Filippo Maria evidently believed that children deserved to be punished for the sins of their fathers.

89. Filippo Maria's ordering of priorities will be familiar to readers of Machiavelli: see Niccolò Machiavelli, *Lettere*, ed. Franco Gaeta (Milan, 1961), 505, for Machiavelli's confession to Francesco Vettori (April 16, 1527): ". . . amo la patria mia più dell'anima. . . ." But the expression of such sentiments had become common currency in Italian political circles at least a century earlier: see Riccardo Fubini, *Storiografia dell'umanesimo in Italia da Leonardo Bruni ad Annio da Viterbo* (Rome, 2003), 102.

90. The reference is to Amedeo, the son of Amedeo VIII of Savoy. According to Biglia, col. 155, Filippo Maria was deeply affected by his brother-in-law's premature death in 1431: "Philippus tam aegre mortem tulit, ut tres menses diem fugiens nullum posset praeterquam de juvene verbum audire" (Filippo was so shaken by the death that for three months thereafter he holed himself up and would hear of nothing that did not pertain to the young man).

91. The reference is to the events of 1439, which ended badly for Filippo Maria Visconti: see chapter 23 above and Cognasso, 333–37. Decembrio is our only source for this and the other anecdotes related in this chapter.

92. Decembrio is referring to talks held between Filippo Maria Visconti and leading citizens of Milan in the wake of the humiliating peace terms

negotiated with Venice at the end of 1426, on which see chapter 18 above. Biglia, cols. 92–94, offers a somewhat different version of the same incident.

93. The reference is to Filippo Maria's efforts, in 1429–30, to erect a chapel dedicated to Sant'Ansano in the Duomo of Siena: see Buganza, "Note," 256–57.

94. Ludovico Gonzaga (1412–78) entered the service of Filippo Maria Visconti as condottiere in 1436. He was restored to the graces of his father, Gianfrancesco I (1395–1444), after the latter deserted Venice and joined the Visconti service like his son: see chapter 23 above.

95. The career of the Ferrarese statesman Uguccione de'Contrari (1379–1448) is detailed in *DBI* 28:534–37. A close collaborator of Marquis Niccolò III d'Este, Uguccione was also much appreciated by the Venetians, due to his frequent involvement in diplomatic negotiations. He gained particular favor with Filippo Maria Visconti in the post-1441 period, when the latter was seeking to improve his relations with Venice: see, for example, Simonetta, 126–27.

96. For Sforza's marriage to Bianca Maria Visconti (1425–68) in October 1441, see above, chapter 23. The machinations Decembrio describes here — e.g., Bianca Maria's sojourn in Ferrara (October 1440–April 1441) and the rumors of her imminent betrothal to Leonello d'Este — are also related in Simonetta, 99.

97. The homoerotic overtones of this chapter shocked Leonello d'Este, the first reader of Decembrio's biography; see Leonello's letter to Decembrio, October 22, 1447, reproduced in the Appendix to the present volume. Decembrio's estranged brother Angelo, author of the *Politia litteraria*, also passed harsh judgment; see his marginal note to chapter 46, as published by Vincenzo Fera, "Filologia in casa Decembrio," in *I Decembrio*, 159: "Capitulum turpitudinis et infamie." Later readers, such as Paolo Giovio, notoriously chimed in. Yet what Decembrio describes here is arguably tame by Suetonian standards: cf., for example, Suetonius, *Tiberius* 43 and 44.

98. See note 5 on the text. The two earlier manuscripts read *cubiculo* (bedchamber); in the last of the three manuscripts corrected by the au-

thor, Decembrio himself filled a blank left by the copyist with the word *thoro* (bed).

99. In his correspondence, Decembrio himself describes Van Calven as a *ducalis camerarius* of exceptional ability: see Genoa, Biblioteca Universitaria, MS C.VII. 46, fol. 23v.

100. For the fiefs and concessions awarded to ducal favorites such as Andrea Birago and Giovanni Antonio Rambaldi, see Covini, "Le difficoltà politiche e finanziarie," 93. On Birago in general, see *DBI* 10:568–73.

101. For the conquest of Bergamo in 1419, see above, chapter 13.

102. Decembrio is referring *inter alios* to Giovanni Carlo Visconti (d. 1427), the grandson of Bernabò Visconti: see above, chapters 8, 11, and 42. After losing control of Monza, Giovanni Carlo turned to Sigismund as his best chance of reclaiming what he saw as his rightful inheritance. Filippo Maria's encounter with Sigismund at Cantù took place in November 1413: see Cognasso, 162–70.

103. Cf. Suetonius, *Augustus* 72.2: "Ex secessibus praecipue frequentavit . . . proxima urbi oppida" (For solitude he preferred to frequent . . . towns near Rome).

104. That is, by Galeazzo II and Gian Galeazzo Visconti, on both of whom see chapters 3 and 4 above.

105. Giulini, *Memorie spettanti*, 6:236, explains how Filippo Maria developed a system of secondary canals linking his favorite residences to a preexisting network of commercial waterways that included the *Naviglio Grande*, a canal that ran (and still runs) from the upper Ticino River into the heart of Milan. Giulini interprets *legia* as referring to a kind of horse-drawn coach or buggy, but according to the *Glossarium mediae et infimae latinitatis* (online at www.ducange.enc.sorbonne.fr), the word actually signifies a small boat. In the present case, the "skiff" appears to have been adaptable for travel on roads.

106. On Filippo Maria's visit to Cremona in 1427, see above, chapter 26.

107. The physical description of the subject is a staple of Suetonian biography; cf. Suetonius, *Augustus* 79: "Forma fuit eximia. . . ." As noted by

Giulio Zappa, *Verso Emmaus* (Milan, 1921), 63–64, there are significant borrowings here from Suetonius, *Tiberius* 68, e.g.: "Corpore fuit amplo atque robusto, statura quae iustam excederet . . . capillo pone occipitium summissiore ut cervicem etiam obtegeret" (His body was large and robust, his height above average . . . his hair hung down so low behind that it even covered up the back of his neck).

108. There are two surviving Pisanello portraits of Filippo Maria Visconti, one being a medal cast in bronze, the other a charcoal drawing now in the Louvre: see *The Renaissance Portrait from Donatello to Bellini*, ed. Keith Christiansen and Stefan Weppelmann (New Haven and London, 2011), 244–48. It is not known to which of these portraits Decembrio is referring, if to either, for Pisanello is also reported to have executed a painted portrait of the Duke of Milan, now lost.

109. On this ban, see chapter 48 above.

110. Food is another standard Suetonian subject; cf. Suetonius, *Augustus* 76: "Cibi—nam ne haec quidem omiserim—minimi erat atque vulgaris fere" (Of foods—for I would not have us omit even this subject—he partook sparsely, and even showed a preference for the most common dishes).

111. The man in question is presumably Giorgio Aicardi, known as "Scaramuccia," on whom see Giulini, *Memorie spettanti*, 6:361–63, as well as the entry in *DBI* 1:514, and more recently Buganza, "Note," 268, 269, 271. The reasons why Filippo Maria was so fond of this Scaramuccia are explained by Enea Silvio Piccolomini in his *De viris illustribus*, ed. Adrian Van Heck (Vatican City, 1991), 4–5, where we learn that as a boy Scaramuccia was with Filippo Maria's brother when he was murdered, witnessed the bloody scene at close range, and was later found weeping over his master's body.

112. Plato repeatedly stresses in his *Republic* (413d, 486d, 490d, 494b, 535c) the importance of memory as a qualification for government. It should be noted that in the late 1430s Decembrio—building on the earlier work of his father (n. 70 above)—produced a widely-read humanistic translation of Plato's *Republic*: see James Hankins, *Plato in the Italian Re-*

naissance, 2 vols. (Leiden, 1990), 1:117–54; Zaggia, "La versione latina," 7–55.

113. Filippo Pellizzone, without a doubt the best-known of the physicians surrounding Filippo Maria Visconti, was among other things the dedicatee of Guarino's *Vita Platonis* (1430): see *L'epistolario di Guarino Veronese*, ed. Remigio Sabbadini (Venice, 1915–19), 2: 88–90 and 3: 269. He was also the recipient of one of the early manuscripts of Decembrio's translation of Plato's *Republic* (Milan, Biblioteca Ambrosiana, R 75 sup.), inscribed "M. Philippo Mediolanensi phisico": see Zaggia, "La versione latina," 22–23.

114. Cf. Suetonius, *Titus* 3.2: "Armorum et equitandi peritissimus. . . ."

115. See chapter 27 above.

116. Vergil, *The Aeneid*, 7.277, as translated by H. Rushton Fairclough (Cambridge, MA, 1969) in the Loeb Classical Library.

117. Legendary mountains traditionally thought to lie somewhere to the far North of the known world; later humanists sometimes identified them with the Ural Mountains.

118. Cf. Suetonius, *Augustus* 83: ". . . ad pilam primo folliculumque transit. . . ."

119. Decembrio alludes here to a deck of Tarot cards designed by Marziano da Tortona (d. 1423/1425). On Marziano's career as Visconti secretary see Baroni, "I cancellieri," 394–95. Though a man of vast cultural interests and an early Dante scholar (see below, chapter 62), Marziano was no miniaturist. The actual painting of the Tarot cards was in all likelihood the work of the artist Michelino da Besozzo (ca. 1370–ca. 1450): see Buganza, "Note," in *Il ducato*, 275–77.

120. Homer, *Iliad* 23.87–88; it should be noted that Decembrio was something of an early Homer enthusiast: he not only translated books I–IV and X of the *Iliad*, but also compiled an accompanying biography of the author. On both the translation and the *Vita Homeri*, see Zaccaria, "Le opere," 22–25, 43–46; and Zaggia, "La versione latina," 27–28.

121. Not to be confused with Giorgio Aicardi, known as "Scaramuccia," listed in chapter 53 above. Scaramuccia Balbo was a trusted secretary and diplomat in the ducal service: see, for example, Simonetta, 178, for his delicate mission to Francesco Sforza in 1447.

122. Decembrio himself wrote an early commentary on the sonnets of Petrarch (now lost) as well as a recently rediscovered *Vita del Petrarca* dedicated to Filippo Maria Visconti: see Zaggia, "Appunti," 349–53.

123. Throughout the 1430s, Decembrio was directly involved in the production of vernacular versions of ancient historians at the Visconti court. During this time he personally translated the *Historia Alexandri* of Curtius Rufus and the *Commentarii* of Julius Caesar. His friend and fellow humanist Antonio da Rho (see below, chap. 63) translated the *De vita Caesarum* of Suetonius. See Zaggia, "Appunti," 189–205, 321–28.

124. On the prolific and learned humanist Antonio da Rho (ca. 1398–ca. 1450), see the entry in *DBI* 3:574–77, as well as David Rutherford, *Early Renaissance Invective and the Controversies of Antonio da Rho* (Tempe, AZ, 2005). Decembrio apparently felt that his friend Antonio had been insufficiently rewarded for his literary efforts.

125. "Franciscus Barbula" is code for Decembrio's archrival and sworn enemy, the redoubtable Hellenist Francesco Filelfo (1398–1481), on whom see the entry in *DBI* 47:613–26. Filelfo's arrival in Milan in 1439 marked a turning point in Decembrio's career, as he gradually lost the cultural supremacy he had exercised at the Visconti court up to that time. Decembrio's bitter remarks here betray his frustration: by the mid-1440s Filelfo had secured the position of preeminence in Milan that he was to keep for the rest of his long life.

126. On Cyriac of Ancona (1391–1452), the inveterate traveler and collector of ancient lore, see the entry in *DBI* 84:361–64, as well as Cyriac of Ancona, *Life and Early Travels*, ed. and trans. Charles Mitchell, Edward W. Bodnar, and Clive Foss (Cambridge, MA, 2015), and idem, *Later Travels*, ed. and trans. Edward W. Bodnar with Clive Foss (Cambridge, MA, 2003). Cyriac had only sporadic contact with Milan, where he seems to have been well received. Decembrio's bile here may be a further effect of his hatred of Filelfo, who was a promoter of Cyriac's prospects:

see, for example, Filelfo's letters to Francesco Barbaro and to Leonardo Giustiniani, December 30, 1443, in Francesco Filelfo, *Collected Letters*, ed. Jeroen De Keyser (Alessandria, 2015), 1:300. Filelfo also maintained a healthy correspondence with Cyriac: see ibid., 63–66, 70, 81, 126–27, 250, 254, 262–63, 316–18, 352–53.

127. Once again Decembrio seems to be settling scores with enemies and rivals; for his hatred of Tommaso Morroni of Rieti (1408–76), see Poggio Bracciolini, *Lettere*, 3 vols. (Florence, 1984–87), 2:303–8 (letter of Decembrio to Poggio, April 14, 1438), 303: "Equidem monstrum quoddam iampridem novi infame, impudicum, Thomam scilicet Reatinum, vita turpi, moribus obscenis . . ." (Indeed I have known that repulsive monster Tommaso of Rieti for some time: he is truly a shameless lowlife of filthy and obscene habits . . .). For a more balanced view, see Biondo Flavio, *Italy Illuminated*, ed. and trans. Jeffrey A. White, 2 vols. (Cambridge, MA, 2005–16), 1:220: "Rieti now boasts Tommaso Morroni, a man blessed with eloquence and an extraordinary memory." It is true however that Morroni failed to find favor in Milan under Filippo Maria Visconti: see Zaggia, "Appunti," 370–75. For his later fortunes there under Francesco Sforza, see Franca Leverotti, *Diplomazia e governo*, 210–13; and *DBI* 77:202–5.

128. Decembrio is presumably referring to the notorious prodigy Ferdinando (or Fernando) of Cordova. Widely regarded as a charlatan, Ferdinando found a valiant defender in Lorenzo Valla: see the latter's *Epistolae*, ed. Ottavio Besomi and Mariangela Regoliosi (Padua, 1984), 232, 258–62. John Monfasani, *Fernando of Cordova: A Biographical and Intellectual Profile* (Philadelphia, 1992), also takes a more positive view. According to Etruscan legend, Tages was the founder of the art of divination: see Cicero, *De divinatione* 2.50–51.

129. Leverotti, "La cancelleria," 51, lists both men as members of the *Consiglio segreto*. On Guarnerio Castiglioni (d. 1460), see Gigliola Soldi Rondinini, "Ambasciatori e ambascerie al tempo di Filippo Maria Visconti (1412–26)," *Nuova rivista storica* 49 (1965): 313–44, at 325–27, as well as the entry in *DBI* 22:161–66. Castiglioni was a correspondent and personal friend of Decembrio's, with whom he shared a love of classical learning; see Elena Maderna, "Una lettera inedita di Guarnerio Castiglioni a Pier Candido Decembrio," *Libri e documenti* 4 (1978): 17–25, and Tino Foffano,

"Inediti di Guarnerio Castiglioni da codici ambrosiani," *Aevum* 81 (2007): 683–703; he was also the dedicatee of one of Decembrio's early literary works, the *Grammaticon:* see Zaccaria, "Le opere," 20. On Guido Torelli (1379–1449), see Rondinini, "Ambasciatori," 334; Simonetta, 13–14, 21–22, 29, 33; Maria Nadia Covini, *L'esercito del duca: Organizzazione militare e istituzioni al tempo degli Sforza* (Rome, 1998), 79, 95.

130. The careers of both Gaspare Visconti (d. 1436) and Iacopo Isolani (1356–1431) began in the period prior to that of Filippo Maria Visconti, under whose reign they nevertheless remained important figures. On Gaspare Visconti, see Rondinini, "Ambasciatori," 316–18. On Cardinal Iacopo Isolani, governor of Genoa from 1424 to 1428, see the entry in *DBI* 62:659–63.

131. On Marsilio da Carrara (d. 1435), son of Francesco Novello, the last Carrara to rule Padova, see the entry in *DBI* 20:693–95. On Antonio Bossi, see *DBI* 13:286–87; Rondinini, "Ambasciatori," 327, as well as Covini, "Per la storia delle milizie viscontee," 37.

132. On Giovanni Corvini d'Arezzo (ca. 1370–1438), see Baroni, "I cancellieri," 385–87; Rondinini, "Ambasciatori," 318–19; and the entry in *DBI* 29:828–32. Corradino Vimercati is listed as a member of the *Consiglio segreto* by Leverotti, "La cancelleria," 51; for his role as secretary and ambassador from 1410 into the 1440s, see Baroni, "I cancellieri," 392–94, and Rondinini, "Ambasciatori," 334–35.

133. For the influence exercised at court by Zanino Riccio (d. 1428), see Baroni, "I cancellieri," 395–97; Rondinini, "Ambasciatori," 331–32. Baroni, ibid., 406–8, also documents the careers of Lanzalotto and Luigi Crotti; the two brothers are listed as members of the *Consiglio segreto* by Leverotti, "La cancelleria," 51.

134. Not too much is known about Siriato; for Lampugnani, see above, chapter 33.

135. The career of Brunoro Gambara da Brescia (d. 1468) is detailed in *DBI* 52:36–37; among other things, he was the husband of the Veronese humanist Ginevra Nogarola (1419–64), who bore him five sons: see Rino Avesani, *Verona nel Quattrocento: La civiltà delle lettere* (Verona, 1984), 60–68. Francesco Landriani (ca. 1410–71) was a powerful figure at the Mila-

nese court: see, for example, Simonetta, 144, 180; Cognasso, 325, 340–42, 349. Decembrio's spiteful comments here are probably dictated by his jealousy of Landriani's success in winning ducal favor.

136. The identity of Giovanni Balbi is uncertain. Both Giovanni Matteo Bottigella (1410–86) and Tommaso Tebaldi da Bologna (1415–75) are on the other hand well-known figures; for details on their careers and further bibliography, see Massimo Zaggia, Pier Luigi Mulas, and Matteo Ceriana, *Giovanni Matteo Bottigella: Cortigiano, uomo di lettere e committente d'arte* (Città di Castello, 1997), 8–12 and passim.

137. Ottaviano Ubaldini della Carda (b. 1423) was the son and successor of the condottiere Bernardino Ubaldini (above, chapter 29); on the latter, also reputed to be the biological father of Federico da Montefeltro, see Simonetta, 9, 14, 151. Cristoforo Torelli (d. 1460) was the son of the aforementioned Visconti counselor and condottiere Guido Torelli: on both father and son, see Covini, *L'esercito del duca*, 79.

138. The career of Iñigo d'Avalos (d. 1484) is profiled in *DBI* 4:636–37. He was among the Aragonese leaders defeated at the battle of Ponza and thereafter conveyed as prisoners to Milan in 1435 (above, chaps. 21 and 31). He remained in Milan for a number of years, becoming a ducal favorite and receiving many honors. Decembrio dedicated to him the second half of his translation of the *Commentarii* of Julius Caesar (on which see n. 123, above).

139. On Ottolino Zoppi, see Somaini, "Filippo Maria e la svolta," 123, and Simonetta, 56. For both Giacomo Lonati and Moretto Sannazzaro (d. 1454), see Covini, *L'esercito del duca*, 75–77.

140. Filippo Maria initially supported the Council of Basel, whose opening session was held in 1431. He later distanced himself from its more radical phases, however, withdrawing his support in 1438–39 when the council deposed Eugenius IV and elected an anti-pope in the person of his father-in-law, the former Duke of Savoy, Amedeo VIII. See now Cristina Belloni, "La politica ecclesiastica di Filippo Maria Visconti e il Concilio di Basilea," in *Il ducato*, 321–66.

141. Decembrio has in mind above all Suetonius, *Augustus* 90, 91, 92, but superstition plays a role in most of the Suetonian lives, e.g., *Tiberius* 69,

Gaius Caligula 61. See in general Andrew Wallace-Hadrill, *Suetonius: The Scholar and his Caesars* (London, 1983), 189–97.

142. Cf. Suetonius, *Augustus* 92: "Auspicia et omina quaedam pro certissimis observabat: si mane calceus perperam ac sinister pro dextro induceretur, ut dirum. . . ."

143. Cf. Suetonius, *Augustus* 90: "Tonitrua et fulgura paulo infirmius expavescebat. . . ."

144. Of the astrologers mentioned in this paragraph, the best known are Pietro Lapini da Montalcino (1401–49) and Antonio Bernareggi (d. 1463/67). On the former, who was professor of astrology at the University of Pavia from 1418 to 1428, see *DBI* 83:524–26; on the latter, who entered Filippo Maria's service as ducal physician in 1440, see Monica Azzolini, *The Duke and the Stars: Astrology and Politics in Renaissance Milan* (Cambridge, MA, 2013), 46–47, 73, 78–87, 254–58. Lanfranco da Parma is presumably Lanfranco Bardone: see Azzolini, *The Duke*, 79, 255. Azzolini provides information on the other figures mentioned here on pages 250–51.

145. The reference is to the famous *Astrarium*, an astronomical clock constructed in the fourteenth century by Giovanni Dondi Dall'Orologio (1330–88): see *DBI* 41:96–104.

146. The location being referred to here is the *Corte dell'Arengo*, the traditional residence of the Visconti rulers of Milan. After the assassination of his brother Giovanni Maria (see above, chaps. 4, 6, 8, and 11), Filippo Maria, like his father, Gian Galeazzo, broke with tradition by preferring, when in Milan, to reside exclusively within the confines of the more isolated and well-fortified Castle of Porta Giovia. His consequent inaccessibility was a source of resentment to the Milanese citizenry: see Evelyn S. Welch, *Art and Authority in Renaissance Milan* (New Haven and London, 1995), 177; Alessandro Ballarin, *Leonardo a Milano* (Verona, 2010), 1:426–29.

147. The typical beginning of the Suetonian death narrative: cf. *Augustus* 97, *Tiberius* 74, *Caligula* 57, *Claudius* 46, *Domitian* 15.2.

148. The *Corte dell'Arengo*, on which see note 146, above. Giulini, *Memorie spettanti*, 6:386, documents the event from an independent source, the *Chronica bossiana*.

149. Again, compare Suetonius, *Claudius* 46: "exortus crinitae stellae, quam cometen vocant" (the appearance of the star with long hair they call a comet).

150. Both Antonio and Giacomo Visconti were early candidates for the succession whose claims were later discarded or downgraded: see above, chapter 40 and notes 83 and 84. On the supposed, but most probably nonexistent, last will and testament of Filippo Maria, the literature is large: for a convenient synthesis, see Francesco Cognasso, "La Repubblica di S. Ambrogio," in *Storia di Milano* (Milan, 1955), 6:388–94, as well as Ballarin, *Leonardo a Milano*, 1:266–72. Decembrio's contention that Filippo Maria named King Alfonso of Aragon as his successor is unfounded. It may be an indication that Decembrio's sympathies lay with the powerful *bracceschi* faction in Milan, which opposed the claims being advanced by Francesco Sforza on the basis of his marriage to Bianca Maria Visconti.

THE DEEDS OF FRANCESCO SFORZA

1. The reference is to the two high points of Sforza's career: his conquest of Milan, February/March 1450, and the peace of Lodi, signed on April 9, 1454. The first accomplishment secured Sforza's acceptance as successor to the Visconti; the second ended nearly thirty years (1426–54) of almost continuous warfare between Milan and Venice, paving the way to a more general peace in Italy via the Italian League, or *Lega italica*, of 1455: see *DBI* 50:7–10.

2. Decembrio alludes here to the entry of the king of Naples, Alfonso of Aragon, into the Italian League. The event went some way toward reconciling old enemies and was sanctioned by the arrangement whereby two of Sforza's children, his daughter Ippolita (1445–84) and his second son Sforza Maria (1451–79), were pledged to marry into the House of Aragon: for details see *DBI* 42:404–10.

3. Lactantius, *Institutiones Divinae* 1.17: "Quid ergo a nobis expetatur amplius? Num eloquentia superare possumus Ciceronem? Minime id quidem. . . ." (What more then is to be asked of us? Are we capable of surpassing Cicero in eloquence? Certainly not . . .). Earlier in his career,

Decembrio had launched a savage attack on Lactantius: see James Hankins, *Plato in the Italian Renaissance*, 2 vols. (Leiden-New York-Köln, 1990), 1:148–53.

4. On the career of the condottiere Muzio Attendolo (1369–1424), who earned the nickname "Sforza" due to his aggressive battle tactics, see *DBI* 4:543–45.

5. Presumably, a reference to Justinus, *Epitoma* 9.8: "Quibus artibus orbis imperii fundamenta pater iecit, operis totius gloriam filius consummavit" (Applying those skills used by his father to lay the foundations of a world empire, the son crowned with glory the completed work).

6. A barb aimed squarely at the prominent humanist Francesco Filelfo (1398–1481), Decembrio's main rival at the Sforza court. By the time these words were written, in 1461–62, Filelfo had completed the first eight books of his *Sphortias*, an epic poem designed to describe the deeds of Francesco Sforza in heroic verse: see now Jeroen De Keyser, *Francesco Filelfo and Francesco Sforza: Critical Edition of Filelfo's 'Sphortias,' 'De Genuensium deditione,' 'Oratio parentalis,' and His Polemical Exchange with Galeotto Marzio* (Hildesheim-Zürich-New York, 2015), xi–xix, xxxiii–xliii, 1–219.

7. Horace, *Ars poetica*, 372–73: "mediocribus esse poetis non homines, non di, non concessere columnae" (neither men nor gods, nor the booksellers' ads have ever allowed poets to be mediocre). In fact, Decembrio was soon to be proven right on this point. In June 1464 the professor of rhetoric at Bologna, Galeotto Marzio, having been asked to express his opinion on the first eight books of Filelfo's *Sphortias*, issued a scathing assessment. Among other things, Marzio accused Filelfo of lacking poetic verve: "magis versificator quam poeta videris" (you come across as a poetaster rather than as a poet). A series of polemical exchanges ensued between the two humanists: see De Keyser, *Francesco Filelfo and Francesco Sforza*, xxix–xxxii, xlvii–l, 299–367 (pp. 307–8 for the passage quoted). On Galeotto Marzio, see *DBI* 71:478–84.

8. Decembrio's account of the birth of Francesco Sforza matches in most details with that given by an earlier contemporary source, Antonio de'Minuti, *Compendio dei gesti del magnifico et gloriosissimo signore Sforza*, ed. Giulio Porro Lambertenghi, in *Miscellanea di storia italiana* (Turin, 1869),

7:95–306, at 139. Minuti completed his *Compendio* in 1458; for his career as an important Sforza bureaucrat, see *DBI* 74:717–19. Minuti, however, has Francesco born "sonate le XXIV ore, poco dreto all'Ave Maria," which would correspond to just after eight p.m. in Tuscany in high summer. This probably explains the words "ut vero alii contendunt, in occasu solis." The astrological allusions in this passage are Decembrio's own.

9. Decembrio's chronology is garbled at this point: Muzio Attendolo took up service with Florence in April 1401; as such, he was sent to join forces with the newly elected emperor Rupert of Bavaria (1352–1410), who had come to Italy to counter Gian Galeazzo Visconti's expanding ambitions in Northern Italy. According to Minuti, *Compendio*, 142, it was during this time that Rupert "concesse a Sforza e a tutta sua casa de Attendoli che portassino per arma el leone d'oro."

10. Muzio Attendolo briefly joined the service of Gian Galeazzo Visconti after the latter's occupation of Perugia in January 1400.

11. As promised in his introduction, alongside the Sforza story, Decembrio mentions "other notable matters" throughout his narrative. The movement of the White Penitents, known as the *Bianchi*, occurred in 1399, the Jubilee in 1400.

12. The eight children born to Muzio Attendolo and his mistress Lucia da Torgiano (1380–1461) included Francesco (1401–66), Elisa (1402–76), Antonia (1404–71), Leone (1406–40), Giovanni (1407–51), and Alessandro (1409–73).

13. Muzio also fathered children from three successive marriages: Bosio (1411–76), born of the first wife; Leonardo (1415–38), born of the second; and Bartolomeo (1420–35) and Carlo (1423–57), born of the third. Carlo pursued an ecclesiastical career and eventually became archbishop of Milan (1454–57).

14. Lucia da Torgiano married Marco da Fogliano sometime after 1411. Children born of this marriage included Corrado da Fogliano (d. 1470) and Bona Caterina (1422–82). Decembrio does not mention a third child, Rinaldo (d. 1445). On Corrado and Rinaldo, see *DBI* 48:462–65 and 482–83.

15. Muzio Attendolo entered the service of King Ladislas of Naples in 1412. By that time Ladislas had for several years been engaged in a highly successful campaign of military aggression aimed at extending his control over the territories ruled by the popes (also called the Patrimony of St. Peter), which were then in a state of considerable disarray due to the Papal Schism of 1378.

16. That is, in the *Life of Filippo Maria Visconti*, chapters 4 and 8. The events referred to occurred between May 16 and June 16.

17. On the career of the famed condottiere Micheletto Attendolo, see *DBI* 4:542–43.

18. King Ladislas of Naples died in August 1414.

19. In November 1414 Queen Giovanna had Muzio Attendolo imprisoned at the instigation of the influential courtier Pandolfello Alopo, who was rumored to be her lover: see *DBI* 2:524. In the following year, with the queen promised in marriage to Giacomo Borbone de la Marche, Pandolfello liberated Muzio Attendolo in the hope of using him to combat his new rival for power. The alliance between the two men was sealed by Muzio's marriage to Pandolfello's sister Caterina.

20. Marco Attendolo (d. 1465) was the son of Muzio Attendolo's sister Margherita: see *DBI* 4:541–42.

21. On Giacomo Borbone de la Marche (1370–1438), see *DBI* 12:491–94. Giacomo's marriage to Queen Giovanna took place on August 10, 1415. Shortly thereafter, Muzio Attendolo was seized and imprisoned for a second time. The Castel dell' Ovo is located by the harbor in Naples.

22. Margherita Attendolo's decisive actions probably saved her brother's life: see *DBI* 4:544.

23. 1416.

24. 1416. On the colorful career of Andrea Fortebracci, better known as Braccio da Montone (1368–1424), famed condottiere and chief rival of Muzio Attendolo in this period of turmoil, see *DBI* 49:117–27.

25. Muzio Attendolo occupied Rome in August 1417. Foschino Attendolo (1392–1452) was, like his bother Marco, a son of Margherita Attendolo: see *DBI* 4:534–35.

26. Oddone Colonna (1370–1431) was elected pope as Martin V in November 1417. He began his journey to Rome in the spring of 1418.

27. Francesco Sforza married Polissena Ruffo (1400–1420) in October 1418.

28. The battle at Viterbo took place in June 1419. Besides Foschino Attendolo, the best-known condottiere among those captured on the day was Manno Barile (1379–1449). A full list of the captives can be found in Minuti, *Compendio*, 239.

29. Decembrio stumbles again on the chronology. The event he relates here occurred not in 1419, as he seems to think, but several years later, in 1423: for a fuller account, see Simonetta, 7–8. The Aragonese courtier and military commander Ramón de Boïl (d. 1458) was not yet active in Italy at this time: another mistake.

30. Giacomo Caldora (1369–1439) was yet another military adventurer involved in the affairs of the Kingdom of Naples. Decembrio is the only contemporary source to mention this marriage.

31. For a detailed account of Muzio's death on January 3, 1424, see Minuti, *Compendio*, 295–98.

32. Decembrio has in mind the famous passage of Livy 1.16.

33. The battle took place on June 2, 1424. Wounded in action, Braccio was carried from the field and died a few days later while undergoing treatment. Decembrio's account appears to lend credence to the belief, widely held at the time, that the death was no accident: Francesco Sforza was rumored to have deliberately pushed the surgeon's blade into his enemy's brain. Later Sforza historians countered such allegations by concocting a quite different story: see especially Simonetta, 19.

34. Both Muzio Attendolo and Braccio were unscrupulous military adventurers out to exploit the turmoil that plagued Central and Southern Italy in this period. Their rivalry continued into the next generation, acquiring significant political overtones in Milan as their followers, nicknamed *sforzeschi* and *bracceschi*, clashed for influence at the Visconti court. The struggle between the two parties intensified after the death of Duke Filippo Maria in 1447: for details see Serena Ferente, *La sfortuna di Jacopo*

Piccinino: Storia dei bracceschi in Italia, 1423–1465 (Florence, 2005). Earlier in his career, Decembrio appears to have harbored sympathies for the *bracceschi*. In the immediate aftermath of the battle of Aquila, he wrote a eulogy on Braccio: see Federico Petrucci, *Petri Candidi Decembrii Epistolarum iuvenilium libri octo* (Florence, 2013), 126–32. Twenty years later he penned a lengthy account of the career of Niccolò Piccinino, the recently deceased condottiere and acknowledged leader of the *bracceschi: Panegyricus in funere illustris Nicolai Picenini ad cives Mediolanenses*, ed. Felice Fossati, in *RIS*, 2nd ser., vol. 20.1 (Bologna, 1958), 991–1009. See too *Life of Filippo Maria Visconti*, note 150.

35. An exaggeration: the young Francesco Sforza shared credit for the victory with the more experienced generals in charge of operations, Micheletto Attendolo and Giacomo Caldora. See, for example, Minuti, *Compendio*, 304–5.

36. Decembrio refers here to the notorious love affair of Ugo (1405–25) and his stepmother, Parisina d'Este (1404–25). See *DBI* 68:61–63.

37. The loss of Brescia in 1426 was a major blow to the prestige and power of Milan in its struggle with the combined forces of Florence and Venice: see Cognasso, 223–33.

38. The battle of Maclodio was fought on October 12, 1427. Note that Decembrio does not mention the presence of Francesco Sforza among the Visconti military forces that went down to defeat.

39. The events listed here all occurred in 1427, except for the Peace of Ferrara, which was signed in April 1428 and which obliged Filippo Maria Visconti to cede Bergamo to the Venetians.

40. Decembrio is trying to put a positive spin on what was an unmitigated disaster. Sforza was in fact ambushed by irregulars and barely managed to escape with his life. The failure of his first solo mission for Filippo Maria Visconti represented a severe setback for the young condottiere: he was subsequently downgraded and relegated to the provincial backwater of Mortara for the next two years. For a more straightforward account of the ambush and its aftermath, see Simonetta, 32–33.

41. Polissena Sforza (1428–49) married Sigismondo Malatesta in 1442. Her mother was Giovanna d'Acquapendente.

42. On the soldier and statesman Tristano Sforza (1429–77), see Maria Nadia Covini, *L'esercito del duca: Organizzazione militare e istituzioni al tempo degli Sforza* (Rome, 1998), 39–40. He married Beatrice d'Este (1427–97), a daughter of Niccolò III d'Este.

43. Decembrio alludes to the balance of power concept that would eventually emerge as the most viable solution to Italy's woes in this period: the classic study is that of Giovanni Soranzo, *La lega italica* (Milan, 1924). For a more recent assessment, see Riccardo Fubini, *Italia quattrocentesca: Politica e diplomazia nell'età di Lorenzo de'Medici* (Milan, 1994), 185–219.

44. Sforza undertook his mission to Lucca in the summer of 1430 with the tacit approval of Filippo Maria Visconti, even though he was technically responding to an appeal for help from Paolo Guinigi (1372–1432). On Sforza's approach, the Florentine forces prudently withdrew to safety; there was no battle and thus no military glory.

45. Like the preceding battle that never took place, this is another gross distortion: Guinigi was betrayed and captured by conspirators in his own inner circle, who then handed him over to Francesco Sforza. A more sober contemporary account of these events can be found in Biondo Flavio, *Historiarum ab inclinatione Romani imperii decades* (Basel, 1531), 450–57.

46. This chapter redounds mainly to the glory of Filippo Maria Visconti and his preferred condottiere Niccolò Piccinino. Piccinino defeated the Florentine forces at the battle of the Serchio on December 2, 1430. Decembrio had already celebrated this famous victory in his 1444 funeral oration for the fallen hero: see *Panegyricus in funere illustris Nicolai Picenini*, 994–95.

47. Niccolò III d'Este (1383–1441) married Ricciarda di Saluzzo (1410–74) in 1429. Their first child, Ercole (1431–1505), was to become Duke of Ferrara in 1471.

48. Decembrio explicitly contradicts here what he had written in his *Panegyric in Praise of Milan*, a work composed in the Visconti period, most probably in 1435. There he had given all credit for the Milanese victory on the River Po to Niccolò Piccinino: see Giuseppe Petraglione, "Il *De laudibus Mediolanensium Urbis panegyricus* di Pier Candido Decembrio,"

Archivio storico lombardo 34 (1907): 22–23, 42–45; and above, *Life of Filippo Maria Visconti,* chapter 20 and note 39.

49. Less biased contemporary sources accord credit for the victory over Carmagnola at Soncino to the senior commander in charge of the operation, Niccolò da Tolentino: see Biglia, cols. 146–47. For a blistering chastisement of Decembrio and other Sforza panegyrists on this point, see Giorgio Giulini, *Memorie spettanti alla storia . . . di Milano* (Milan, 1854–57), 6:314.

50. Sigismund received the iron crown as king of Italy in Milan on November 25, 1431. Decembrio's designation of Sigismund as emperor here is anachronistic, for he was in fact crowned emperor only later, in Rome on May 31, 1433. See the *Life of Filippo Maria Visconti,* chapter 32, where Decembrio had more accurately styled Sigismund king of the Romans at this point in his career.

51. The expedition to the Marches was undertaken in connivance with Filippo Maria Visconti, even though (as had been the case with Lucca in 1430) Sforza was no longer officially on the latter's payroll. The Marches were an integral part of the papal state: Filippo Maria's strategic move was calculated, under the guise of enforcing the dictates of the Council of Basel, to cripple the power of the Venetian pope, Eugenius IV. See Cognasso, 299–301.

52. Suetonius, *Julius Caesar* 37. By all accounts, Sforza met with little or no resistance: the populations welcomed him as an alternative to their rapacious and corrupt papal governors.

53. The Sforza conquest of papal territories in the Marches and in Umbria put tremendous pressure on Pope Eugenius IV. The pope therefore negotiated an agreement whereby Francesco Sforza became Standard-bearer of the Church. This agreement, signed at Calcarella in March 1434, put Sforza at odds with his erstwhile employer Filippo Maria Visconti. But Decembrio's chronology is wrong (the year is 1434, not 1433), and his sequencing of the events is jumbled and confusing. The battle fought near Tivoli, for example, took place after, not before, the deal struck at Calcarella.

54. Angry at Sforza's betrayal at Calcarella, Filippo Maria Visconti unleashed his condottieri (including the *bracceschi* Niccolò Fortebraccio and Niccolò Piccinino), with orders to march against him.

55. By mentioning Federico da Montefeltro (1422–82), Decembrio is suddenly jumping ten years ahead, to the time in the mid-1440s when the newly installed lord of Urbino helped Sforza to restore control over his wayward subjects in Central Italy.

56. Decembrio had suggested quite the opposite in his 1444 funeral oration for Piccinino: see *Panegyricus in funere Nicolai Picenini*, 997. On the turbulence in Rome—in fact, an armed insurrection against the pope that forced him to flee the city disguised as a Benedictine monk—see Anthony F. D'Elia, *A Sudden Terror: The Plot to Murder the Pope in Renaissance Rome* (Cambridge, MA, 2009), 40–41. The most detailed contemporary account is that provided by Biondo Flavio, *Historiarum ab inclinatione Romani imperii decades*, 481–85.

57. Possibly a reference to the *Opuscula* Decembrio was collecting into a single volume in the early 1460s. The volume was intended for Borso d'Este and included four of Decembrio's previously published historical writings, namely the *Panegyric in Praise of Milan*, the *Life of Filippo Maria Visconti*, the *Funeral Oration for Niccolò Piccinino*, and a *Compendium of Roman History*. For a description, see Pyle, "Harvard MS Richardson 23," 191–98.

58. See *Life of Filippo Maria Visconti*, chapters 21 and 31.

59. Another leap forward in time, here to 1450: see below, chapter 39.

60. This chapter, even more explicitly than the previous one, is largely devoted to illustrating the sagacity of Filippo Maria Visconti. Decembrio's concluding words constitute an admission that the narrative has somewhat unaccountably veered off course.

61. On Sforza's occupation of Bologna, see Cognasso, 310. The operation was the result of a peace agreement between Filippo Maria Visconti (who had been supporting the anti-papal elements in the city) and Pope Eugenius; it had nothing to do with any military skill on Sforza's part.

62. Like his sister Polissena (note 41 above), Sforza Secondo (1435–91) was born of Francesco Sforza's extramarital relationship with Giovanna d'Acquapendente.

63. After freeing Alfonso of Aragon from captivity, Filippo Maria Visconti pledged his support for Alfonso's claim to the throne of Naples, whereas he had previously supported the opposing claims of the House of Anjou. One result of this shift of allegiances was the passage of Gaeta (where Filippo Maria had stationed a garrison) into Aragonese hands. Isabella's valiant efforts on behalf of her husband are described by Bartolomeo Facio, *Rerum gestarum Alfonsi regis libri,* ed. Daniela Pietragalla (Alessandria, 2004), 191–217. See too Somaini, "Filippo Maria e la svolta," in *Il ducato,* 118, 123, 127, 148, 151.

64. On the papal condottiere Baldassarre Baroncelli da Offida (1380–1436) and his plot to capture and kill Francesco Sforza, see *DBI* 6:434–35. A detailed account can be found in Simonetta, 64–67. Unlike Simonetta, Decembrio does not mention Offida's "accidental" death in custody a short time later: the would-be assassin was struck a mortal blow on the head by a falling roof tile while taking his exercise in the prison yard.

65. Decembrio has considerably embellished a minor incident, on which see Simonetta, 68. Note too that Francesco Sforza, having signed on to serve as commander of the Florentine and Venetian forces (November 27, 1436), will henceforth find himself fighting on the side of the enemies of his future father-in-law, Filippo Maria Visconti.

66. See *Life of Filippo Maria Visconti,* chapters 21, 22, 23.

67. Drusiana Sforza (1437–74) married the condottiere Giacomo Piccinino (1423–65) in 1464. For details see *DBI* 83:172–74.

68. Decembrio's narrative quietly skips over two years of inactivity here (1437 and 1438), picking up the story in February 1439, when Francesco Sforza signed a new contract with Florence and Venice. The omission is meant to mask the fact that under his previous contract (see above, n. 65) Sforza had consistently and controversially refused Venetian orders to cross the River Po, avoiding thereby any direct action against Milan, where he continued to nourish hopes of securing the succession to the

Visconti. Sforza's change of heart in February 1439 was due to the break-down of his secret negotiations with Filippo Maria over the consignment of his future bride, Filippo's daughter Bianca Maria: see Cognasso, 322–35.

69. The principal actions described here took place in late 1439: Cognasso dates the battle fought at Tenno November 9, Piccinino's entry into Verona November 17, and Sforza's arrival in Verona November 20: Cognasso, 335–37. See also above, *Life of Filippo Maria Visconti*, chapter 23.

70. In his *Memoirs* (*De temporibus suis*), Leonardo Bruni provides an eyewitness account of the panic caused in and around Florence by the rampaging troops of Piccinino in 1440: see Leonardo Bruni, *History of the Florentine People*, ed. and trans. James Hankins and D. J. W. Bradley (Cambridge, MA, 2001–7), 3:390.

71. Cognasso, 339, dates Sforza's victory at Soncino June 14, 1440; he also cautiously accepts that the idea of keeping Sforza's army in Lombardy, rather than bringing it down to Tuscany to defend Florence against Piccinino, stemmed from Cosimo de'Medici. Close ties of cooperation had indeed existed between Cosimo and Francesco Sforza ever since the mid-1430s, when the latter had signed on as Florence's chief condottiere (above, nn. 65 and 68). In fact, Cosimo and the Florentines were to be instrumental in helping Sforza realize his ambitious plan to become the successor to Filippo Maria Visconti: see Riccardo Fubini, "L'età delle congiure: I rapporti tra Firenze e Milano dal tempo di Piero a quello di Lorenzo de'Medici," in *Florence and Milan: Comparisons and Relations*, ed. Sergio Bertelli, Nicolai Rubinstein, Craig Hugh Smyth, 2 vols. (Florence, 1989), 2:189–239, at 189–90, and idem, *Italia quattrocentesca*, 84. Another sign of this Medici-Sforza collaboration comes later in Decembrio's text, when he highlights the presence of the prominent Florentine diplomat Angelo Acciaiuoli at the ceremony marking Sforza's installation as ruler of Milan in 1450 (see below, chap. 39).

72. The battle of Anghiari was fought on June 29, 1440. It resulted in the comprehensive defeat of the Visconti forces under Niccolò Piccinino. Francesco Sforza was not involved; the glory of victory belonged to the commander of the Florentine armies, Micheletto Attendolo.

73. According to Simonetta, 105–10, Sforza's position at Martinengo in the summer of 1441 was a desperate one: his siege operations were not delivering results, while Piccinino's arrival on the scene had closed off his escape route; it was Filippo Maria Visconti whose sudden change of heart broke the deadlock. On the condottiere Giacomo Gaivano, see *DBI* 51:313–16.

74. Sforza's marriage to Bianca Maria Visconti in October 1441 marked an important milestone in his career: he had now become lord of Cremona and son-in-law to the Duke of Milan. The marriage was accompanied by yet another settlement of the long-standing territorial disputes between Milan and Venice: by the terms of the Treaty of Cavriana (November 1441), the border between the two states was stabilized along the River Adda, meaning that Filippo Maria acknowledged Venetian possession of both Bergamo and Brescia.

75. Niccolò III d'Este died on December 26, 1441. Alfonso of Aragon took Naples on June 2, 1442. The latter event represented a new threat to Sforza, whose loyalties had always lain with the claims of the House of Anjou to the Kingdom of Naples.

76. Dismayed by the increasing ambitions of his new son-in-law, Filippo Maria Visconti forged a triple entente with King Alfonso and Pope Eugenius, the intent of which was to divest Sforza of the lands he held in Central and Southern Italy. Sforza lost his possessions in the south, but his initial losses in the Marches and in Umbria were temporarily made good thanks to victories over Niccolò Piccinino at Monteloro and over Piccinino's son Francesco at Montolmo.

77. Galeazzo Maria Sforza (1444–76) was destined to succeed his father as Duke of Milan in 1466: *DBI* 51:398–409. This time around, Decembrio edges closer to the correct name: see above, *Life of Filippo Maria Visconti*, chapter 38 and note 79. At the time of writing (1461–62), Galeazzo Maria was Count of Pavia and was expected to marry Dorotea Gonzaga (1449–67). The marriage never took place, however, due both to political complications and to Dorotea's early death: see *DBI* 57:707–8.

78. Ippolita Sforza (1445–84) married Alfonso II of Aragon (1448–95) in 1465: see *DBI* 2:331–32.

79. The battle of Casalmaggiore was fought on September 28, 1446. The defeat effectively destroyed Filippo Maria Visconti's military capacity. The way now lay open for the Venetian forces to march on Milan itself: they set out immediately, halting only with the onset of winter.

80. Decembrio has once again stumbled on the chronology: the revolt of Fermo had occurred in the previous year, on November 24, 1445. The move threatened to put an end to Sforza's state in the Marches. This time, Sforza's efforts to recoup his losses were unsuccessful: the year 1446 ended with the failure of his siege of Gradara.

81. Sforza nevertheless remained officially in the service of Filippo Maria's enemies, Venice and Florence. The agreement mentioned here between the two men, each equally suspicious of the other's motives, was signed in February 1447 and kept secret.

82. The Venetian pope Eugenius IV died on February 23, and the humanist Tommaso Parentucelli became Pope Nicholas V in the following month.

83. Filippo Maria Visconti died on August 13, 1447. According to Simonetta, 178, Sforza received the news at Cotignola two days later.

84. See *Life of Filippo Maria Visconti*, chapter 71.

85. The Venetians rejected the attempts of the new Milanese government to obtain a cessation of hostilities. They took possession of Lodi on August 16 and Piacenza on August 19.

86. No, he had not. Filippo Maria had made his daughter heir to his patrimonial lands only; he expressly excluded the possibility that she might succeed him as legitimate ruler of the duchy: see Francesco Cognasso, "La Repubblica di S. Ambrogio," in *Storia di Milano* (Milan, 1955), 6:389. Decembrio was well aware of this fact, as can be seen from the more honest account given of the matter in *Life of Filippo Maria Visconti*, chapter 71.

87. In September 1447, Sforza took control of Pavia in his own name, not in the name of the Milanese, on whose behalf he was supposed to be fighting. The move revealed the condottiere's true colors and caused considerable consternation in Milan, where the government immediately and

unsuccessfully sought to negotiate a separate peace agreement with Venice, hoping thereby to divest itself of Sforza altogether. See Simonetta, 191; Cognasso, "La Repubblica di S. Ambrogio," 410.

88. An eyewitness account of the horrors perpetrated by Sforza's troops at Piacenza (November/December 1447) can be found in the chronicle of Antonio di Ripalta, *Annales Placentini*, in RIS 20 (Milan, 1731), col. 896. The sack of Piacenza subsequently became a byword for the cruelties and sufferings visited by Christians upon Christians: see Biondo Flavio, *Italy Illuminated*, ed. and trans. Jeffrey A. White, 2 vols. (Cambridge, MA, 2005–16), 2:18–19. Even Sforza apologists felt obliged to detail the crimes, though they also attempted to exonerate their leader himself from any direct responsibility: e.g., Francesco Filelfo, *Sphortias* 3.655–800, in De Keyser, *Francesco Filelfo*, 72–76; Simonetta, 211.

89. As pointed out above, in note 87, Milanese suspicions of Sforza and the consequent overtures to Venice had already come into play after the Pavia incident, in September 1447. It was the breakdown of negotiations with Venice, not a popular uprising, that led the Milanese government to accept an uncomfortable marriage of convenience with their headstrong generalissimo.

90. Sforza's successful surprise attack on the Venetian fleet at Casalmaggiore occurred on July 17, 1448. For a detailed account of the action, see Simonetta, 220–24.

91. See Livy 2.10.

92. The victory won at Caravaggio, September 15, 1448, became a centerpiece of Sforza historiography. For an extended description of the preliminaries, the strategy, and the battle itself, see Simonetta, 226–41.

93. This picture of conditions in post-Caravaggio Milan has the weight of eyewitness testimony behind it: indeed, from September 1, 1448, Decembrio was not only resident in the city, he had assumed the office of secretary to the government. On his role in this capacity, see Borsa, "Pier Candido," 362–66.

94. The outcome of the battles fought at Casalmaggiore and Caravaggio meant that Venice, having sustained major losses, was now ready to cut a deal either with the government in Milan or with Sforza. Sforza had the

more convincing case: by the Treaty of Rivoltella, October 18, 1448, Venice not only recognized Sforza's claim to Milan but also promised to lend him logistical and military support in his quest to conquer the duchy. Sforza for his part conceded Bergamo, Brescia, Crema, and most of the Ghiaradadda to the Venetians: see Cognasso, "La Repubblica di S. Ambrogio," 421–25.

95. One can only guess at the reasons behind the welcome Sforza received in Piacenza (October 23, 1448) after his sack of the city less than a year earlier.

96. According to Simonetta, 259, while at Abbiategrasso, Sforza ordered his men to divert the waters of the Naviglio Grande, the canal by which food supplies entered Milan. The plan was to starve the city into submission.

97. Abbiategrasso capitulated on November 22, 1448; the other acquisitions mentioned here came about early in the following year: Cognasso, "La Repubblica di S. Ambrogio," 427–30.

98. On Roberto Sanseverino (1418–87), the son of Sforza's sister Elisa, see Covini, *L'esercito del duca*, 98–99. Dolce Orsini dell'Anguillara (1401–50) is profiled in *DBI* 3:301–2. Dolce's son-in-law Orso Orsini (d. 1479) was also the author, toward the end of his life, of an important treatise on the art of war: *Governo et exercitio della militia*: Covini, *L'esercito del duca*, 52.

99. Decembrio here provides a thumbnail sketch of developments that followed in the wake of Sforza's separate peace with Venice, signed on October 18, 1448 (see above, n. 94). One result was the defection to Milan of the Sforza condottiere Carlo Gonzaga (d. 1456). Gonzaga's plans were far from clear, but he appears to have aspired to lordship over the city: see *DBI* 57:693–96. His coming coincided with an intensification of the ongoing power struggle between the so-called Guelf, or people's party, and the aristocratic Ghibellines, who had to this point held the leading role in the city's governance. A popular, Guelf-led government gained power in January 1449 and shortly thereafter accused the Ghibellines of conspiring to deliver the city to Francesco Sforza. A series of arrests and executions followed, with the Guelfs bent on using their power

to eliminate their rivals: see Cognasso, "La Repubblica di S. Ambrogio," 430–32.

100. Worn out by increasingly chaotic party strife and fearing for his own safety, Carlo Gonzaga eventually (September 11, 1449) struck a deal with Francesco Sforza that involved him handing over the strategically located town of Lodi.

101. For a graphic description of the famine that gripped Milan at this point, see Simonetta, 334: according to Simonetta, the starving Milanese were eventually reduced to eating not only dogs and cats but even rats and other things "disgusting and repugnant to humankind."

102. On March 6, 1449, the Milanese government signed an agreement with Ludovico of Savoy (1413–65) whereby the latter would undertake to defend the city in return for territorial concessions. Ludovico's military intervention was ill-timed and poorly executed; his forces were soundly defeated on April 20: see Cognasso, "La Repubblica di S. Ambrogio," 433–36.

103. It was in fact Decembrio himself, acting in his capacity as secretary to the Milanese government of the day, who on March 24, 1449, penned official letters to the French king, Charles VII, as well as to the dauphin Louis soliciting their help. The letter to the dauphin, the future king of France, Louis XI, is published in *Archivio storico lombardo* 61 (1934): 648–50. It exhorts the dauphin to join forces with Charles d'Orléans and Ludovico of Savoy to aid Milan against the advancing enemy, namely Francesco Sforza. The letter heaps abuse on Sforza, branding him as a traitor and accusing him of aiming to establish tyranny over Lombardy. The correspondence was intercepted by Sforza agents and helped make Decembrio *persona non grata* in Milan after the Sforza takeover in 1450: see the account of the affair given by Simonetta, 258, and the Introduction, xxx–xxxi. Decembrio's remarks here thus have the flavor of a palinode, while also dovetailing nicely with Sforza's own cautious policy in regard to France.

104. The reference is to a speech made by the imperial agent, Enea Silvio Piccolomini, in the summer of 1449, during his second mission to Milan. According to the account contained in his memoirs, Piccolomini at-

tempted on this occasion to persuade the Milanese to accept the emperor as their rightful ruler, promising them military aid if they did so: see Pius II, *Commentaries*, ed. Margaret Meserve and Marcello Simonetta, 3 vols. to date (Cambridge, MA, 2003–), 1:82–93. Unlike the speech "Est mihi non parum" that Piccolomini had made almost two years earlier on October 21, 1447, during his first mission to Milan (see now the edition by Michael Cotta-Schønberg, available in the HALSNS database), the full text of the speech of 1449 is to my knowledge no longer extant.

105. This is the only record we have of the proposed Milanese mission to the emperor, and Decembrio's refusal to undertake it. The passage is a significant indicator of Decembrio's desperate efforts, in the early 1460s, to rehabilitate himself in the eyes of Francesco Sforza. By invoking the fact that his father, Uberto, as secretary to his namesake Pietro di Candia, had played a significant role in securing the imperial investiture for the first duke of Milan, Gian Galeazzo Visconti, in 1395, Decembrio was underscoring his own adherence to Sforza's claim to recover the ducal title: see now Jane Black, *Absolutism in Renaissance Milan: Plenitude of Power under the Visconti and the Sforza* (Oxford, 2009), 84–93; and the Introduction, xxxvi–xxxvii.

106. The chronology is skewed: Decembrio's narrative here returns to events that transpired earlier in the year. On Carlo Gonzaga's victory at Monza in March 1449, see Simonetta, 275–77. Francesco Piccinino deserted Sforza and rejoined the Milanese on May 1: see *DBI* 57:172.

107. The agreement was signed on September 24, 1449: see Cognasso, "La Repubblica di S. Ambrogio," 438–39.

108. On the possible identity of Francesco Visconti, to whom Decembrio dedicated his treatise on the immortality of the soul, see Kristeller, "Pier Candido Decembrio," 289–90.

109. On the lord of Rimini and condottiere Sigismondo Pandolfo Malatesta (1417–68), see *DBI* 68:107–14, and Anthony F. D'Elia, *Pagan Virtue in a Christian World: Sigismondo Malatesta and the Italian Renaissance* (Cambridge, MA, 2016): he had signed on as commander of the Venetian forces on November 26, 1449.

110. Giacomo Piccinino (1423–65) had taken charge of the Milanese defenses after the death of his elder brother Francesco on October 16, 1449. Both men were sons of Niccolò Piccinino and thus natural rivals of Francesco Sforza: see *DBI* 83:171–75.

111. According to Cognasso, "La Repubblica di S. Ambrogio," 447, the uprising took place on February 25, 1450, and was followed the next day by Francesco Sforza's first entry into the city.

112. Francesco Sforza's initial entry into Milan on February 26, 1450, consisted of a brief and hastily organized visit; it did not include the consignment of the ducal insignia. The latter were conferred only after protracted negotiations, in the context of Sforza's triumphal entry into the city on Sunday March 22: see Alessandro Colombo, "L'ingresso di Francesco Sforza in Milano e l'inizio di un nuovo principato," *Archivio storico lombardo* 32 (1905): 33–101, 297–344. Decembrio appears here to have conflated the two entries into one.

113. Decembrio touches here on two themes that one finds constantly reiterated in the encomiastic literature regarding Francesco Sforza: his clemency and his post-1450 status as the Milanese *pater patriae*. See, for example, Francesco Filelfo's *Oratio parentalis*, in De Keyser, *Francesco Filelfo*, 243, 246, 251–52, 273, 288. For the theme of *clementia Caesaris* and its ancient sources, see Peter Stacey, *Roman Monarchy and the Renaissance Prince* (Cambridge, 2007). Decembrio's coverage of Francesco Sforza's career thus both begins and ends with the theme of clemency, a princely virtue that ostensibly links the former condottiere to the preceding Visconti dynasty: see above, chapters 1, 12, 23, and 39.

114. Sforza's offers of peace were conditional on the Venetians ceding the crossings on the River Adda, which they had occupied during the previous war. When the Venetians refused, Sforza proclaimed he could not allow them "to hold the keys to his house": see Paolo Margaroli, *Diplomazia e stati rinascimentali: Le ambascerie sforzesche fino alla conclusione della Lega italica* (Florence, 1992), 120–21.

115. The alliance with Florence, July to August 1451, was something of a foregone conclusion, given the earlier Florentine support for Sforza's occupation of Milan. Sforza's ties with Florence proved instrumental in

securing the adherence of France in February 1452, providing a necessary counterweight to Emperor Frederick III, who continued to regard Sforza as a usurper: see Margaroli, *Diplomazia*, 234–63.

116. Frederick's descent into Italy early in 1452 caused considerable consternation in the Sforza camp but ultimately proved to be without long-lasting effect: see Fabio Cusin, "Le aspirazioni straniere sul ducato di Milano e l'investitura imperiale (1450–54)," *Archivio storico lombardo* 63 (1936): 277–369. The emperor's marriage to Eleanor of Portugal took place in Rome on March 16, and on the same day he received the Italian crown normally conferred in Milan or in Monza, much to the dismay of the Sforza entourage.

117. Venice opened hostilities on May 16, 1452. The action coincided with an offensive from the west by Guglielmo di Monferrato and with aggression from the south initiated by Giberto da Correggio. Both men were intent on using the leverage afforded by the Venetian campaign to extend the territory controlled by their seigniorial families. Sforza was consequently under severe pressure during the opening phases of the campaign: see Franco Catalano, "La nuova signoria: Francesco Sforza," in *Storia di Milano* (Milan, 1956), 7:30–44.

118. Catalano, "La nuova signoria," 45–58, confirms that Venice, stunned by the double blow of the fall of Constantinople (May 29, 1453) and a major Sforza victory at Ghedi (August 15, 1453), was first to sue for peace. Constantine XI, not John VIII, was the last Byzantine emperor.

119. See notes 2, 77, and 78, as well as chapter 29 above.

120. Among Sforza's younger children, Ludovico Maria (1452–1508), nicknamed "il Moro" because of his jet-black hair and dark complexion, was destined to become the most famous. He was to rule the Duchy of Milan from 1480 to 1499, initially as regent for his nephew and later in his own right. His fame today is largely due to his having been the patron and protector of Leonardo da Vinci, who was resident at the court of Milan from 1482 to 1499. Ascanio Maria (1455–1505) became prominent as a cardinal of the Church (created 1484): he played a crucial role in the election of Rodrigo Borgia as Pope Alexander VI in 1492. Of the three other children listed here, Filippo Maria (1449–92) remained out-

side of politics; Elisabetta (1456–72) and Ottaviano (1458–77) died in their teens. All of Sforza's children enjoyed the full benefits of a humanistic education.

121. Decembrio here puts a positive spin on the reconstruction of the Castle of Porta Giovia, stressing its essentially ornamental character. The castle had been dismantled after the death of Filippo Maria Visconti in 1447. Francesco Sforza ordered it to be rebuilt in June 1450. The project was controversial, however, insofar as the castle's military function suggested to the Milanese populace that their city was being held by force of arms: for particulars, see Evelyn S. Welch, *Art and Authority in Renaissance Milan* (New Haven and London, 1995), 175–90; Patrick Boucheron, *Le pouvoir de bâtir: Urbanisme et politique édilitaire à Milan* (Rome, 1998), 199–218. Machiavelli later condemned Francesco Sforza's decision to rebuild the castle as impolitic and counterproductive: see *The Prince*, chapter 20; *The Discourses*, 2.24.

122. The symbolic importance of Sforza's restoration of the Corte dell'Arengo can hardly be overemphasized. Located in the heart of Milan, in close proximity to the famous Duomo, the palace had been abandoned by the reclusive Filippo Maria Visconti, who preferred to reside in the heavily fortified Castle of Porta Giovia (see *Life of Filippo Maria Visconti*, chap. 49). Francesco Sforza deliberately set up both his administration and his residence in the Corte dell'Arengo, hoping thereby to heal the rift that had developed between city and prince under his predecessor: for details, see Welch, *Art and Authority*, 203; Boucheron, *Le pouvoir de bâtir*, 206–7; Alessandro Ballarin, *Leonardo a Milano*, 4 vols. (Verona, 2010), 1:426–28.

123. Along with the *Ospedale maggiore* (oddly not mentioned here) and the widening and paving of the city streets, the canal of the Martesana was part of a comprehensive campaign of public works undertaken by the new regime in the 1450s: see Boucheron, *Le pouvoir de bâtir*, 259–62. The focal point and prime beneficiary was to be Milan itself; improvements in the city's infrastructure were meant to mark a departure from the neglect that had characterized the rule of the last Visconti (e.g., *Life of Filippo*

Maria Visconti, chap. 35). Decembrio presents the canal of the Martesana as a public good, implying a sharp contrast with the waterways of Filippo Maria Visconti, constructed as they had been for the private delectation of the prince (*Life of Filippo Maria Visconti,* chap. 49).

APPENDIX

1. On the authoritative character of this manuscript, which belonged to Decembrio and contains numerous notes and corrections in his hand, see Zaccaria, "L'epistolario," 97–98; Zaggia, "Appunti," 201. A detailed description can be found in *I manoscritti 'G. Gaslini' della Biblioteca Universitaria di Genova,* ed. Oriana Cartaregia (Rome, 1991), 66–69.

2. To our knowledge, these three letters first appeared together in their complete versions in Ianziti, "Pier Candido Decembrio and the Suetonian Path," 261–63. Previous editions were based on the faulty Milanese manuscript (Milan, Biblioteca Ambrosiana, I 235 inf., fols. 8v–9v, 40v) and/or presented only selections: see, for example, Carlo De' Rosmini, *Vita e disciplina di Guarino Veronese e de' suoi discepoli* (Brescia, 1805–6), 1:109–10; Cinquini, *Lettere inedite,* 25–27; Vincenzo Fera, "Filologia in casa Decembrio," in *I Decembrio,* 163–64.

3. Genoa, Biblioteca Universitaria, MS C.VII.46, fol. 6v.

4. Porto, a small village in Ferrarese territory, was the site of one of the favored country residences of the itinerant Este court: see Marco Folin, "Le residenze di corte e il sistema delle delizie fra Medioevo ed età moderna," in *Delizie estensi: Architetture di villa nel Rinascimento italiano ed europeo,* ed. Francesco Ceccarelli and Marco Folin (Florence, 2009), 86, 88, 90, 95, 100, 107, 111, 116.

5. Genoa, Biblioteca Universitaria, MS C.VII.46, fols. 6v–7r.

6. Genoa, Biblioteca Universitaria, MS C.VII.46, fol. 32r.

7. The reference is to Pisanello's famous medal portrait of Decembrio, on which see Luke Syson and Dillian Gordon, *Pisanello: Painter to the Renaissance Court* (London, 2001), 36, 118; Susan Gaylard, *Hollow Men: Writing, Objects, and Public Image in Renaissance Italy* (New York, 2013), 8–9.

Bibliography

LIFE OF FILIPPO MARIA VISCONTI

EDITIONS OF THE LATIN TEXT

Georgii Merulae Alexandrini, Antiquitatis Vicecomitum libri X. Duodecim Vice-comitum Mediolani principum vitae, auctore Paulo Jovio. Philippi Mariae Vi-cecomitis Mediolanensium Ducis Tertii vita, auctore Petro Candido Decem-brio. Milan, 1630.

Philippi Mariae Vicecomitis Mediolanensium Ducis Tertii vita, auctore Petro Candido Decembrio. Edited by Ludovico Antonio Muratori. In *RIS*, vol. 20, cols. 981–1020. Milan, 1731.

Vita Philippi Mariae Tertii Ligurum Ducis. Edited by Attilio Butti, Felice Fossati, Giuseppe Petraglione. In *RIS*, 2nd ser., vol. 20.1, 1–438. Bolo-gna, 1925–35.

TRANSLATIONS

Leben des Filippo Maria Visconti und Taten des Francesco Sforza. German translation by Philipp Funk. Jena, 1913. The life of Visconti is on pages 1–56.

Vita di Filippo Maria Visconti. Italian translation by Elio Bartolini. Milan, 1983.

DEEDS OF FRANCESCO SFORZA

EDITIONS OF THE LATIN TEXT

Annotatio rerum gestarum in vita Francisci Sfortiae IV Mediolanensium Ducis. Edited by Ludovico Antonio Muratori. In *RIS*, vol. 20, cols. 1021–46. Milan, 1731.

Annotatio rerum gestarum in vita Illustrissimi Francisci Sfortie Quarti Mediola-nensium Ducis. Edited by Attilio Butti, Felice Fossati, Giuseppe Petra-glione. In *RIS*, 2nd ser., vol. 20.1, 441–989. Bologna, 1935–58.

TRANSLATIONS

Leben des Filippo Maria Visconti und Taten des Francesco Sforza. German translation by Philipp Funk. Jena, 1913. The life of Sforza is on pages 57–96.

STUDIES

Battistella, Antonio. "Una lettera inedita di Pier Candido Decembrio sul Carmagnola." *Nuovo archivio veneto* 10 (1895): 99–135.

Borsa, Mario. "Pier Candido Decembri e l'umanesimo in Lombardia." *Archivio storico Lombardo* 20 (1893): 1–75, 358–441.

Cinquini, Adolfo. *Lettere inedite di Pier Candido Decembri*. Rome, 1902.

I Decembrio e la tradizione della 'Repubblica' di Platone tra Medioevo e Umanesimo. Edited by Mario Vegetti and Paolo Pissavino. Naples, 2005.

Ditt, Ernst. "Pier Candido Decembrio: Contributo alla storia dell'umanesimo lombardo." *Memorie del R. Istituto Lombardo di Scienze, Lettere e Arti, Classe di scienze morali e storiche* 24 (1931): 21–206.

Fumagalli, Edoardo. "Una nuova lettera di Pier Candido Decembrio: Nota sulle biografie di Filippo Maria Visconti e di Francesco Sforza." In *La storiografia umanistica*, edited by Anita Di Stefano, Giovanni Faraone, Paola Megna, and Alessandra Tramontana, 1:333–46. 2 vols. Messina, 1992.

Gabotto, Ferdinando. "L'attività politica di Pier Candido Decembrio." *Giornale ligustico di archeologia, storia e letteratura* 20 (1893): 161–98, 241–70.

Ianziti, Gary. "Pier Candido Decembrio and the Beginnings of Humanistic Historiography in Sforza Milan." In *After Civic Humanism: Learning and Politics in Renaissance Italy*, edited by Nicholas Scott Baker and Brian Jeffrey Maxson, 153–72. Toronto, 2015.

——. "Pier Candido Decembrio and the Suetonian Path to Princely Biography." In *Portraying the Prince in the Renaissance: The Humanist Depiction of Rulers in Historiographical and Biographical Texts*, edited by Patrick Baker, Ronny Kaiser, Maike Priesterjahn, Johannes Helmrath, 237–70. Berlin, 2016.

Kristeller, Paul Oskar. "Pier Candido Decembrio and His Unpublished Treatise on the Immortality of the Soul." In Paul Oskar Kristeller, *Studies in Renaissance Thought and Letters*, vol. 2 (1985), 281–300, 561–84. 4 vols. Rome, 1955–86.

Lentzen, Manfred. "Die Rivalität zwischen Mailand und Florenz in der erste Hälfte des 15. Jahrhunderts: Zu Pier Candido Decembrios *De laudibus Mediolanensium urbis*." *Italienische Studien* 9 (1986): 5–17.

Petraglione, Giuseppe. "Il *De laudibus Mediolanensium Urbis panegyricus* di Pier Candido Decembrio." *Archivio storico Lombardo* 34 (1907): 5–45.

Petrucci, Federico. *Petri Candidi Decembrii Epistolarum iuvenilium libri octo* (Florence, 2013).

Ponzù Donato, Paolo. "Il *Bellum Alexandrinum* e il *Bellum Africum* volgarizzati da Pier Candido Decembrio per Inigo D'Avalos." *Interpres* 31 (2012–13): 97–149.

———. "Il *Bellum Alexandrinum* e *Bellum Africum* volgarizzati da Pier Candido Decembrio per Inigo D'Avalos: Edizione critica." *Interpres* 32 (2014): 7–112.

Pyle, Cynthia Munro. "Harvard Ms Richardson 23: A 'Pendant' to Vatican Ms Urb. Lat. 276 and A Significant Exemplar for P. C. Decembrio's *Opuscula historica*." *Scriptorium* 42 (1988): 191–98.

Schadee, Hester. "The First Vernacular Caesar: Pier Candido Decembrio's Translation for Inigo d'Avalos with Editions and Translations of Both Prologues." *Viator* 46 (2015): 277–304.

Simonetta, Marcello. "Esilio, astuzia e silenzio: Pier Candido Decembrio fra Roma e Milano." In *Roma donne libri tra Medioevo e Rinascimento: In ricordo di Pino Lombardi*, 81–107. Rome, 2004.

Viti, Paolo. "Decembrio, Pier Candido." *DBI* 33 (1987), 488–98.

Wylie, J. Hamilton. "Decembri's Version of the *Vita Henrici Quinti* by Tito Livio." *English Historical Review* 24 (1909): 84–89.

Zaccaria, Vittorio. "L'epistolario di Pier Candido Decembrio." *Rinascimento*, 2nd ser., 3 (1952): 85–118.

———. "Pier Candido Decembrio e Leonardo Bruni." *Studi medievali*, 3rd ser., 8 (1967): 504–54.

———. "Pier Candido Decembrio traduttore della *Repubblica* di Platone." *Italia medioevale e umanistica* 2 (1959): 179–206.

———. "Sulle opere di Pier Candido Decembrio." *Rinascimento*, 2nd ser., 7 (1956): 13–74.

Zaggia, Massimo. "Appunti sulla cultura letteraria in volgare a Milano nell'età di Filippo Maria Visconti." *Giornale storico della letteratura italiana* 170 (1993): 161–219, 321–82.

———. "La traduzione latina da Appiano di Pier Candido Decembrio: Per la storia della tradizione." *Studi medievali*, 3rd ser., 34 (1993): 193–243.

———. "La versione latina di Pier Candido Decembrio della *Repubblica* di Platone." *Interpres* 13 (1993): 7–55.

———. "Linee per una storia della cultura in Lombardia dall'età di Coluccio Salutati a quella del Valla." In *Le strade di Ercole: Itinerari umanistici e altri percorsi*, edited by Luca Carlo Rossi, 3–125. Florence, 2010.

Zappa, Giulio. "La Vita di Filippo Maria Visconti di Pier Candido Decembri." In *Verso Emmaus: Scritti d'arte e di storia di Giulio Zappa*, edited by Franco Bianchi and Carlo Vicenzi, 47–69. Milan, 1921.

Index

☙❧

Abbiategrasso, 91, 93, 177, 227, 229, 309nn96–97; castle of, 5, 63

Acciaiuoli, Angelo, 239, 305n71

Acquapendente, Giovanna d' (concubine of Francesco Sforza), 181, 199, 300n41, 304n62

Adda (river), 17, 31, 33, 217, 231, 243, 245, 247, 283n74, 306n74, 312n114

Adige (river), 31, 199

Adolf of Nassau, 272n5

Adriatic coast, 35

Adriatic Sea, 7

Africa, 47

Aicardi, Giorgio (Scaramuccia), 101, 288n111, 290n121

Albenga, 29

Albergati, Niccolò (cardinal), 25

Alberico da Barbiano (the younger), 43, 280n58

Alessandria, 13, 59, 179, 229

Alexander the Great, xxi, 153

Alexander V (pope; Pietro di Candia), 233, 311n105

Alexander VI (pope; Rodrigo Borgia), 313n120

Alfonso of Aragon (king of Naples), x, xxx, xxxv, 21, 27–29, 33, 45–47, 149, 193, 209, 277n43, 281n64, 295n150, 295n2, 304n63, 306nn75–76

Alfonso II of Aragon (duke of Calabria), 306n78

Alighieri, Dante. See Dante Alighieri

Alopo, Caterina (sister of Pandolfello), 163, 298n19

Alopo, Pandolfello, 163, 298n19

Alps, 35

Ambrose of Milan (saint), xvi

Ambrosian Republic, xvi, xvii, xviii, xxvi, xxvii, xxix, xxx, xxxii, xxxiii, xxxiv, xxxv, xxxvi, xlv n20, xlviii n45, l n50, 149, 213–19, 223–27, 229–37, 261

Amedeo (Prince of Piedmont), 79, 285n90

Amedeo VIII (duke of Savoy), xxx, 25, 179, 285n90, 293n140

Amidano, Vincenzo, xl, xli, lii n63

Ancona, March of, 189, 197, 209, 302n51, 302n53, 306n76

Ancona, marquisate of, 191

Angera, 3, 272n2

Anghiari, 31, 203, 205, 278n46; battle of, 205, 305n72

Anjou, House of, 304n63, 306n75

Annoni, Giorgio, 41, 279n52

Ansano, Saint, chapel dedicated to, 286n93

Anthony, Saint, 137

Antonio da Rho, xlvi n27, 127, 290nn123–24

321

Publication of this volume has been made possible by

The Myron and Sheila Gilmore Publication Fund at I Tatti
The Robert Lehman Endowment Fund
The Jean-François Malle Scholarly Programs and Publications Fund
The Andrew W. Mellon Scholarly Publications Fund
The Craig and Barbara Smyth Fund
for Scholarly Programs and Publications
The Lila Wallace–Reader's Digest Endowment Fund
The Malcolm Wiener Fund for Scholarly Programs and Publications